Onc Ioscow

'Funny and motivational. For anyone who has ever run a good 5k parkrun and thought – what if…'

'*Chariots of Fire* meets *Day of the Jackal* – superb!'

'As close as you'll ever get to *feeling* those two races in 1980. A love letter to an era of athletics and two legends who inspired a generation.'

'The sheer audacity of it... Relentlessly surprising.'

'Captures the tension, jeopardy, and agony of a middle-distance race like no 'normal' sports book ever could.'

'An *outrageous* finish as stunning as an Ovett kick.'

'The subliminal thriller scenes never go where you expect. *The Bourne Identity* written with PG Wodehouse glee, heavily disguised as a sports book. Or vice versa.'

'The fastest first chapter you'll ever read.'

The Coe – Ovett Novel

ABOUT THE AUTHOR

Richard Weaver has run in three World Masters 800m finals. He was a five-year-old playground sprinter when the 1980 Olympics took place. During the writing of this book he was living in Moscow. He has never worked for the British Secret Service and is not especially handsome. If this is a novel it's his first.

Once Upon a Time in Moscow

The Coe – Ovett Novel

RICHARD WEAVER

ISBN: 978-1-3999-6310-7

Sometimes I run and don't even feel the effort of running. I don't even feel the ground. I'm just drifting. All the agony and frustration, they're all justified by one moment like that.

Steve Ovett

Eight athletes enter the arena. Feeling their spikes finally dig into the track is a relief after such a long wait in the call room. Dusk is falling. They look up and see rows of spectators rising to the heavens. The eye of the world is watching. Nerves. A sheen of sweat glints off their muscles in the floodlights. Empty legs. Fear. Their only comfort is that the track is dark red, the same familiar colour as back home, except for the new-white brightness of the lane lines. The runners wait behind each staggered start around the bend, taking their last deep breaths and last thoughts before they go. Central Lenin Stadium. This is it. Once upon a time in Moscow.

Lane 1	Nikolay Kirov	USSR
2	Steve Ovett	Great Britain
3	Agberto Guimarães	Brazil
4	Detlef Wagenknecht	DDR
5	David Warren	Great Britain
6	José Marajo	France
7	Andreas Busse	DDR
8	Sebastian Coe	Great Britain

Each athlete is young slim and handsome with a chiselled renaissance beauty. Eight physical specimens. The backside of their split-shorts curves outwards around mighty glutes; the equine power which will drive them around two laps of ferocious racing. The backs of their thighs have a thick rectangular bulge as if their hamstrings are gift-wrapping a house brick. Every inch of physique is loaded up for impending violence. A grenade of muscle packed around each shoulder but whip-thin arms. Their faces are gaunt with hollow shade beneath each cheek bone and an emaciated edge to the jawline. These men are in their athletic prime.

Sebastian Coe is the 800 metre world record holder.
Coe is the favourite.

Coe is drawn in lane eight with no one outside him to run off at the start. Lane eight is the worst. You can't see anyone for the first seventy, eighty, ninety metres. It's a bad lane draw, made worse in a big race when you're riddled with nerves, which Coe is. Millions are watching on television sets back in the UK and around the world. The only people who don't think Coe will win are the people who think Ovett will win.

```
Threeman. Embedded Moscow, Russia 2019.
Sleeper asset. Operational capability: RED3
```

All eight runners have dared to dream of gold. Although right now, in their spikes and their race numbers, the gold medal is a useless thought: too far away. They block out victory. They try to ignore the ninety thousand spectators and the fact that this single moment has defined every waking-sleeping-eating-training hour of their life for the last four years. Or more. Eight years. Ten. Ever since they laced up their first pair of junior spikes. Instead of thinking of the occasion, they reduce the race into one much smaller thought: one tactic, a training memory, a coach's words, a pace feeling, or just the familiar red colour of the track. Any crumb of focused positivity will do. You can't really decide what this thought is beforehand, it just comes. Maybe it doesn't even matter exactly what you think, but make it simple and repeat it to yourself over and over again.

Choose one:
Make it hurt early – Relaxed – Fifty-two split – Follow Coe

None of the runners are confident. Especially not Coe. The pressure is affecting pathways between tendons and muscles which absolutely must be in sync. Physical confusion. Others might have it too. On the start-line the nerves are acutely uncomfortable, oppressive, almost debilitating. The athletes all know they're sprinting themselves into a world of pain; a world which needs to be frightening and physiologically catastrophic if they're to have any chance of winning. Confidence in an 800m race is only a relative quantum of fear. Sometimes it helps to be the most scared. Adrenaline might be worth one second. Fear might take you through a half-gap that disappears the moment you see it. Steve Ovett is the only athlete on the start-line who's been in an Olympic final before.

The air is warm and still. An expectant ether. The Moskva River continues its never-ending horseshoe around Central Lenin Stadium. Across the water in the sloping woods of Vorobyovy Gory the darkling sparrows have fallen silent.

```
Ops capability RED3: hand-to-hand combat,
advanced linguistics, identity transposition
[polymorphism], weapons-trained, military
service or has prior criminal conviction for
violence-related offence.
```

Above the treetops on the plateau of the escarpment, the Moscow State University skyscraper soars upwards, tapering into a concrete needle with a single gold star on top. Eight athletes. Seven will lose.

```
Threeman latest contact made with Station R
on September 3, 2021. At drop location #2.
```

Outside the stadium Lenin stands ten metres tall on his plinth. One hand thoughtfully holding his lapel, the other gripping his trusty cap down by his side. He gazes sideways heroically into the egalitarian future, his coat-tails billowing in the winds of Soviet history. But he's exhorting an absent rabble. The concourse is deserted. Today his proletariat are all track fans inside the stadium, a sea of enthralled faces watching Coe, watching Ovett, watching their man Nikolay Kirov. The collective gaze of ninety thousand thickens the gravity at track level. Tension. Crowd chatter drops to only hushed murmurs. These in turn quieten as the moment of truth arrives. The starter marshall is ready. A crescendo of silence.

The 1980 Olympic 800 metre final.

Vnymanye. The starter raises his pistol. The athletes step up to their line and crouch in standing start position, eyes focusing down on the small stretch of track ahead, ready to launch themselves into one-minute-forty-something seconds of tactical chaos and cumulative physical horror. You can't remember pain race to race, but you try to recreate it on the start-line, to embrace it, to prepare your body to sprint into it. And beyond it. To win you have to dare to die.

BANG!

The eight athletes catapult out of their positions in unison. Legs driving. Arms pumping from the shoulders. Aggression. The spectators in the front-row seats gasp at such awesome acceleration over the opening strides. Two full laps at *that* speed?! The eight proud coaches cross their fingers or offer a silent prayer. And from his commentary position deep in the stands the unsung hero of the tale opens his account.

Tremendous roar around the stadium as they go on their way.

Guimarães goes storming off in lane three. Kirov, spurred on by the home crowd, closes the stagger quickly on Steve Ovett. Warren runs hard for fifty metres then the bend eats him up. Wagenknecht. Marajo. Busse starts cautiously out in lane seven but with close tabs on Coe. Sebastian Coe starts equally cautiously out in lane eight.

At the start of the back straight they break from their lanes. Guimarães appears to be ahead. Just. The runners now swoop like kamikaze bombers towards lane one. Busse and Coe stay wider longer. Warren and Kirov surge to get a cleaner position at the front when the pack forms. Wagenknecht, the towering East German, is halfway down the order, but as the pack narrows the race already seems to revolve around his giant frame in a central position. Andreas Busse, also big, tracks exactly along with Coe, keeping him wide on his right shoulder. Coe and Busse are still wide and two metres behind the pack as it starts to come together. Busse keeps Coe in the outer lanes for as long as possible. The textbook move if you're six-foot-four and drawn in lane seven inside the world record holder.

Isolate him wide. Make him feel lonely.

The pack attempts its first knot. They all want the outer half of lane one, sitting on the leader. But if you go hard for that position you might end up with the lead itself. Nobody particularly wants that, even though the leader is guaranteed a clear run and lane one around the bends. Where is Coe? The others aren't expecting to land the lead today. Coe will come floating through to the front and smash the first lap, they all think. This hasn't happened yet.

Instead, as they converge the leader might be Guimarães, or Warren, whichever one goes boldly for the inside lane in the next few strides. Wagenknecht on a natural path towards lane one is veering sideways into Ovett's space.

Bosh!

Wagenknecht takes a heavy flicked elbow from Ovett and lands his next stride back out in lane three. Marajo has to swerve wide to avoid contact. Busse and Coe, still drifting in, both avoid the bumping. Wagenknecht accelerates to regain ground and tucks in safely onto the line of lane one-two. An excellent recovery. He is now midway down the bunch and just ahead of Ovett.

As they approach the second bend the pack flanks out: a half chevron of migrating geese. Everyone wants to be on a right shoulder, ideally of the leader, to overtake if – *when* – they need to. Nobody feels secure of their race position. You never can be on the mad first lap. It's extra distance running in lane two around a bend, but often a fair sacrifice for tactical freedom. Wide minimises danger and maximises opportunity, but wider is further and therefore also dangerous. And wide… wide just *feels* horrible.

After the fast start, and the surges for position off the break, and the jostling, the pace softens just a fraction. Sebastian Coe hasn't taken it out after all. No one has planned for this.

```
Threeman leaves his apartment. Walks to the
metro. The sky is blue with wispy streaks of
cloud. Moscow. An October morning. 2021.
```

No Coe ahead as a target. So the best race position is now on the right shoulder of Agberto Guimarães. The Brazilian leads. The second-best position might well be being the leader himself: lane one with clear track ahead. These are the positions you have to work hardest to get, and they're even harder to protect. Are they worth it on the first lap? You might pay later but so might everyone else behind. In the pack they'll be playing Russian roulette in and out of boxes, getting chopped, having to check strides, working against shoulders, and fending off any friendly elbows flying around. The deeper you are in the pack the greater the risk. Although the inside half of lane one is the shortest distance. Tactics. The faster you are the easier your tactics.

```
The red line to Vorobyovy Gory. Thirteen
stops through town. Threeman assesses the
passengers opposite him. Threats?
```

But tactics are not just about where to position yourself in the pack. Distribution of effort is as important as race position. In an 800m race the fastest runner doesn't always run the fastest. Sebastian Coe has a personal best two seconds quicker than anyone else in the field. Two seconds! That's a fourteen-metre head start. The only time Coe and Ovett have raced each other, in Czechoslovakia at the 1978 Europeans, Coe blitzed the first lap from the front. Ovett sat on him until the final straight and outsprinted him. Tactics. But neither of them won the race because East Germany's Olaf Beyer distributed his pace better and beat both favourites in the last fifty metres. *The Thief of Prague*. Tactics. Coe has this memory fuzzying the picture in his race computer. That's why he's not in the lead. The conundrum of strategy has a million variables once the race starts. Eight runners fighting for position every stride. Best to eliminate thoughts. Tactics should be synapses, instinctive reactions with a trigger mechanism faster than your brain. All your brain wants to do is override speed and avoid pain. Opportunities come and go in the blink of an eye. You have to feel it. Do it. And have done it. Before it becomes a decision. The art of the 800m racer.

200 metres run.
Coe is comfortable in sixth place.

The pack curves into the top bend. No wind today. Tucking in is not a factor. In their flanked-out formation everyone has a tactical option except for Steve Ovett who's at the back and badly blocked. He can't move up in lane one which is a dead-end box behind two runners: Kirov and Guimarães. Ovett realises he's not good – not good at all. Synapses. He looks wider again for scope to manoeuvre, but the tight pack is more bodies than air now. Another nudge won't work. He has nowhere to move into. Halfway around the second bend Ovett is in seventh place and firmly shut in.

Coe's wide run off the break was a blessing in disguise. He wasted no energy in the early jostling and is now in a decent position, albeit on the outside line of lane two around the bend. Each lane wider you lose three-and-a-half metres on one full bend, so the pack squeezes in laterally as much as arms, shoulders, hips, and trail legs allow. Although he's wide, Coe has a clear run to improve his situation, if his instinct today chooses.

Vorobyovy Gory. As the carriage doors start to close Threeman walks off the train. Checks platform. Front tail or back tail? Clear. He walks to the metro exit and takes the steps down to the Moskva embankment. The fisherman? Check. Dog-walker? Not yet.

After such a quick start Guimarães is suddenly wary of how much work he's done to get the lead. He doesn't want to help everyone with a fast slipstream or ruin himself for the second lap (no wind is still a headwind at 800m pace) so he eases off a touch. Warren is alongside Guimarães and feels it slow. He doesn't want the lead *yet* and also eases off. Wagenknecht just behind takes his foot off the gas too. Even a tiny fraction less effort slows the pace of a pack significantly. No one expected a tactical race, but with renowned front-runner Coe being unexpectedly cagey that's exactly what this has become.

On the second bend they clamp together.
The tactical cards have fallen for now.

In the lead it's Guimarães in the green-and-yellow of Brazil. Second is Warren in the white Great Britain vest with one red hoop and one blue hoop around the torso. Despite being the second slowest qualifier for this final, Dave Warren has landed himself the perfect race position on the right shoulder of the leader. He should attempt to stay exactly there for as long as he can.

In third, directly behind Warren, is Wagenknecht running in lane one-two. Detlef Wagenknecht presents a major obstacle to anyone wanting to come past either side, or anyone running in the wake of his trail legs. Fourth is Busse, tight on his compatriot's right shoulder, running dead centre of lane two. He widens the muscular phalanx of East German blue in the crucial race positions. Are the DDR boys running as a team? Negative. Impossible to premeditate where they would each end up, or what Seb Coe would or wouldn't do. They're running the race as it pans out. It's mere happenstance that they're both huge, are both now alongside one another, and are both causing a significant tactical problem for the two race favourites.

```
Threeman puts his rucksack down on a grass
slope near the riverbank. Then heads
upstream. Slow and easy. Like any other
Saturday morning jogger.
```

The moustachioed Kirov, with that dark flowing mane, is equal fourth in lane one. He has shoulder room around him for a relatively free run. Nobody wants to fight Kirov for his poor position, completely boxed behind Guimarães and Dave Warren, neither of whom are likely to win. Kirov also has seventy-five kilos worth of Wagenknecht pinning him in from the right.

```
Red sweatshirt as agreed. Adidas track
trousers. He jogs past the fisherman, then a
dog-walker with a whippet on an extendable
lead. Threeman pats the dog on the head. The
dog owner smiles - job done.
```

In sixth position is Coe, forced to run wide but he's clear of trouble. With Busse on his inside shoulder Coe cannot tuck further in unless he accelerates, which his synapses are telling him it's too early to do. The extra distance around one bend won't cost a runner of Coe's supreme quality. Not now the pace has slowed. His world record gives him a two-second tactical cushion on everyone else in the field.

```
To: Nevis. Routine contact made with
Threeman. All okay signal reciprocated. All
Moscow field assets have now reported in as
per monthly protocol. From: Station R
```

Steve Ovett is inside Coe, level in sixth but in an infinitely worse position, with a wall of bodies in front of him and more on his right shoulder. José Marajo in the blue vest of France is at the back in eighth place.

Dusk has become a deep indigo night.
A shooting star streaks across the Moscow sky.
But for whom?

Ovett is in serious trouble. Stone dead behind the pack. Kirov is the block directly ahead of him in lane one. Wagenkecht is blocking diagonally in front to the right. And Busse is now running tight to Ovett's right shoulder barring the sideways escape. Ovett still has a metre of space to move up in lane one, but that would lead into an even narrower box behind three runners: Kirov, then Guimarães and Dave Warren. The tactical options seem to be getting worse with every stride for Ovett. It's unthinkable to drop further back and move out to extricate himself. That would take him behind and even wider than Coe. And in any case, Marajo has just moved up inside Coe, sealing the box into which Steve Ovett has got himself. Wearing a straitjacket, padlocked in chains, stuffed into a cast-iron bank safe, Houdini plunges into the icy river. The only option is to wait and hope. Ovett's one saving grace is that he has run an even pace into such a dreadful spot. The others have burnt some of their matches with subtle surges, or wider runs, to achieve their better race positions. The pack enters the home straight for the first time. 300 metres run. The crux of the race is how long they stay in the clamped bunch like this.

Coe is well clear of trouble on the outside of the pack. Here on the home straight, running wide is not damaging for him at all. In fact, even this early in the race Coe can make a killer move on Ovett if he sees it. If he looks. Or feels it.

Now. If his synapses trigger? They don't.

Twenty metres more. The opportunity is right there. Thirty metres. Forty. Halfway down the home straight. Still! He can absolutely bury Ovett. It's all set up. If a chess grandmaster advances a Coe white rook to the front of the race, it would leave the Ovett black king in checkmate at the back of the pack. Even allowing for it to open up, Coe can get four or five – maybe six! – metres on his most dangerous rival before the bell if he wants it. The pack would accelerate and string out. Ovett would eventually get a run but only around heavy traffic. For Coe a long finish is do-able off this pace. It hasn't been super-quick.

Coe makes no move.
The world record holder waits.
Passive.

The clamp remains. Almost a whole lap of effort is now creeping into the legs. Even at this relatively slow pace (for them) the effects are building. Harder to breathe. Already the heaviness. Everything is screaming at you to back off. With every stride you need more courage to stay aggressive, to stay foolhardy. Coe makes a decision and stays alongside Busse, where he's been all race, and where at the moment his brain says he's okay. Everyone just about has a position with an option. Everyone can feel and create their immediate future in the race. Everyone but one. One person still absolutely *has* to find an answer.

Ovett.

Halfway down the home straight he tries to force a run between Kirov and Wagenknecht. No proper gap exists unless Ovett narrows his arms forward into it and makes one. He attempts this but doesn't succeed in prizing it open for himself. With nine-millimetre steel spikes flicking up in front of him and a high risk of tripping against trailing legs, Ovett backs off. Sensing a quickening of the pace might happen towards the bell, he resists a second attempt to crowbar himself through. Ovett has to resign himself to the tactical dystopia. Though ghastly, the only option is to settle in lane one just inside Wagenknecht, and gamble on the breakout.

```
To: Gyllyngvase. All quiet in R. Babies
sleeping soundly. Be a shame to wake them,
chum. From: Nevis
```

Meanwhile out in lane two, with every stride nearer the next bend, Coe's width in sixth place is becoming more perilous. Wide right now is okay, but wide again around the third bend adds yet another three-and-a-half metres to his race. His theoretical pre-race cushion is disappearing. Busse nudges ahead of Coe by half a shoulder. As the race approaches the bell only Marajo is in a worse position than Coe or Ovett. Everyone else is somehow and in some way good. The leaders up front have all run hard but they're only halfway.

DING! DING! DING!

400 metres run. A slow split. Only 54.5 seconds. Almost scarier than a fast split. They all know it's going to be an insane burn-up now on the second lap. The clangs of the bell are always loud so close to your left ear. They startle every race into action. Now you can think of gold. Now you absolutely have to think of gold. Who wants it? At this point everyone can still reach out and touch it – even Marajo in last place if he has a Dave Wottle finish. At the front Guimarães pushes hard into the bend, but the pack reads it and accelerates on him as one solid bloc. No tactical change for ten metres, twenty metres, twenty-five metres.

Then Warren kicks. Superbly bold.

A huge move from the young Brit to surge two metres past Guimarães on the bend. No one has told Warren he can't win. And a surprise attack for gold might be the best way to win a miraculous bronze. Or an epic fourth. He has cashed in his perfect race position early, but with 370 metres to go Dave Warren is now leading the Olympic 800m final.

The shape of the pack morphs. Dramatically.

With over a lap of effort in their legs the synapses are operating fractionally slower now for some. Split-second reactions to this move will determine the rest of the race. Warren moving ahead and into lane one opens up the front of the pack. Nikolay Kirov instantly kicks out of his box and moves wider into the space alongside Guimarães. His synapses also take him on past the Brazilian. Adrenaline is rampaging through the Kirov veins. He now has a clear run through on Warren in the lead. It's a brilliantly instinctive move from the Soviet champion, racing perfectly the tactics in front of him. But not all tactics are in front of you, and when you take you also give.

Kirov has just opened the front door for Ovett.

Ovett's tactical synapses fire immediately. I'll have that! He accepts the gift. His move into the gap happens faster than the double DDR option to surge and re-box him. The Ovett cadence increases, his stride lengthens, the shoulders relax, as he purrs into new-found freedom. The panther is uncaged.

But having glided smoothly inside Wagenknecht, does Ovett then push to get on Kirov straight away? No... He tempers his surge to hold Wagenknecht wide on his right shoulder (and right elbow) around the rest of the bend. This means anyone – Coe – needing to move up on the outside will now be forced to run the bend in lane two-three to pass the hulking Wagenknecht. Only when Ovett is out of the bend does he accelerate onto the shoulder of Guimarães. Tactical genius. Into equal third. Ovett is in the mix.

Sebastian Coe enters the back straight at the back of the pack which is now rapidly stringing out. Coe has missed the big accelerations. Or did his width negate his own attempt at a surge? Somehow he's lost a metre-and-a-half on Busse. Coe is even behind Marajo who's moved up the inside line, sucked into the vacuum left by Ovett. Now Coe is in last place and has run another entire bend out in lane two. His reign as race favourite ended fifteen strides ago and he still doesn't seem to know it.

300 to go.
The drip feed of lactate into their legs increases.

Kirov is flowing now, overtaking Warren and moving into a one-metre lead. Nikolay Kirov. His heart pounding inside his red CCCP vest. He pours it on down the back straight extending his lead to two metres. Two-and-a-half. Kirov has three metres. The race is all about Kirov.

Ovett passes Guimarães and then Warren, into second place in dynamic pursuit of Kirov. Behind this move the two East Germans are forced to stay wide because Dave Warren is suddenly fading. They are in the scrap to overtake him which also involves Guimarães in lane one-two brushing shoulders with Warren. A nasty mess at a crucial time in the race. Any sparring of shoulders will kill your rhythm, kill your speed, especially on the brutal second lap. Wagenknecht and Busse tussle in lane two while drawing onto Guimarães. With the last bend in sight, lane one is out of bounds until you get past Dave Warren.

Lactic.

Warren's body is reacting to his incredible efforts so far. It senses the catastrophic lack of oxygen and is trying to help him by producing lactate for energy. But his body can't process this energy source fast enough and so it turns into lactic acid. He feels the acid starting to burn as it seeps deep into his leg muscles, gradually poisoning them, making them stingy, leaden, and less responsive. His sprint training has been designed to help him delay and buffer this inevitable effect, but his body can only do so much after such a strong kick. Lactic. It hurts. Stride on stride he is losing power to drive off the track. His legs will not lift as high. He can't get the back leg forward quickly enough to achieve the same turnover he had only twenty metres ago. Lactic. He pumps his arms harder from the shoulders to generate some leg cadence. This extra effort tailspins him even further into oxygen bankruptcy. Lactic. It won't go away.

Like quick-drying cement.
It pours into his thighs. Painful. Heavy. Slow.

Warren drives through the horrific burn because he knows everyone else will get it too. But he gets it first and is now a sitting duck in lane one. Kirov and Ovett have buried him and are pulling away into the distance. Warren's technique is starting to disintegrate. Guimarães also moves ahead of him. Wagenknecht and Busse are about to do the same. Helpless. Nothing will stop him running backwards. In the biggest race of his life Dave Warren gave it a tremendous go, but if you get it wrong… it's a long way home. *Da svidanya.*

250 metres to go.

The front of the race is beautiful. The full majestic power of Ovett is now on display. A masterclass of arrogance and control. Utter disdain for the over-excited Kirov move. With a clear run now, all Ovett has to do is track Kirov and pull gradually onto his shoulder. The pack has been obliterated. Kirov leads but went hardest and earliest. Ovett is covering the move all the way down the back straight with smooth calculated speed. This is on. And he knows it.

Steve Ovett … those blue eyes like chips of ice.

Seven metres behind the leaders, Seb Coe finally realises that sleeping during the Kirov and Ovett moves has left him a long way adrift. The race for gold has started and Coe is nowhere near it. In the Christopher Nolan movie, Ovett has been spliced into the next scene, jump cut to an alternate reality, in the future, showing in an IMAX cinema several metres further up the track. Coe is Alfred Hitchcock still in his pyjamas. Realising the unfolding disaster, Coe tries to get himself back into the race. He's still wide and still struggling to get past Busse and Wagenknecht before they enter the last bend. Horrible.

Kirov leads in his home Olympics, doing the unthinkable, the impossible. He maintains his victory push as the final bend approaches. Ninety thousand cheers ring out for the hero with the hammer and sickle emblazoned on his chest. The pride of Byelorussia. His thighs are pumping furiously like steel pistons on the Minsk-Moskva Ekspress. But his spikes sink deeper into the track with every stride. Such a hard kick. So early. If he hasn't timed it right the sluices will open and the entire Soviet Bloc supply of quick-drying cement will pour into his legs.

200 to go. Kirov drives. 180 metres. The crowd spurs him on through the unbearable heaviness. 160 – drive!

Nikolay Kirov. *Molodyetz.* This is his moment. The dream came true. All the training, all the sprint reps, all the pain was for this one chance. At the top of the final bend Kirov is leading the Olympic final in front of a home crowd. He has asked the ultimate question. Now, can he see the tears of pride in the eyes of his coach? *Davay Kolya, Davay!* Can he hear the roars of his comrades willing him on for an astonishing upset? *Vperyod!* Or can he hear only the cold beating heart behind his right shoulder? Ovett. Natural born killer.

On the last quarter of the bend Ovett is lining up Kirov with every silky stride. Increasing his turnover to a cadence Kirov can no longer match. Pressurising. Imposing his supremacy. Looking for the first giveaway, the sign, that first mechanical chink, any subliminal change in the Kirov technique as it starts to break down: something in the arms, the shoulders, or a tiny wrench of the neck. Only one ragged movement and Ovett knows.

They start the slingshot into the home straight. The crowd rises. The sprint finish is on. Behind them, a long way behind, Sebastian Coe has launched a blistering attack, picking off several places around the last bend into fourth place, onto the shoulder of Guimarães, but still with an awful lot to do to get on Ovett and Kirov. At the front of the race there remains only one last act. Ovett unleashes.

The timing is as cruel as it is immaculate. The kick itself starts on the bend five strides before, but the acceleration draws him onto Kirov only at the exact moment they both hit the home straight. Just as the noise of the crowd erupts for the final push. Just as the mirage of the finish line appears in front of them for the first time. Just as Nikolay Kirov finally dares to believe he can win. The most exquisite moment to kill.

100 metres to go.

Ovett is level. Mesmerising rhythm now. His leg speed increases as his arms and shoulders click smoothly into sprint overdrive. Savage determination etched across his face. Kirov somehow responds and for five strides Ovett is shoulder to shoulder with the Soviet vest. Then every stride takes something out of Kirov. An inch. Two inches. Three inches up on Kirov is enough to rip out his racing heart. All eyes are on Ovett as he stretches his lead to half a metre. With sixty metres to go Ovett has daylight. In five more strides it's total demolition.

And Ovett hits the front!

Two metres. All guns blazing now. The effortless power is there. Muscles firing in glorious coordination. Every stride detonates Ovett further clear. Three metres. The more he relaxes the faster he goes. With thirty metres to the finish line Ovett is on his own sprinting to victory. His spikes barely seem to touch the track. He has the speed. He has the class. It's going to be gold for Great Britain.

Ovett wins.
Coe second. Kirov third.

Threeman

★

Moskva. An October morning. The sky is pale blue with wispy streaks of cloud. A scent of autumn leaves breezes down off the woods and along the river. I put my rucksack with my racing flats on the slope by the embankment. Mine is only the third bag. I'm early. Downstream on the riverbank road there are two slim figures in tracksuits. Out over the water a black-headed gull floats serenely, almost motionless, using only deft wing angle to maintain its height. Wavelets on the Moskva lap against the riverbank wall. Wind. Enough to be a factor. I'll sit on someone. Like Ovett would.

I start my stopwatch and head slowly towards the metro bridge. A rubberized jogging path extends along the side of the pavement, softer and grippier than the tarmac. The familiar dark red of a running track stirs memories of a thousand interval sessions. Stay relaxed. Today is only a tempo. First week of the winter programme. For sociability I'm running it in the Gorky Park 5k parkrun. I probably won't talk to anyone but the atmosphere and colours of the other runners will stimulate me. Even the joggers.

The park is lined by the Moskva River on one side and sloping woodland on the other. An isolated sliver of tranquillity away from the bustle and 'issues' of the city. In Moscow life Gorky Park has always symbolised wholesome and playful pursuits. Even in the grimmest days it was an apolitical haven. Today too. Walkers. Runners. Rollerbladers. My warm-up is slow. No rush to get the stiffness out of my feet. Let it happen.

A fisherman leans against the river railings in a hooded camouflage suit and white tennis shoes. His line is cast far out into the Moskva straining with the current.

There's a light bend in the end of his rod. Puffing away on a cigarette he wages silent chess against the unsuspecting carp.

Ahead of me is a morning walker with a dog, a dark grey whippet on an extendable lead. It bounces effortlessly along on four slimline calves. His fur has a sleek sheen and is taut around his lithe racing frame. Majestic. It stops to sniff the iron railings. As I jog past he switches his curiosity to me. I reach down and pat his head. *Molodyetz*. He trots along with me for eight strides until, unfairly for us both, his lead runs out and he gets yanked to a standstill.

The embankment road passes under Luzhniki Bridge where it's much colder out of the sun. The bridge has a metro station on one level and a three-lane highway on top. The metro platform has glass sides so you can see out over the Moskva. Legs already looser. Body temperature rising. Nice. I take a sharp left up the side of the bridge. A flight of two, four, six, eight… ninety-four steps rises past the metro entrance and into the woods of Vorobyovy Gory. Sparrow Hills. The sweeping horseshoe escarpment which guides the Moskva through a giant meander in the south-western quadrant of the city. I trained in Vorobyovy Gory all summer. Perfect for hill reps.

Underneath my red Puma sweatshirt my t-shirt starts to cling to the first patches of sweat on my skin. Even jogging slowly I feel fast in my super-lite track trousers: expensive Adidas ones with a slim-fit taper and ankle zips up the side. Under these I'm already in my race shorts. My stopwatch says five minutes jogging time. I want a long warm-up today, almost a run in itself before the race. Except today isn't a race, just a disciplined sociable tempo.

In the woods the path turns to the right up a constructed section with steps made from railway timbers. The Lydiard Steps. They rise diagonally across the slope to the very top of Vorobyovy Gory. The section is three-hundred metres long. Hard running if you sprint it which normally I do. Sixty-eight seconds is my fastest time up the Lydiard Steps. Today I take them leisurely, enjoying the gazelle-like spring to reach each higher step.

Another runner passes coming the other way.
I nod. He opens a palm. *Zdrastye.*

```
To: Nevis. See attached [ciphered]. An
unscheduled drop received today by Threeman.
From: Station R
```

At this pace there are three foot-strikes between each step, one of which is a stuttered half-stride, and the drive up to the next step is off a different leg each time; a quirky ragtime stride pattern which distracts me from the effort. Only at the top does a wave of breathlessness hit me.

Always good to blow out the cobwebs before a tempo.
To nail it from the start if you need.

My first wear of these new Mizunos today and loving them already. Wave Sky 3s in the silver-and-white space odyssey colour scheme. Weight: 320-grams. A middle-distance athlete can never own enough pairs of quality flats. These are only for base mileage. Heavy and supportive. The new foam has that instant return off the foot-strike. That cushioning will last me about four months. Maybe five. After that I'll wear them casually.

Legs feeling awake now. I start to anticipate the sensation of running fast *against* people. At the top of the woods is a main road. Ulitsa Kosygina. I turn right and jog past the cable car station. Parked on the kerb is a mobile coffee kiosk with steam and a thick espresso aroma wafting out of the hatch. I'll have that! I take two big sniffs for stimulation. Bouncier.

Crossing Kosygina takes me onto the palatial concourse of *MGU*. Moscow State University. Now I'm on soft grass. A lawn with landscaped flowerbeds extends six-hundred metres to the skyscraper. It's further than it looks because *MGU* is so huge – two-hundred-and-forty metres up to the single gold star. My feet are enjoying the give of the grass. I run sideways facing inwards then turn and face the trees, alternating every five steps, and switch, and again, for circulation through the bones of my feet and more springiness in my calves. Training volume this week has been low. I should be fresh as a daisy. Could probably smash it today. Or just rhythm it and see.

MGU is magnificent and sinister in equal measure. A neo-gothic skyscraper designed for Stalin as a personal statement at the height of his terror. Forty-two storeys, built by prison labour, it stands in solitude on the highest point in Moscow. The tapering silhouette and five-pointed star on the central spire was the logo for the 1980 Moscow Olympics.

Ovett. Will I run majestically today?

At the *MGU* steps I do twenty press-ups then jog back along the other side of the lawn. Stopwatch says thirteen minutes. Thirteen easy minutes. The grass here is flat and mown tight enough for some pre-race drills: high-kneed skips, walking lunges, and heel flicks. Waking up the fast-twitch.

`To: Gyllyngvase. Rather important you walk your dog, chum. Tomorrow. The lake. See you at 14:00. From: Nevis`

The Gorky Park parkrun is five kilometres along the Moskva embankment, straight out and straight back, but in an arc following the giant river bend. There's a U-turn at halfway which is coned and marshalled. The wind gets channelled around the arc by the hills so we'll get the headwind for the whole first half. The route is almost completely flat and therefore popular, attracting a hundred or so runners every Saturday. Most of them are only keep-fit joggers but there are usually half-a-dozen quality runners. Long-distance road specialists mostly. Sometimes an 800-metre physique with that extra edge of power. I'll slipstream one of the endurance boys. On the way back I can just technique it with the wind behind – I'll fly along. Today is only a loosener to launch into the winter programme. 5k fitness is the bread and butter. The essential aerobic base required to cope with the rigours of middle-distance interval reps. In nine months it's the World Masters Athletics Championships. July 2022 in Finland.

Yeah.

This gives me forty-one weeks of training. Two-hundred-and-eighty-seven days. If I make it to the start line it will be my fourth World Masters, and probably my last. The niggles are becoming injuries more often nowadays and they last longer. Gets harder to achieve the required momentum. Emotionally far riskier slimming to race weight each season. This is my last roll of the dice. I'm in the M45 category now (male: 45-49). I've never won an individual medal but have reached two 800m finals and two 1500m finals. I came fifth in the 800m in Porto Alegre. Last time in Malaga I was knocked out in both the 800m and 1500m semi-finals. Too fat. And too fucking slow. In Finland I'll be ready.

EXT. Black Park, South Buckinghamshire.

Daytime. Woodland surrounding a lake. Autumn colours. A man in glasses and a zipped-up parka coat is sitting on a bench on the edge of the lake. He is of stout build. Early 50s. A thick thatch of greying hair. NEVIS. Next to him in the middle of the bench is a Tupperware box with foil-wrapped sandwiches and an apple. He is holding a remote control console with which he is carefully manoeuvring a model warship towards some ducks in the middle of the lake.

A second man appears. This man is wearing an expensive wool overcoat, long and single-breasted. Saville Row suit beneath his coat. Silk tie. Polished city shoes. He is taller [and slicker] but of about the same age. GYLLYNGVASE. He sits down at the other end of the same bench.

They don't greet each other. Nevis applies intermittent dabs to the console controls. A short time passes in silence as both men watch the model warship making its furtive approach to the ducks. Then --

GYLLYNGVASE: Which one is it today?

NEVIS: HMS Venturer. Type-31 Inspiration class frigate. Scale miniature. Ministry of Defence just commissioned five of the real thing. Despite my report saying we needed twelve.

GYLLYNGVASE: What's so good about them?

NEVIS: Anti-submarine technology. [a beat] I'm trying to steer those ducks all the way up to the other end of the lake without scaring them. Good test of stealth and manoeuvrability. Push too hard and they fly off.

GYLLYNGVASE: A naval sheep dog herding unsuspecting waterfowl.

NEVIS: Exactly. How was the M40, chum?

GYLLYNGVASE: Fine. Any excuse for half an hour of Classic FM in the Aston -- What's so urgent to report?

NEVIS: Help yourself to a sandwich, Alec. You'll find a rather nasty little USB in the cheese and pickle. From Moscow. What we've been fearing.

At the end of the *MGU* lawn I cross back over the main road and jog up to the escarpment lookout, a stone balustrade on the edge of the slope. From here I can see down over the trees of Vorobyovy Gory to the Moskva. The meander in the river is much smaller from this height. The opposite bank is dominated by what is now called Luzhniki Stadium, another architectural monument of the Soviet 1950s; a giant oval of sandstone with a colonnade wrapped around supporting its half-dome roof. Despite major renovations, the stadium is the same as when it was constructed in the fifties, except at the Moscow Olympics in 1980 there was no roof. In those days the sky still belonged to the people. An open bowl stadium meant that every ray of sunlight was sucked into the vortex of athletics history.

Tsentralny Stadion Imeni V. I. Lenina.
This is where it all happened.

The Clash. Sebastian Coe versus Steve Ovett. For nine days in the summer of 1980 the world stood still, as Moscow became the epicentre of a drama the like of which athletics had never seen before, nor has it since. A rivalry which towered over the Olympic Games like the *MGU* skyscraper itself. The plot unfolded not just over one race, nor over the two middle-distance races, but over four whole years. Two athletes on a collision course of relentlessly converging fates. The Clash of the Titans had to happen and it could only happen here in Moscow. Central Lenin Stadium was the unavoidable endgame.

Sweat trickles down the back of my t-shirt.

Today is October 2, 2021. Many things have changed in Moscow since the days of the USSR. Many things have not. Or have reverted. It's been complicated and is getting rather more so. Layered over the turbulent Soviet history is a modern but schizophrenic society. Flourishing business and refreshing youth culture juxtaposed with throwback centralised power. A watertight KGB police state disguised by capitalist trimmings. On the surface you can't see it, especially if you don't want to. The city is so beautiful. And all the beautiful people I know despise Vladimir Putin, always carefully referred to as 'our government'. The shadow is systematically thrown, deeper and darker, as history eats itself and mutates. I mostly choose not to look. My Moscow is special. It might be okay. He might not be psychotic.

```
To: Prime Minister. It seems you were right.
New intelligence coming out of R very ugly.
See attached from Station R source
[deciphered]. As per our last conversation,
I'm afraid. Plum Tree planning massive
invasion of U in the spring, or earlier.
Wants the whole thing - not just Donetsk and
Lugansk. Kyiv from the north through Belarus
and the coast with fleet from Sevastopol. He
might have gone nuts. Or might always have
been nuts. Pardon my French, but this is
going to be the full shit show. Sir. Liaise
with Washington absolute soonest. From:
Gyllyngvase
```

The longer history of Moscow is an easier theme to take in. It drips down the painted walls of Red Square, sings out from the Bolshoi, reflects off the oblique angles of modernist concrete, wafts through warrens of apartment blocks. The turbulence and terror is distant enough, safely processed by time, so that I can savour my personal historical thread of choice. And here standing at the *MGU* lookout is a golden seam of history – athletics history. For all its complications, what Moscow will always have, especially when inhaled from this spot, is the middle-distance ether. Olympic vapours of breathable glory and of mystifying failure. The race oxygen lingers along with wisps of the two spirits who left part of themselves here forever.

Steve Ovett and Sebastian Coe.

On separate missions to win the same two gold medals.

Between them they held every middle-distance world record in the book: the 800m, 1000m, 1500m, the mile, and the two-miles. Coe and Ovett had been destroying all the other contenders for three seasons – mercilessly, majestically – but they had specifically avoided racing each other for two whole years. One of them was the best. But who? Strength. Speed. Tactics. Nobody knew who had the edge. Their rivalry was based upon mystery and conjecture even with new electronic timing systems.

When Ovett and Coe finally raced head-to-head at the Moscow Olympics, the whole world watched. July 1980. The two global superpowers wore white track spikes, split-shorts, and Great Britain vests. Athletic supremacy stood above war and ideology. People only wanted to know who would win the race.

Those blue eyes like chips of ice.

I jog down through the woods of Vorobyovy Gory. Back on the embankment I'm at ground level with Central Lenin Stadium, now larger than life just across the river. This 5k is no longer an easy loosener, especially when I see all the other runners milling around at the start line. I'm primed for an aggressive race.

Follow Coe. Or Kirov.

I take off my track bottoms and change into my Saucony racing flats. 218 grams. Turquoise mesh uppers, neon pink laces, and white soles. Garish. A deliberate contrast to my plain gym-grey t-shirt. Bright shoes make me run faster and the runner behind me knows it. I want him demoralised by the flashes of turquoise and the magi-white soles as they flick up in his face. Mesmerising rhythm. He can only stare at the inevitability of his fate. My slimline calves. Smooth calculated speed. The Great Britain Masters split-shorts with the Union Jack insignia. And yes! The egg-shaped head with the Ovett balding pattern. An eerie simulacrum. The more I relax the faster I go. The runner behind feels extra weight in his legs. He runs on gamely, but emotionally he has already caved in to my supremacy.

The joggers stand and chat. I side-step my way through to the front of the field. All the good people are up by the organiser in the hi-viz jacket. At the start line I smile at the other runners. Everything about it. Fucking bring it on.

I note three super-slim lads in their late teens in split-shorts. Whippets. With their youth advantage they'll definitely beat me, and they're welcome to it – I wish them well. No, I'm looking for the pretenders... the gnarled bastards my age, but less handsome. Or smug fuckers in their thirties who think they're more handsome than me. Probably in a new running vest, or calf guards, or a fancy sports watch. I scan for signs anyone has splashed out on kit because they think they're a big deal. Targets. After the first kilometre it will be obvious who I have to beat. The organiser invites us forward and we line our toes up between the start cones.

The Gorky Park 5k.
Vnymanye. KLAXON!

We're off. The stampede charges along the embankment towards the metro bridge. Yes, I'm up into my running nicely and in amongst the leaders. The three young whippets cruise effortlessly ahead. Great to see. I let them go. Behind them are two lads in their late twenties (or early thirties?) quick but not as quick as the whippets, and they're running side by side. I accelerate for ten strides and tuck in behind them, out of the wind, feeling for the slipstream, feeling. *There.*

We pass under the metro bridge at 200 metres run. The patter of footsteps is thinning out as the front of the race strings out into ones, twos, and in our case a group of three. We're on the service road five metres inland from the river railings. There's a two-way cycle lane but the only cars that drive here are park ranger vehicles. I settle into the rhythm required to sit in behind my assigned pacemakers.

This is faster than my recent normal pace. But do-able.

On the left he's wearing a 'MOSKVA MARATHON' t-shirt in red. His mate on the right is in Adidas yellow: a golden yellow like the brick road. Yellow has a much better running style. Springier, over the top of the tarmac. Marathon Man is taller and stronger but scrapes along the road like Groucho Marx chasing a buxom waitress. Or was it Karl Marx? But crap form is not necessarily a sign he's a crap runner. 5k takes all sorts. His early cadence is impressive. Both of them have lean shoulders and slim waists, but Marathon Man's calves are chunky.

The wind whips around them. This slipstream is a definite advantage. No idea why they're side by side and not working together. A gentlemanly pact? Maybe they don't know it's an international field today. Yellow Brick

Road looks round. So does Marathon Man. In their rear-view mirror they have Ovett. Rogue stealth. The Steve McQueen Ford Mustang in *Bullitt.* Just oozing danger. The looseness of my old t-shirt against relaxed shoulders. Extra easy, empty face. Ice.

I look back myself, casually, to assess the pretenders. Behind me two others have tagged on to our bunch. One is in an orange t-shirt. Medium-height, slim build, with a fluid style. The orange top is New Balance. Clockwork Orange is sitting on me. Clever. Very clever indeed. The other guy is wearing a black vest with 'PROPAGANDA' written across it in retro Soviet font. In my split-second glance back I don't have time to process both their running forms, so I paint in Propaganda by numbers. What is he? Expensive flats I expect, but does the same loop and distance every training run. Never does weights. Or speedwork. Hips too low. Not a threat.

The wispy clouds have disappeared leaving the October sky entirely blue. A great day for the race. The *human* race.

The Vorobyovy Gory woods slope down to the left edge of the road. On our right is a line of beech trees along a grass verge. The route becomes a tunnel under the overhanging branches. The sunlight glows yellow through the tint of the autumn leaves. Yellow like the floodlights of a capacity Zurich. Oslo. Or Crystal Palace.

On the grass verge this side of the tree trunks is an inviting two-foot-wide dirt track. No. I stay on the tarmac behind the energy-saving shield which Marathon Man and Yellow Brick Road are providing.

My breathing has found a rhythmic sweet spot. Ankles are loose. Quads powerful. A giant tube of galvanized steel stands at the side of the road. The elephant leg. It's the pylon which holds up the cable car over the river. Across the water we're opposite Central Lenin Stadium. The middle-distance ether. I breathe in a quintillion oxygen molecules, one of which was there at the 1980 Olympic 800m final. It must have drifted over from the bowl of the stadium and been up and down the Moskva River thousands of times since. Only a slight down-draught on that July evening and it might have been gasped in by Ovett as he kicked out of the box. I get it instead. As it passes through my lungs into my bloodstream it releases a feral surge of energy.

The pace is fast but I'm super-comfortable.

Beep-beep. Yellow Brick Road and Marathon Man look at their fat stopwatches. Garmin? Whatever. Their beeps are the one-kilometre split: the stadium meridian line. I already know this is the one-kilometre split because I measured it two weekends ago, but I don't look at my watch. If this is as fast as it feels I don't want to know. Just race it. Synapses.

The leading three whippets have taken out a great lead on us, easily a hundred metres ahead already. Awesome. One of them has lost ten metres on the front two. At least he was brave. Strain in my breathing. Aerobically I'm entering the furnace. This needs to be happening already. Racing is about hurting early but then controlling the escalation.

I'm super-comfortable with the discomfort.

Marathon Man moves up onto the dirt path. Yellow Brick Road follows behind him in single file. I veer right to get on the train and take a default look back. Clockwork Orange is four metres back looking solid. Propaganda is eight metres behind but still in touch. I was right about him: good but not class.

```
To: Nevis. Intel corroborated by Langley.
White House acknowledging the extent of the
shit show. Pentagon already operational. As
are we. Prime Minister requests situation
report on embedded field assets in R. From:
Gyllyngvase
```

Is this uphill? We seem a couple of metres higher above river level now. Sneaky false flat. We're back on the tarmac again. We only went onto the dirt track to avoid the huge puddle which fills the road at that point. A fat drainage pipe requires hurdling. We then run a stretch of tarmac which is badly pitted. I'm at the stage where it annoys me having to think about different foot-strikes, but my mind also welcomes the distraction from the mounting battle for oxygen. Yellow Brick Road tucks in behind Marathon.

The first pang of distress in my quads. Fucking enjoy it.

Our route is a long crescent around the outside of the river meander. The scenery barely changes. The race is getting grittier as the monotony and pain ratchets up. Trees. Tarmac. Pace. As our angle on the crescent changes a hundredth of a degree each stride, the glass skyscrapers of the Moscow City district get closer and shift left into our eyeline. For a whole kilometre this is the only variation we get. Yellow Brick Road is metronomic. The footsteps behind tell me Clockwork

Orange is close. In 500 metres we'll reach the halfway U-turn – a free look at the opposition. Will there be clues? Another gap opens in the tree line on our right. The walkers way over on the opposite bank can see us as we pass a sign written in five-foot-high white letters, Hollywood style:

'SCHASTYE V PARKYE'. Happiness in the park.

Yes, at this pace. Happy with my form, and delighted that Marathon Man is doing all the work. Two whippets power past us in the opposite direction on the other side of the trees. They're flowing downwind. Our group has 150 metres to the race marshall at the turn. He's clapping the third whippet through. Then he claps and cheers us as we approach. The five of us are in single file:

Marathon Man leads.
Yellow Brick Road – Ovett – Clockwork Orange.
Then Propaganda.

The marshall shouts the halfway split. I check my watch. The shout is spot on. He must have been in radio contact with the starter. It's quick but I can handle it. We accelerate back into our rhythm. The downwind must be worth fifteen seconds. Twenty if you're a track legend. We're now on an esplanade directly alongside the river. The iron railings on our left side are the only thing between us and the blue-brown waves of the Moskva. The black-headed gull reappears, this time lower to the water patrolling for fish. On the other side of the tree line to our right, we see the dribs and drabs of the rest of the field. Ones. Twos. No one else has a pack of any sort. We are five.

Slipstreaming is no longer a factor. We move out from a line into a pack. Yellow Brick Road drops a metre. Propaganda is now on my shoulder. With ten smooth strides Clockwork Orange moves up next to Marathon Man. I'm running close to the railings for the shortest inside line of the meander, and to exploit the gravitational pull of the river.

We overtake an open barge with six cone-shaped piles of earth. We're faster than it, despite it being in the centre of the downstream current and fifty metres inside us on the stagger. The Moskva eventually feeds into the Volga. Those piles of earth could be destined for anywhere from here to Stalingrad. Every inch of this race is being fought over. Bullet by bullet, shell by shell, we're all being reduced to rubble.

```
EYES ONLY:
The Prime Minister and Alec Gyllyngvase

As requested. Our sleeper assets in Moscow.

 Ophelia        Embedded 1997      AMBER
 Winterfold     Embedded 2015      RED3
 Ingot          Embedded 2011      RED1
 Applecross     Recruited 2016     RED3
 Threeman       Embedded 2019      RED3
 Pythagoras     Recruited 1980     AMBER

Further information available but not
advisable. With respect. Tight loops and all
that. From: Nevis
```

Two kilometres to go. Marathon Man fires the next shot. Clockwork Orange goes with the nudge. They gap us by eight metres. I move up to Yellow Brick Road who is breathing much harder now. Noticing this distracts me from the fact that I am too. His arms are less compact than three minutes ago. Chinks. Marathon Man is looking increasingly effective. Time to tag on. Goodbye Yellow Brick Road. Propaganda reads the move and follows with me.

I don't focus specifically on bridging the gap. Stay easy. Just flow and let it happen. It's no bad thing if Marathon Man has started to believe it's a two-horse race. Guess what, mate? There are four horses still in this and one of them is a middle-distance thoroughbred. Have they all sussed yet that I've got the biggest finish? It's not like you can hide it. Even my old grey t-shirt says class. Especially the old grey t-shirt. Too arrogant to need a newer one.

Steve can run the first lap of an 800m in 52 seconds and he's relaxed. A lot of the top 800m runners can run a first lap in 52 but they're not relaxed, and that's the difference. When Steve runs he's very relaxed.

Harry Wilson – coach of Steve Ovett

With 1.5km to go I feel like dropping a bomb and losing Propaganda. Psychologically I can bury him with an effortless surge to get on the other two. Except it will be nasty effort, but he won't know how much. Even if he follows, just seeing – witnessing – my flow tells him he has no chance in the final shake-up. One less to worry about in the big finish. Let's do it. I change up to 1500m mode and *relax* for twenty strides and glide up onto the shoulder of Orange. Propaganda grinds his gears and falters with the pressure. Inevitable. If he backs off and regroups he'll still run a great time. And he can tell his girlfriend he ran with me for most of the race.

Marathon Man – Clockwork Orange – Ovett.

The sunshine transforms the normally dark woods into a patchwork of ochres, russets, and syrup browns. Central Lenin Stadium is just ahead to our left on the opposite bank. The cable car gondolas are now moving left and right about a hundred metres ahead of us. 1km-ish to go. Should I go here just for the bravado? No. Aerobically I'm already well into the red. My lungs feel top heavy in a way that reminds me why 5k is definitely not my distance. Fuck. The blubber is tightening around my waist. Too fat. And ugly. I'll stick to the gameplan. One stride at a time. Just sit on the bastards.

Marathon Man surges. Ovett and Clockwork Orange read it. Not to follow this time would mean certain defeat. It's not punchy enough to create a gap but it ramps up the stakes considerably. We're all gasping for each breath now. These guys have got serious pain thresholds. Respekt. My quads are far less bouncy now. It's getting grimmer with every stride. No enjoyment left anywhere, only the masochistic buzz of keeping up with the pace, of staying in the mix, of knowing this might be on. Central Lenin Stadium. The elephant leg pylon stamps on an ant to our left. A cyclist on a carbon Orbea flies past on our outside. She's hardly pedalling. The downwind favours my superior running form, the majestic Ovett flow.

Marathon Man tries yet again. Of course he fucking does. Not a surge to get rid of us, just a statement increase in speed to hurt everyone regardless of whether he wins, which he now might well do. Clockwork Orange seems comfortable with it. Am I? No. But I'm on it. If

Marathon Man has more gears I'm in big trouble. Has Clockwork got a kick?

Stay smooth. A pleasure cruiser on the Moskva passes us in the opposite direction. It has a glass roof so even the passengers below deck can watch Ovett 2.0 run in the Gorky Park 5k. Am I cruising here? Yes and no. I have one more gear but it's the Big One and only available in the last 200 metres. Until then I'm on the aerobic cliff edge at the mercy of these endurance specialists. Marathon Man probably hasn't laced up a pair of track spikes since he was fifteen.

Nearly there. 500 metres to the metro bridge. 700 to go. No wait. It's 750 including the width of the bridge itself. Maths in pain is hard but my sprint legs can always measure to 200 metres out. Or 220 for a Düsseldorf. If I'm still level with them at the far side of the bridge I've fucking won this. I dig in with every stride to last until then.

600 metres to go.
Clockwork Orange kicks.
The long finish!

Fucking hell. He surges clear. It's daring and stylish and Marathon Man cannot go with it. Clockwork has some impressive leg speed. Horribly, I have no option but to accelerate and get on him. This is high risk. I can no longer hide behind a mask of cool arrogance – I'm eyeballs out here. Back yourself. We're opening up into some serious finishing pace, unleashing the arm drive. It's all over for Marathon Man behind. Ancient history. Fuck off.

The metro bridge. The marshalls and the cones of the finish line are in view. If I unleash the fury this early I won't make it all the way, but I need to kick just to stay on him. His balance at this speed is outstanding. We enter the endgame.

Clockwork Orange – Ovett.

Then all of a sudden he eases off, and instinctively so do I. We float the last 150 stride for stride and finish together, side by side. We've done the hard work. No need to blitz a sprint finish. The penny drops – Clockwork Orange is a middle-distance man too. Neither of us wants to waste a hamstring or an aorta winning a training run in October. The only important victory was us both beating Marathon Man. We finish equal fourth behind the three whippets.

Battered. A few metres beyond the coned finish line I retch twice into the undergrowth by the road. Nothing comes out. Marathon Man finishes fast and ugly fifteen seconds behind. Yellow Brick Road and Propaganda annihilate each other in a photo finish. Impressive guts from both of them. I stretch my hamstrings off. Other runners then the joggers eventually start streaming in. They get resounding claps from the organisers. I drink some tea from my flask then walk-jog along the embankment. Clockwork Orange drinks some water from a bottle, puts the bottle in his bag, and walk-jogs in the same direction. I gesture to cool-down together and we jog chatting about the race. One of the teenage whippets cruises alongside and joins us. His skin is taut around his lean racing frame.

– Did you win it? I ask.

– *Da*, he replies just matter-of-factly. No flicker that it's even a thing. Class.
– *Molodyetz*. Good lad.

Ten minutes of jogging flushes out the calves. I eat a banana, finish my tea, then put on my track bottoms. A good day at the office, as Apollo says. I'll message him my time later.

Endorphins release themselves, whizzing through my post-race psyche. I feel beautifully slow ambling up the steps from the river to the metro. The privilege of middle-distance runners is that between training sessions we can move around like snails. Seb Coe said that. Vorobyovy Gory is in the south-west of Moscow on the red metro line. I live ten miles away in the north-east of town, also on the red line. The distance is nothing on such an efficient metro system. Only twenty-eight minutes. Trains come every two minutes with on-the-dot precision even at weekends. I stand on the platform and wait. A digital clock above the far end of the tunnel shows the time since the last train left. I watch the digits tick up.

1:56
1:57
1:58 – my 800m personal best. Aged 39. Handsome.
1:59

The train arrives and the doors slide open. Vorobyovy Gory metro station has glass sides overlooking the river. I sit on a west-facing seat so I can see Central Lenin Stadium, now in close-up just across the riverbank and over some trees. Four decades have passed since the 1980 Olympic clash between Sebastian Coe and Steve

Ovett, but here in Moscow it feels like only yesterday. The carriage doors close and my train accelerates into the future, hurtling down the tunnel towards the 2022 World Masters Championships.

Comrade Nyet

★

Two weeks later.

EXT. A nature reserve.
Near Pinewood Studios, South Bucks.

Daytime. We see a wooden bench in the partial shade of an oak sapling, overlooking a stream. Seated on the bench are Nevis and Gyllyngvase. Surrounding the bench for the observable distance are wildflowers, long-stemmed grasses swaying, and various colourful insects. Home counties nature at its finest. The sound of birds chirping.

Gyllyngvase is tall and classically handsome, with a cut-glass British accent, an urbane Cary Grant type, a kempt Brad Pitt, a Ryan Gosling [if available] or other Hollywood alpha of similar untouchability.

Nevis is also cut-glass [if anything more so] but his face, build, and general style are more agricultural. An off spinner turned unflappable umpire.

GYLLYNGVASE: [surveying] This is all new.

NEVIS: They've done a good job with the landscaping haven't they.

GYLLYNGVASE: What was it before?

NEVIS: Just ugly farmland with no footpaths. Such a waste. The film studios decided they were going to expand and threw the kitchen sink at a planning application. The chair of the local residents' association is a personal friend, and I floated the idea that it would be rather nice if Pinewood contributed to the local scenery with this little spot -- outstanding natural beauty and so on. They agreed.

GYLLYNGVASE: Idyllic. And right next to your house.

NEVIS: Permissive access to the nature reserve is indeed favourable for adjacent homeowners. It's called working the system. One of my many small hobbies.

GYLLYNGVASE: [smiles] Nice for the birds, anyway.

NEVIS: And the newts -- what brings you here, chum?

The conversation switches to business. Nevis remains calm and emotionless throughout, as if none of the information is new to him. Gyllyngvase has a hint of angst [or perhaps professional pressure?]

GYLLYNGVASE: Yes, it's all getting rather serious. [sighs] We need to act. Confirmation from the top. Prime Minister is insistent. Pentagon on the same page too. All avenues must be pursued for the removal of Plum Tree.

NEVIS: Tricky.

GYLLYNGVASE: Extremely. It's assumed the only likely possibility of effective removal is termination.

NEVIS: A very reasonable assumption.

GYLLYNGVASE: Implications of any official involvement would be severe. Let's face it, chum, this would be catastrophic. Although Langley brains already assess the situation as heading to catastrophe mid- to long-term.

NEVIS: Because NATO won't let him win on the

ground.

GYLLYNGVASE: Weapons technology given to the Ukrainians virtually guarantees he won't. Already a massive cache on its way. More hi-tech hardware than you can shake a stick at. Way more than we can ever admit, although Plum Tree will work it out soon enough. Plan is to let the Russian Army in a bit. Make Plum Tree think they're doing okay. Make them overextend. Then fuck them -- but very slowly.

NEVIS: Until it makes Plum Tree go so bonkers he decides to use the nuclear option to get it done.

GYLLYNGVASE: Yes, unfortunately intel from Langley is strong that he's considering this. A first strike is ready to go from the Americans.

NEVIS: That would need to be conclusive.

The significance of the word hangs in the air. A beat. Then --

GYLLYNGVASE: Apparently planned as such. Can you fucking imagine? They'll do it but clearly they're desperate to prevent this at all costs. As are we, chum. So the Prime Minister asks with greatest urgency to please explore all options available to your... to our assets. If we can remove Plum Tree from the picture then sanity might eventually prevail.

Two dog-walkers pass on a gravel footpath nearby. The topic of conversation is changed while the footsteps crunch into the distance.

GYLLYNGVASE: Is that a chalk stream?

NEVIS: It is. Clear as gin. The sticklebacks love it. If we sit here long enough we'll see a kingfisher dive in for lunch. The swallows prefer the dragonfly -- and mind your feet, we're in the protected amphibian corridor.

GYLLYNGVASE: Any mammals?

NEVIS: Us. And water voles but they're shy. Occasionally a fox, although they're not specifically catered for. And look up there. Nesting boxes for the bats.

Steven Michael James Ovett was born on October 9, 1955, eleven months before the arrival of Sebastian Newbold Coe. In his teens Ovett from Brighton matured early and became a freakish junior athlete. An absolute specimen on the Sussex County scene. He dominated at the 400m, middle-distance, cross-country, and broke local long jump records. Meanwhile Sebastian Coe, a southerner based in Sheffield, was a later developer but his trajectory was being masterminded by a supremely patient coach – Peter Coe, his father. Nobody knew at the time but even in youth the two fates were converging.

The young Steven Ovett dominated his peers clocking up umpteen age-group victories, exuding Olympic promise with every swashbuckling performance. Everyone on the circuit knew how good he was, including the Great Britain selectors who were eager to blood him in international competition as soon as possible. Steve was aggressive, stylish, and strong, with natural speed. A fearless racer. Ovett loved running and loved winning.

Coe's early steps to the Olympics were quieter, under the radar, but projected year-on-year to each decimal place in Peter Coe's forensically prepared training programme. Sebastian Coe barely featured in any UK rankings until he was eighteen but was hitting every performance progression the coach set. Peter knew he had a world-beater. Seb was lightly built but beautifully balanced, aggressive, with natural speed. A fearless front-runner. Coe loved running and hated losing.

Nevis points. Gyllyngvase looks up at three wooden bat boxes in a mature sycamore. The walkers have passed. Business can continue.

GYLLYNGVASE: Any of your chaps got anything on whether he's ill. And if so, how long he's got?

NEVIS: Rude health, alas. Occasional Paracetamol. And Viagra we're told -- not a crime in itself, one hopes.

GYLLYNGVASE: Any number two if we did get him?

NEVIS: We don't think so. Nature of the beast, chum. Hard to say if this is good or bad. Better the devil you know? Not sure this applies if the invasion happens. Successor would probably all depend on timing. If there's a window for any of our chaps to do something, unlikely we would have the luxury of variable timing. But someone will inherit the red button. If we kill Plum Tree it will trigger a response. Probably Berlin or London. You know that.

GYLLYNGVASE: Both are under threat anyway if he goes nuclear first. The most dangerous option is to do nothing, so the Prime Minister suggests balance of risk should not a factor in planning. However, he says any 'clean' options would be of maximum interest. Assisting a Russian national to carry out the deed is considered highly desirable. At all viable?

NEVIS: It would be the cleanest of the unclean. Viable? Yes and no. Splinter factions do undoubtedly exist but they're almost certainly infiltrated by the FSB. Very likely if we want it done we'll have to pull the trigger ourselves.

GYLLYNGVASE: Are any of those six assets in Moscow a situational match for involvement?

NEVIS: They all are. It's not a wholly new contingency. Agents are briefed on this topic from time to time. Ideas may already exist. But the overall chances of success are low to very low. As you can imagine, manoeuvrability and communication in the field will soon be extremely limited.

GYLLYNGVASE: And access to the target is all but zero.

NEVIS: The likelihood of escape and extraction are also slim. Best to manage the PM's expectations -- but nevertheless, as you say, the option must be pursued. We will get on the case. Operation Plum. I like it. Hopefully we can get him leg before wicket.

GYLLYNGVASE: Communicate the order to the assets immediately. How soon is as soon as possible?

NEVIS: I took the liberty of anticipating the plan. With respect. Signals are on their way to all assets as we speak.

Preobrazhenskaya. On long runs I wear my retro Adidas track top because I need zipped pockets for my key, phone, passport, and metro card. It has a high collar in case it's cold, but my weather app says twelve degrees, so I can wear lite track trousers. My socks have thick woven undersoles to add extra cushion to my Mizuno flats. All set.

The elevator clunks down from my eighth-floor apartment. As the lift doors open, the rat who lives under the stairs is standing sentry on the bottom step. He sees me and scurries into his hidey hole. I drop a cube of cheese for his breakfast as I leave. It's eight o'clock. The sun is up and already warming the air. I turn left out of my building and run south-west into town along Bolshaya Cherkizovskaya. Starting slowly. Barely a jog.

Preobrazhenskaya Ploschad is a crossroads of three-lane roads plus tram lanes. As usual my feet are stiff and painful first thing. The steps of the underpass help as early variation in foot-strike. I spring two steps at a time back up to street level at the new business high-rise Preo-8, then continue past my local Starbucks, the Tajikistan restaurant, Burger King, and Sberbank. I feel a lightness around my shoulders today. 74.8kg on the scales this morning. Not race weight but not disastrous for October. The steep downhill to the river helps my rhythm.

Matrossky Bridge crosses the Yauza. With high walled sides the Yauza looks like a canal here. Four miles downstream it flows majestically into the Moskva. If I had a speedboat with enough fuel, I'd be strolling into Kazino Emperyal in Baku within seven days. I admire your luck, Mister? Ovett... Steve Ovett. In fact, it would take way more than seven days. Epic meanders on the Volga. Zebra crossing. Look left. Pavement step. Spring up. Looser feet now.

Up from the bridge I jog past a fat man in flips flops. He's gambling on the early morning sun. His pot belly is sticking out of a grey tank vest which matches his grey gym shorts and grey socks. He's walking a grey pitbull. The dog has an affectionate go for my ankles. I swerve with a balletic hip sway and a one-two quickstep, then launch back into my full stride. The move clicks me nicely into a higher gear. Both sides of the road here are lined with Khrushchev-era eight-storey apartment blocks like mine. All identical in plain beige brick. No frills, apart from the security rat guarding the hallway. Nine minutes. The Brothers Znamensky Olympisky Centre and then the Old Fire Tower. Sokolniki.

This is the first time I've run into the centre of Moscow. Been living here two years – two happy years. I'm following the route of the red metro line. Today is only about mileage. Easy pace. Bouncing along. Strengthen the tendons. Heart rate elevated but nothing crazy.

At Krasnoselskaya there are billboards promoting political candidates for upcoming elections. I rarely follow the Russian news. Too busy running, and not interested in the one-eyed government angle which pervades all media. Not sure how I feel about these billboards. They do represent different political parties. I guess the reason the sham is so clever is because a nominal sub-stratum of politicians have actually been elected. With the fallback that it can be rigged if need be. Or unwanteds removed. Shot: Nemtsov. Or imprisoned: Navalny. I don't dwell on it. I'm only a runner. Twenty minutes. Komsomolskaya.

An incline. At the top is one of the seven sister skyscrapers: the symmetrical tapers of the Red Gate Building. It's not as tall as *MGU* but covers the same theme of Stalinist vertigo. These days it's all posh flats but in the USSR days it was government ministries: grey-suited apparatchiks, pencils and ledgers on their desks, filing cabinets containing Five-Year Plans, a well-thumbed copy of Marx strategically in view, preferably leaning against a small bust of Lenin. Idealism. Dutiful Soviets. Constantly looking over their shoulder. To purge or to be purged? The aura is chilling even on a warm Sunday morning.

Krasnye Vorota. An underpass. Smaller backstreets. The Le Corbusier statue. Thirty minutes in. Chistye Prudy metro.

In the coffee bars on Myasnitskaya customers sip lattes at window seats. A karaoke bar is turfing out revellers. They're not rowdy but they won't be running 10k today. Starlite Diner is already dishing up eggs and hash browns American style. Several of the bars on this street are open 24-hours. Moscow never sleeps.

Lubyanka. I'm now in the eye of central Moscow turning right to pass Lubyanka itself: the KGB headquarters. The FSB nowadays. Different letters. Same protocol. The grandfather of one of my loveliest students is a famous KGB operative: a jovial anglophile who writes spy novels. Moscow has nothing if not duality. Lubyanka is a thuggish stone lump which dominates its square on the northern side. Eight floors but it feels much bigger. The blood-curdling screams from history cannot escape its walls. The first two floors are built with monstrous granite blocks each bigger than a man – any man, no one was safe. The stone is natural grey darkened with a grubby layer of post-communist soot. Like Putin himself. The upper floors are painted eggnog yellow with pastel rhubarb for the baroque flair around each window. A heavyweight boxer in lipstick. The top floor has no windows. Depending which history book you read, this floor is where the prison of the secret police used to be. Now converted into an espionage museum, so they say. Lubyanka fascinates me. Especially the bad shit. But only the old bad shit.

On the corner of Lubyanka I take the underpass to the top end of Nikolskaya, my pedestrianised home straight. This is the tourist zone, so I favour the shaded side of the street for a clearer run. After forty-six minutes I arrive in the wide-open splendour where the sunshine glints off every magical cobblestone.

Krasny Ploschad. Red Square.

Just over nine kilometres distance in the legs. After some hamstring stretches up against a concrete bollard, I decide to time myself on a perimeter lap of Red Square. I speculate on what the course record is and wonder if the two politzia standing on the corner of *GUM* department store will approve of an attempt to shatter it? The pink Kazan Cathedral behind me is chiming out bongs for the Orthodox Sabbath. I reset my phone's running app and line my toe up with the edge of the stone kerb, crouching into start position with my finger poised on the stopwatch. A race for the ages this one. *Chariots of Fire* with a Gazprom flame. GO!

Tremendous roar from the crowd as they go on their way.

The first twenty metres is cobblestones and annoying tourists milling around in the way. This corner of the square is always the busiest; nearest to the metro, to the entrances of *GUM*, and to the Nikolskaya cafés. I dodge the people and spring up onto the flat paving on the short north side, running within touching distance of the National State Museum. This was founded in 1872 to promote Russian self-awareness and history. The ornate brickwork is painted the colour of dried blood.

Red Square is not a square. This short side of the rectangle is only seventy metres. Back down on the cobbles, my first left turn is beneath the Nikolskaya Tower, soaring into the sky with a five-pointed star on its spire twinkling ruby red for luck. I make a wish. Viable? Two more politzia in black uniforms and Kevlar bodywarmers are walking up from the gardens of Aleksandrovsky Sad. They're tooled up to the nines. I drop my pace to look less like a dangerous fugitive.

The Eastern Kremlin Wall stretches the entire length of the back straight. The wall is dark pastel red, the exact red of an outdoor running track. From the cobbles, long rows of stone plinths rise up towards the wall; terracing for dignitaries during military parades. The front row plinth is tight to the track just like at the Bislett Stadium, Oslo. At the base of the Kremlin Wall a line of firs marks the medieval necropolis beneath. These trees always seem deliberately undersized to accentuate the grandeur of the Kremlin. It works.

At the mid-point of the back straight is a step-pyramid in shiny brown quartzite. Lenin's Mausoleum. Built on a layer of sand to protect it from the vibrations of tanks parading past and – later – parading nuclear missiles. Here lies the founding father of Red Russia. Lenin was probably an outstanding 800m runner in his youth. Opportunism: if there wasn't a gap, he made a gap. The cubism of the mausoleum is incongruous among the medieval towers and churches. Maybe why it exudes such obscene levels of gravitas, and yes cruelty. The two politzia guarding Lenin are talking to each other and don't notice me run past. I'm an invisible man, a vapour, just a harmless nobody, Comrade Nyet on his world record mission. This back straight must be at least 300 metres long. Brutal. My ankles and calves are battling the vindictive cobbles, but each time they flex into yet another beautiful all-conquering stride. Weapons of world destruction rumble over these stones every Victory Day on May 9. Today it's my Mizuno Wave Sky 3s.

I drive on. World record pace is a knife-edge.

Steve Ovett ran most of his record attempts behind the metronomic pacemaking of Bob Benn of Croydon Harriers. Benn was a guru of even lap times and staunchly faithful to his mate Ovett; always happy to sacrifice his own race for the privilege of leading out the Big O. The mere presence of Benn and Ovett on the same start-sheet suggested a fast one. I tuck in behind the imaginary Benn who today is also a guru of uneven cobbled surfaces.

Slightly uphill for eighty more metres. The cemetery of

honour for Soviet heroes has a row of busts and headstones at the foot of the Kremlin wall. I take an ice-cool tactical glance over my right shoulder. From the cemetery a familiar granite face sneers back at me. The bushy moustache. That badger of hair. *Those* demonic eyes. Stalin! I drive my quads to the crown of the hill. Absolute power.

Beneath the clock of the Spasskaya Tower I turn left. There's no course marker on the ground to say so, but this is the halfway mark. I speed up as the ground falls away downhill to St Basil's Cathedral. The iron gate of the church garden marks the apex of the top bend. The nine asymmetric towers of St Basil's each have a spectacular onion dome on top. Each dome is decorated in a different two-tone motif. Postcard from Moscow. The motifs are the same colour combinations used for cross-country spikes. Apart from the blue-and-white dome which feels more like an 800m spike.

CATHEDRAL GUIDEBOOK [excerpt p.2]

The famous onion domes of St Basil's Cathedral are constructed around a hollow internal frame with a thick wood exterior, apart from the dome of St Martyrs Cyprian and Justinian which has a thinner ceramic surface [painted tsarist blue and white].

The top bend is a sharp turn back up the hill. After crossing the exit road at Ulitsa Ilinka I can finally get off the cobbles and onto the flush paving of the *GUM* promenade. On the flat surface my neo-effortless flow returns. Bob Benn peels away into the middle-distance ether. Another outstanding display of pacemaking from the Croydon man.

The lonely run now against the unforgiving finger of the watch.

More police. It dawns on me that all the pairs of politzia in Red Square have been male-female combinations. The new paradigm of Soft Power? Attract. Seduct. Co-opt. I'm not convinced. The list of political opponents exiled, or in prison, or dead would suggest that soft is the new hard. As a mere guest I don't pass judgement, but there do seem dark rumblings down in the south-west of the country. And beyond. One of my IELTS students is from Donetsk.

I get no disapproving stares or politiza whistles to stop me running. I even get an admiring look of co-opt from the blondinka on patrol outside *GUM*. It's unfair that she'll think this is my actual race pace. I ran 9.2km to get here as well, Olga. If that's your name? In your ribbed Kevlar. You minx.

Ovett drives on – a really majestic full stride still.

Only 200 metres to go. Along *GUM* department store I tick off the distance shop by shop; a succession of posh displays for luxury Western brands. From the Cartier window a diamond-encrusted wristwatch twinkles hello. According to my Casio F-91W (£12.99 from Argos) I'm inside the record beyond doubt. *GUM* lines the entire length of my home straight. Every metre is excruciating effort. Dior. Armani. Louis Vuitton. More proof, if any were needed, of the Marxist-Leninist failure. In a truly utopian society these boutiques would be Brooks, New Balance, and Ron Hill.

All guns blazing now. Each stride takes me closer to the record books. The finishing line is the Kazan Cathedral at the end of the *GUM* promenade. With a desperate kick in the last ten strides, I finally breast the finishing tape, just before an appropriate Kazan bong. I stop my watch. Phew! Insane cobbles, and not just each stone; the whole surface of the square undulates on a stride-by-stride basis. I drop my hands to my knees and gasp. Solo time trials are always the worst. I check my phone GPS app...

Red Square measures exactly 800 metres.
3:14.44 – *the world record has gone!*

Until an accredited statistician proves otherwise, I'm taking it. The happily married politzia couple, with their his-and-hers taser belts, see me out of breath and looking at my watch. They seem unfazed by me enjoying Red Square for middle-distance training. The medieval architects obviously had elite athletics in mind when constructing the 800-metre layout. Another good day at the office – or – pie and chips! Another of Apollo's end-of-session sayings.

I do miss the gang back home. Hey ho.

Amazing sunshine as I walk through Resurrection Gate and down past the Zhukov statue. The hero of Stalingrad looks different today. They recently replaced the old statue with a new one of him astride a more impressive-looking horse: more equine power. I stretch my glutes against a wall overlooking the lawns and flowerbeds of Aleksandrovsky Sad. Even with a torso of evaporating sweat I'm not cold.

Seb Coe still holds the world record for 800 metres on a cinder track. 1:44.98 at Loughborough in 1981. Now only forty years later I hold the official IAAF world record for a cobblestone track.

And Steve Ovett gives Sebastian Coe his answer.

Winterfold

★

Park Olympisky Derevny. The site of the Olympic Village for the 1980 Games is three stops south on the red line from Central Lenin Stadium. A jog from Yugo-Zapadnaya metro. Today it's all flats. Sixteen-storey apartment blocks arranged around courtyards along a central boulevard. Nine blocks lining the left side of the boulevard and nine blocks lining the right. The athletes on the undercard of Moscow 1980 were as equally split down the middle about who was going to win The Clash of the Titans. There were two sides to the same street and you either lived on one side or the other. Bolshaya Ovettskaya. Or Prospekt Coe.

PRIVATE DIARY - A.C. NEVIS [unpublished]

Entry from 23rd October 2021

<u>Who?</u> Ophelia. Winterfold. Ingot. Applecross. Threeman. Pythagoras.

<u>How?</u> Access to Plum all but zero. Only possible option in all this mess is Winterfold. Nobody else stands a chance. The future of everything is in your dark world - it has to be you, Winterfold.

Note to self: acknowledge the pressure you're feeling. Must relax and vary perspectives. Hobbies more important than ever.

Approaching completion of HMS Dauntless. 1:150 scale and she's a beauty. Today sandpapered the balsa and painted the hull in fire retardant. Sea Viper missiles to be simulated with toy fireworks. Will scare the ducks shitless if they fly off [chuckle]. Next steps: paint exterior of hull in dazzle camouflage and complete topside shell.

```
Delivery of motor and remote console due
next week. Can house motor as on HMS
Venturer.

Must write to MoD friend to thank him for
the design spec. Invaluable. Exciting to add
a Type-45 to my fleet. Destroyer class. The
bigger picture.

Gyllyngvase is up to it with his secretary.
Fucking careless.
```

Next to the Olympic village an urban park was created for the athletes to relax in. Or train in. I already have a decent sweat on as I trot through the park gates. Everything about the landscaping says elite training venue. A thin lake with a tarmac path (measuring 2.5km) curves around a valley. Paths of various gradients criss-cross the slopes. Three humpback footbridges pinch into the lake for runners to reach their next incline. As I cross one of the bridges a dog-walker the size of Geoff Capes launches a pink ball for his Jack Russell to chase. The ball bounces in front of me with the dog racing after it at top speed. His claws go clickety-click over the tarmac like four-mill spikes on a competition-grade Mondo.

The vibe of international athletics is everywhere. The Olympic rings feature in the iron detail of the bridges, and the metal railings are configured with the Moscow 1980 logo. There's even a sitting duck – Dave Warren superbly bold – happily sunning itself on a wooden platform in the lake. In the hot Olympic summer this was where the athletes came to jog off their races, to run out the adrenaline. The Ovett ether is potent. I smash twelve reps from the humpback bridge up to the bike hire hut. Forty-seven seconds each. On my toes. Driving.

Aggressive. Majestic.

The Clash of the Titans story started four years earlier at the Montreal Olympics in 1976. Sebastian Coe didn't get selected. Steve Ovett did.

Despite being only twenty, it was not even Ovett's first major championships. At eighteen he had silvered in the 800m at the 1974 Europeans in Rome. The Great Britain selectors had no doubts thrusting this sublime talent onto the biggest stage of all, and in both middle-distance events. In 1976, of the two future titans only Ovett got the benefit of learning, through bad luck and through bad mistakes, what the Olympic Games were all about:

pressure – back-to-back days of races – qualifying heats – tactical instinct – danger – semi-finals – the ferocity and desperation of every runner – focus – the ability to de-focus and de-pressurise – sleep – dealing with insomnia – coping with boredom in the Village – not over-eating in the canteen – not watching races or other sports – tapering for freshness – but keeping your legs ticking over with a familiar volume of running – abnormal spikes of performance arousal – crazy endorphins – every high followed by a low – the quest for mental equilibrium – the ability to walk out for the final in peak emotional condition – expectation – ignoring pressure – embracing pressure – the long call-room wait – seeing other people's pressure – entering the arena – rows of spectators rising up to the heavens – the horrible hushed buzz of excitement everywhere – millions of eyes on you – nerves – rivals – doubt – pressure – fear…

You can't learn it from a textbook or from one-off race meets in Oslo or Zurich. Steve Ovett felt it all and absorbed it all in Montreal 1976, and did so without any external expectation to win, without a deadly arch rival, and without the biggest media frenzy in track and field history following him around everywhere he went. Seb Coe in his first Olympics four years later would face a steeper learning curve.

The 1976 Olympic 800 metres was won by Cuban sensation Alberto Juantorena. For the final Steve Ovett drew lane eight, a considerably worse draw than usual. The IAAF was trialling the 800m event off a two-bend staggered start – a daft system which massively favoured the inside lanes and front-runners. Out in lane eight Ovett had to run blind for 300 metres and guessed wrongly at the pace. As they broke from lanes in the home straight he was well behind the leaders. Trying to recover ground too quickly he lost his usual sting for the second lap. Lesson #1: smooth calculated speed.

Juantorena led for the whole race, apart from just after the bell when Sriram Singh asked the ultimate question. Singh would fade from medal contention but ran an Indian national record which lasted forty-two years. Juantorena, resplendent in his all-white Cuban vest, white split-shorts, and knee-length basketball socks, retook the lead with 300 metres to go. With his long strides he stretched his rivals to the limit down the back straight. Rick Wohlhuter of the USA held on and pressurised with a superb attack off the last bend. But Juantorena opened his legs and showed his class, powering away to a stunning victory. With a strong finish Ivo Van Damme of Belgium passed Wohlhuter to win silver in his first Olympic Games. Ovett rallied down the straight to finish a creditable fifth, just behind West Germany's Willi Wülbeck. Despite the occasion and a good finishing time

Ovett walked away with mixed feelings:

Going down the last back straight all I remember was feeling miserable. I was dying from that far out! But you just keep trying so I came out of the last bend, pushing as hard as I could, pumping my arms to keep loose. I ran a personal best (1:45.4) but it was probably one of my least satisfying races.

By contrast it was an awesome and brilliantly judged performance from Juantorena. He represented a new species of 800m runner. Six-foot-three with a racehorse physique. Codename: *El Caballo.* Juantorena loved to run from the front, and with such a raking stride length he was not only quick but exceptionally difficult to run closely behind. In a rare double Juantorena also won the 400m in Montreal. With his power and aggressive pace distribution he took the 800m into new territory; having a super-fast split in your locker was now essential to compete. Yes, the two-bend staggered start (only ever used at the 1976 Games) did favour his front-running style, preventing anyone slipstreaming him on the first lap, but you couldn't argue with his time in the final. A new world record.

Juantorena confirmed his superstar status the following year by lowering the world record once again. He also won a magnificent 800m shoot-out (off a one-bend staggered start) against Kenyan rival Mike Boit in the 1977 IAAF World Cup. Significant because the well-fancied Boit had missed the Olympics due to a Kenyan boycott. The 1977 season rubber-stamped Juantorena as the undisputed two-lap king. But Moscow was a long way off for El Caballo and hamstring issues were beginning to affect his training. In two incredible seasons he had raised the standard and profile of the 800m event, but alas Juantorena was not to be a factor in the next Olympics. By 1980 he was twenty-nine and opted to only run the 400m in Moscow.

Van Damme (22) along with Wülbeck (21) and Ovett (20) were the athletes with youth on their side and energy to burn. They were the protagonists set to define the next era of 800m running. They each returned from the Montreal Games with priceless experience to set up long and illustrious careers. Ivo Van Damme also had two Olympic medals in his kitbag: silver in the 800m and an equally impressive silver in the 1500m.

After my inclines I can feel my right hip. Time to stop. Less is more at M45. Especially if you've just turned forty-seven. Great session but I think I'll walk to the metro now. In the south-western corner of the park is a white church with three golden onion domes. It's playing religious music on hidden speakers attached somewhere to the outside walls. In the church garden there's a tall, bearded cleric dressed in black robes pruning a rose bush between some graves. As I walk up the steps out of the park a cold seam of air whips up off the lake. In December 1976 Ivo Van Damme was killed in a car accident at just twenty-two. Belgium mourned. The sport mourned. A truly generational talent lost. One lane in the 800m qualifying heats in Moscow would now be tragically empty.

Who wants to live forever? Run as fast as you can.

Fifty Years Of October

★

Prospekt Vernadskovo. The metro exit comes out through a shopping centre with a Burger King on the left and a 24-hour McDonald's on the right. My nostrils flair at the meaty tang of hamburgers as I take the small flight of steps down into the park. I could demolish a Big Mac right now, or even a rare Whopper-Big Mac double, but there is business to take care of. The 50-Years-Of-October Park 5k.

Runners are gathering inside the park on a promontory of wooden decking. About twenty people so far, all in fast-wicking tops, skin-tight leggings, and bright running shoes; some almost as bright as mine. The promontory is set on the edge of a slope and has a toboggan run built off the side of the decking. An adjacent path up the same slope is the home straight for our two-lap course. Hilly!

```
To: Station R. Threeman will be at the
designated signal point at the agreed time.
Wear strictly the running gear stipulated.
He knows the drop, nothing extra required.
Exercise extreme caution. From: Nevis
```

I leave my rucksack on a bench. My warm-up jog takes me to a covert path. I prefer to do my track drills in professional privacy. No point signposting that I might be the dangerman. Today I also do some lateral steps with a resistance loop around my ankles. Stability work for that hip from Thursday. Only a niggle. Everyone in the M45 category will have similar.

In the summer I did this 50-Years-Of-October parkrun. I also walked it to measure it and verify the five kilometres – it's fifty metres over distance. The route is two identical laps on the tarmac park paths, which are shared with dog-walkers and cyclists. I take off my tracksuit.

Race kit: turquoise Saucony racing flats, navy split-shorts, and a matching navy New Balance tee. In one-colour navy I don't look as 'leggy' when I tuck my t-shirt into my shorts. It's not an issue for track races where it's normal to tuck in and where long quads are an important intimidation factor. But here in civilian Moskva life there are attractive Russian females who are generally not drawn to balding stick insects, even ones with a huge finish. Alas my variant of handsome plays to a somewhat niche audience.

5k is an awkward distance for a pure 800m runner. I don't have the range of a Saïd Aouita or a Hicham El Guerrouj. Today I could lose to a significantly inferior runner who happens to specialise in longer road stuff. He'll never know I can destroy him on the track because he never runs a track race. I'll have to work super-hard here just to maintain the hierarchy. I'm not feeling the usual arrogance. Training volume has accumulated in the legs now. Hills aren't my strength. How did that happen on the scales this morning? Those fucking KitKats.

On the start line I take a shadowy position one row back from the main contenders. They all seem to know each other. A clique of banter. I spy three or four impressive physiques but no one crazy young. There might just be something in this for me. The organiser lines the front row up with the cones.

Vnymanye. GO!

The guy who takes it out is in *Spider-Man* arm-warmers.

Get on him. Not too close – there's no wind. Tucking in three metres behind him, I immediately start to siphon off his early rhythm into my own legs for free speed. He's tall with a long torso which means he'll have a big engine. Seems talented: cadence and aggression. His black running vest frames strong shoulders. Wide hips in baggy black trail shorts with three zips. Black calf-guards. Asics flats of only moderate brightness. He's all in black apart from *those* arm-warmers. In his slipstream I'm only seeing the back of his head. Can't judge his race face. But I clocked him at the start line. Late thirties – maybe only mid. Was that his glamorous wife he was talking to by the benches earlier? Probably just his sister.

We pass through the park's central hub, a roundabout where several of the paths come together like spokes on a bicycle wheel, or like a spider's web. In the centre of the roundabout there are four metal artworks of giant hands. The middle two hands are a red and a blue but are only outlines of hands, so that people can walk – or run? – through the palms… but no, we swing out between two orange marker cones to the right of the island of hands. I follow Spider-Man as he exits the roundabout onto a weaving downhill path. Fast this.

On the twisting bends Spider-Man demonstrates his well-balanced running form. With his barrel torso and bustling style, he's an arachnified John Walker. Such a shame he's ruined his 'New Zealand' kit with effete calf guards and the embarrassing arm-warmers. We're still descending. Downhill favours my 800m turnover. Each stride I get a flash of Saucony turquoise, the half-seen swoop of a kingfisher, which reminds me what a sensational runner I am.

Spider-Man isn't *fast* fast. But this is tasty for a 5k.

We've run one kilometre. Lots of turns. Awkward and gamey – a mini grand prix circuit through the birch trees. There's a definite racing line if you know the direction of the next turn. I remember some from my previous run here. Spider-Man knows them all. He skirts the apex of each bend perfectly. Feels like we're absolutely smashing it. The scenery of the park streaks past in subliminal items. Pond. Bronze memorial to the Great Patriotic War (WW2). Outdoor ping pong table. Row of poplars. The basketball courts. Dog-walker with an extendable lead. Dog.

Spider-Man is unrelenting. I wonder how far behind third is? Don't look. Eyes ahead and drive. Stay on this fucker. The mid-section of the loop is flatter. One tree-lined straight runs directly towards the *MGU* skyscraper only a mile away. The 1980 Olympic logo right there in stone. Daring anyone to ask the ultimate question. Discipline. Just sit. At this pace all I'm capable of is sitting.

Breathe. We must be at the lowest point of the loop. Race dynamics? I'm worse uphill. With his size he must be too. Surely? Except the gradient starts up low and even. He can still churn out the same pace – or almost. He isn't gunning it quite as hard. I survive bend to bend and somehow cling on when he nails it on a punishing 500-metre straight through some lindens. Dig deep! Finally, the turns come again and take the edge off his flow. I'm on him but in trouble.

Struggling to maintain rhythm.
Struggling aerobically.

Struggling for… *class.*

The ascent winds up the grassy park slopes through a corridor of trees. The Formula 1 circuit transforms into a Pyrenean cycle climb, the Col de Peyresourde scaled down for a 5k running contest. Cruel gradient. Each percent I feel in my quads. His eight spider-quads are eating up the ground. One turn is a right angle. I drive through the apex and out into the straight. The next turn is almost a hairpin. Shorter steps in. Increasing stride-length for the majestic drive out. That hurts.

I'm way too deep, way too early.
Fuck him – he might crack too.

We pass a lake on our left. The final slope of the first lap looms ahead. Gradient? For the next two hundred metres it's nine percent. Then for the last fifty metres it kicks up to about fifteen percent – or more. It's so steep there's a flight of steps to the side for walkers. There are two black-and-yellow rumble strips across our path to slow down descending cyclists. The first strip messes up my foot-strike. I slam into the bump and lose all push off. Ffff! I sort my stride pattern out for the second strip and power off its leading edge. The climb is hideous. It rips the guts out of my stay-strong mentality. Hamburgers from the shopping centre offer a macabre stench to the agony. I take two nasal inhales of beef as we roll over the top. The zing might help. We're side by side as we approach the start-finish line. Halfway.

Spider-Man gets cheers: *Davay Dima, Davay!*
Nothing for the Big O – so it's like that is it?

No one-lap-to-go bell either, but there's no need to

startle the race into action. This is already a bleak war of attrition. On the flat path the burn from the climb gradually eases. My legs are still there, just, but a wrecking ball has smashed into my aerobic. I check my split. I'm massively up. On *this* course?! Fuck.

Behind us I hear the organisers roar on third place through halfway. About eighty metres back? Need to focus. This is all about concentration. Got to work here to earn that majestic rhythm. On pure technique I dominate the next two hundred metres of path. A satisfying riposte to the partisan organisers. The giant hands are approaching. On the first lap they were a mere curio, an easy landmark of four hundred metres gone. Now they seem grotesquely symbolic. Hands up who's hurting? Me. We take the coned route to the side of the roundabout. It irritates me again that we should be running *through* the hands. Which colour hand would Spider-Man have run through, red or blue? His shit costume is both.

Into the weaving descent. Two hooded crows pick at a morsel of carrion in the middle of the path. Our foot-strikes don't even distract them from the carcass. Both birds are wearing the same grey-and-black uniform of the Waffen SS. Heavy trench coats and beaks. They work over the flesh. At 5k pace it's impossible to identify their victim. Maybe an unfortunate frog who never made it between ponds. Or a recently murdered mouse.

Dare I look back to see who's in third? No. Never show your weakness. Spider-Man keeps the pace high. Am I chipping away at his bulletproof psychology? Two kilometres to go. I have a kick finish. He doesn't. He needs to get rid of me and he knows it. Lo and behold, he puts in a massive surge. Fucking aargh!

Five metres. Stay cool. I back off to maintain my form. Technique! It might be a bluff. He has ten metres. Twelve. Shit. He's backing up his move. I'm so hot the sweat is pouring off my head and through my eyes. Why the fuck does he even need those arm-warmers? Only to get inside my head. To lure me into his spidery web, then present my carcass on a plate to the dude gaining on me in third place.

Spider-Man is twenty-five metres up. On the *MGU* skyscraper straight I cave in and let him go to protect second place. Now then... Who's the fucker in third? This is going to be a major effort to regroup. Third has all the momentum. I have an apocalyptic differential on my split, damage I will inevitably pay for. Drive the legs. Strategically I veer wide on the next bend, so that without turning my head my body will be angled for a sly glance back to check out third. A quick one. Eyes only.

Damn! He clocked me. He knows it's on.

He's fifty metres back. Maybe only forty-five. In black leggings and a grey long-sleeved top. One of Spider-Man's mates from the start line. Late thirties. Hybrid beard slash wrap-around sideburns. Wolverine! Thin as a rake with a loping style but a good clippy cadence. A little bit of Thomas Wessinghage about him. I power out of the next bend to demonstrate my class. Glorious high knees and relaxed arms. Classic Ovett.

It might just psyche Wolverine out seeing it.
Seeing… *him.*

We hit the uphill half of the loop. The last quarter of pain. I need to make Wolverine work for every one of those forty metres. The linden tree straight which I didn't like on the first lap, I like even less now. It couldn't come at a worse moment in my race. The perfect place to reel someone in – or be reeled in. I can see Spider-Man eighty metres ahead now but behind me is the problem. Wolverine's footsteps have been within earshot for some time. Now I have to listen to them. On this gradient with 3.5km run, I can feel the heavy corset of flab around my waist, plus two thick slabs of meat lain across my shoulders. And my fucking tits jiggling about. You fat shit! This is weight I now have to drag uphill. The flab tightens around my stomach bringing me ever closer to being sick. Aerobically I'm fucked. Any attempt at arm drive to generate speed goes immediately to my lungs.

Relax but drive. The middle-distance paradox.

Wolverine must be hurting too. Do I back off and tag onto him? Switch the pressure. No! Banish that thought. The distance ahead is my biggest weapon. An Ovett surge right now would bury Wolfie. A few seconds imagining the audacity of the move keeps me pushing to the next bend. Into the Col de Peyresourde again. One kilometre to go. The straights are now shorter. Advantage me. Shorter sections to keep him gapped. More bends means he sees my awesome profile more. Psyche the fucker out.

He works the short sections better than I do. Annoying.

Up ahead Spider-Man hasn't extended his gap by much after all; a hundred metres at most. For the rematch that could be important. Maybe he was bluffing after all. The thought of crushing Spider-Man in the blockbuster sequel gives me a ten-second energy boost in my current skirmish with Wolverine.

Quads! Except it's all so fucking aerobic. I heave for oxygen. None. I drive through the emptiness. Whoever thought such a barren planet could sustain human life? Wolverine is close enough for a strike. He can smell blood: Type O. Imagine the glee with which he'll tell the story of his race to Spider-Man.

– When did you break him?
– At the *MGU* straight. You?
– Just reeled him in all second lap. Piece of piss.

Horrible. The path delivers us up to the lake. Nearly home. The lake is 200 metres long, to be followed by the killer slope, to be followed by a flat fifty-metre curve to the finish line. Within touching distance. Wolverine surges up alongside me. Shit.

Great tactics. Knows I would annihilate him in a pure sprint. Has to work me over before the finish. Used the lake to target me, didn't he. He gets to me right at the far bank. Do I kick immediately to break him? If it was flat I would, but the fifteen percent uphill bit is yet to come. We pass a green crash mat barrier at the end of the toboggan run, then we start the murderous final slope. Hamburger Hill. Bullets rain down on us from the top of the ridge. I'm taking direct hits. Scorched flesh and lactic ketchup everywhere. Do I know where and when to work the slope? Wolverine must surely know it better. I'll wait for his move. We're side by side as we hit the fifteen percent.

Wolverine – Ovett.
He kicks off the leading edge of the first rumble strip.
I *knew* he fucking would!

I respond. But it's not my usual leg speed kick. Just some kind of a workhorse endurance kick. All disappointment. With each uphill stride an inferno engulfs my quads. Driving up the stairwell of the burning building in fireman's coat and boots, heavy hose over my shoulder, gas tank empty on my back, with pick-axe ready to crash through the rooftop door for oxygen. Calling up every last reserve of flexion from my ankles, feet, even toes, but it's no good. I need spikes. And a tartan track to grip into and explode off each stride. With panache! Here on the tarmac at fifteen percent gradient, it's all too… it's all too fucking grindy.

Wolverine does me.
Even in his 285-gram Asics he does me.

I don't have the eye of the tiger to fight back and scare him on the flat. It's only fifty metres anyway. Not worth it in a training run. You can fucking have it, mate. I ease off and roll into the finish.

Spider-Man wins.
Wolverine second. Ovett third.

At the cones I slow down gradually, suck it up, and just walk on through: upright, hands-on-hips, blank training-run face. Give him absolutely nothing to feed on for next time. He's having a fucking laugh if he thinks he beats me off an even split.

Despite the irritating defeat I fist bump Wolverine and

Spider-Man. I even give them both a cheery *molodyetz*. Then set off on a cool-down while they wait around to clap in their shit mates. Nice to see but I have no stake in the other finishers. I jog to the giant hands and do four reps of 100-metre fast strides. Speed. The much bigger picture.

After strides and stretches I'm back at my kit. On top of my rucksack there's a flyer for a 10k race. Interesting. Could be good mileage. I change out of my sweaty t-shirt. Two female finishers notice. Top class Russian cougars with lithe figures and live needs – my absolute *spezialnost*. Both are wearing pink Nike hoodies. The brunette spies my torso out of the corner of her eye and zeroes in. Of course she does. Blondie also gets involved and less subtly too. Even takes her sunglasses off for closer inspection. I tense my abs. And what the heck I'll give them ten press-ups. Easy. No hurry with the fresh t-shirt. Let them download every last chiselled edge. I love a bit of cougar action. Filthy older women. Except I'm in the M45 category now and these two sorts are younger than me. How did that happen?

```
To: Nevis. All assets have received the
order. Drop went like clockwork. Irina and
Viktoria request future involvement if
similar is required. From: Station R
```

There's a coffee kiosk right by the finish. I buy a bottle of water which I neck. Followed by a hot chocolate chaser with an extra dash of cold milk. Large first slurp. Aah! That hits the spot. The 10k flyer? Could be a worthwhile training run. Looks a good race route but it's in May – ages away. I'll read the rest at home. Before leaving I thank the whole team of race marshalls with individual fist bumps. One of the cougars is hanging around so she gets one too. The main organiser guy is effusive. He insists it's thanks to me for coming. *Spasibo vam!* Which is kind of… yeah, appropriate.

```
To: Gyllyngvase. All assets have received
and acknowledged the order. Might get
requests for hardware or documentation.
Three pre-existing extraction options in
place: north, south, and south by southeast.
From: Nevis
```

On the metro home I drift into deep post-run zen. No emotions. Just an empty space to let the mind and body recover. Only occasional flashes forward to the next training cycle. Training to dismantle Wolverine. Hurting more. Getting tougher – street tough. Handle-yourself-in-a-back-alley tough. Taking on the mugger at his own game. Raining it down on his face. *Hurts your fists this, doesn't it!* I also visualise a slow-motion replay of me taking Spider-Man apart up Hamburger Hill.

See you in five weeks, gentlemen.

The Natalya Rites

★

Krylatskoye Kholm. In the north-west of town. Off-road trails. Fifty minutes on the metro but the terrain is worth it.

To: Gyllyngvase. Winterfold dead. Thought that was our best chance as well. Situation had been highly precarious for several months. Traffic accident - so they clearly wanted us to know. Unfortunately not possible to release her full story at this delicate stage. Another soul sent skyward in our ghastly world, chum. From: Nevis

My trail shoes have a grid of rubber talons for maximum traction in the mud. From my base camp in a wooded dell I do a medley of reps up different paths. Leg strengthener? *Kholm* translates as steep hill. At the very top on one side is a ski station. From there I can see the 1980 rowing lake at Vodny Stadion and the Olympic Velodrome. The 8km tarmac road around Krylatskoye Kholm park staged the road cycling.

To: Nevis. Sorry to hear. Stay ghastly, chum. From: Gyllyngvase

Great session. In the dell there's a holy spring with a stone shrine above it. As I'm putting my tracksuit back on, a babushka is filling up two five-litre bottles. They'll be heavy. I offer to carry them back up the hill for her. She declines, showing me a rickety trolley, but says thank you and touches the cross around her neck and blesses me. An extra tenth of a second in the World Masters semi-final? I'll take it.

OBITUARY - Kathleen Imogen Tilly Snow

With sadness we report the death of Flight

Officer Kathleen 'Kitty' Snow in a road traffic collision in Moscow. A skillful and determined officer, she will be remembered throughout the RAF and other sections as a devoted friend with an overwhelming warmth of personality. Kathleen attended Wycombe Abbey school and graduated from Winterfold College, Oxford in modern languages in 2010 [French, Mandarin, and Russian]. She passed through RAF Cranwell in 2012 and was then stationed at RAF Lossiemouth flying Tornados. After three years Flight Officer Snow, with the full blessing of the RAF, switched to an external civilian-based role. Initially foreseen as an interim assignment, she developed this posting into one of utmost strategic importance. Her valour and sacrifice were beyond duty in unique circumstances. A citation will undoubtedly now be completed to award her the Conspicuous Gallantry Cross posthumously. For those who might have considered they lost touch with their friend Kitty, she spent the last several years operating in Russia, where she was known as Natalya Shakalova - Natasha to her friends.

On my way back to the metro I walk through residential Krylatskoye, a sprawl of high-rise blocks, all identical, white with blue trim, built in the *Perestroika* era. The last glimmer of Soviet hope. The district is geometric and soulless.

To: Nevis. Concerned about general cleanliness out there, chum. Any possibility Winterfold situation means any other assets might be compromised? From: Gyllyngvase

Krylatskoye was where the final scene of *The Bourne*

Supremacy was filmed. When Bourne apologises to the teenage daughter of the couple he assassinated on his first mission. Will I have the same humanity to face the stricken families of my M45 800m rivals? Your husband, I killed him. I annihilated him in a sprint finish. In Finland. It was my first gold. I'm sorry.

`To: Gyllyngvase. Negative, chum. Winterfold operated on entirely solo protocol. Sleeper role. Executive and exclusive duties, one might say. Last thing we heard she was only one bedpost away from the top job. A chemically induced heart attack would have been the easiest solution imaginable. Our lab had done a special job on some blue pills for his extra oomph. From: Nevis`

If Only Once to Wonder

★

After Montreal 1976 the new four-year Olympic cycle began. Ovett was known. Coe was still only a prospect. The earliest opportunity to enter the Moscow equation was the following indoor season. In March 1977 Coe lined up for the final of the European Indoor Championships in San Sebastian. Following the snub from the Olympic selectors the previous summer, this race was laced with context for Coe and his coach.

Coe's physique had matured. At twenty years old he was now stronger, tougher, and much faster. The Peter Coe regime consisted of low mileage and lots of track speedwork. At the time the norm for elite middle-distance runners was seventy miles a week. Some top guys did even more. Peter limited Seb to fifty miles to keep his athlete fresh for the fast track sessions. This structure was feeding through to outstanding training times. Indoors is always a chance for up-and-coming athletes to gain valuable exposure to international competition. The Coe intention went beyond merely gaining experience. They expected to win and to do so in style.

Indoor 800m races have only six runners but they are a nasty physical business. Athletes have to fight for positions with only fifty-metre straights to pass on, and eight tight bends, seven of which could be in a pack. It's usually a full contact affair. At a slim five-foot-nine Coe knew there was no point trying to muscle out the race. Instead, he demonstrated his growing aplomb by taking it out from the gun. He got the lead off the break and kept it. Some digging in was required on the third lap but from the bell he pulled away for a classy victory in his debut international championships. They call it winning the hard way – from the front. Seb Coe relished this masochistic approach and it seemed to suit him. The winning time was even within touching distance of the indoor world record. San Sebastian indeed.

Indoor championships are not given the same weight as outdoors. Rightly so – the big guns only peak in the summer. Nevertheless, for Coe this was an important breakthrough, and a post-it note to selectors and rivals that he could no longer be ignored. Steve Ovett had been impressive at the 800m for three seasons already. The message now from young Sebastian Coe was clear: there were two kids on the block.

★

Bizarrely, a world did exist before Sebastian Coe and Steve Ovett were middle-distance legends. This is a surreal concept for M45 runners born in the mid-70s. Our generation has only blurred childhood memories of this adjacent pre-universe: a dimension lost in time, moons ago, devoid of majestic form and finishing panache. Before Nike Pegasus. Before silky-textured tracksuits. Before world records were thrown around by Ovett and Coe like confetti.

Heading into the summer season of 1977 the focus of the UK athletics scene was still the gritty endurance of Brendan Foster, whose bronze in the 10,000 metres had been Britain's only track medal at the Montreal Olympics. For the previous generation Big Bren had been a long-distance legend, a Geordie giant of the track. But for the Ovett Generation, well… we thought Foster ran ugly, grimacing too much, with his head rolling around when it started hurting. He didn't have the stylistics that mattered. Elsewhere there was Geoff

Capes, the bearded behemoth in the shot-put circle, with a hop-step-spin-and-launch landing his projectile twenty-one metres away. Thud! Capes was indeed a legend to Generation O but only as the world's second strongest man. He tossed cabers, lifted atlas stones, and pulled ten-tonne trucks for us, but he usually lost to Bill Kazmaier.

In 1977 the silky futurism of Coe and Ovett had yet to arrive. Bjorn Borg won his second Wimbledon title with a plywood racket. United won the Cup in a matte Admiral kit. Red Rum, a stayer on soft going, won his third Grand National. There was bunting and tea parties in the street as Queen Elizabeth II celebrated her silver jubilee. Ma'am. Twenty-eight million viewers tuned into Morecambe and Wise on the telly – not a repeat. Until August… Elvis was alive. Viva Las Vegas. Jimmy Carter became the thirty-ninth President of the United States.

The suave man-about-town drove a fawn Morris Marina with faux-leather seats and a traffic light air-freshener dangling from the mirror. Moustaches were in. Sideburns were standard procedure. Chaps wore extravagant flares, shirts with four-inch collars, and kipper ties. They smooched with their ladies on an avocado velour sofa while listening to vinyl albums by Leo Sayer. Or Rod Stewart. Hot Chocolate. In 1977 only early signs of the proto-modern world were there. Technology had only just begun. Two nerds calling themselves Apple Inc. sold their first personal computer. The maiden test flight of the space shuttle blasted off from Cape Canaveral. A quirky science-fiction western with unknown actors and ace 'lightsabers' was released in selected cinemas. Despite the new hope British society floundered, unsure of itself, betwixt eras and identities, waiting for a spark. Politics was a shambles. Generation Ovett didn't much care, we were still on the swings in the park, but for older Coe voters 1977 was the year Margaret Thatcher, as leader of the opposition, gave a rousing anti-Soviet speech. It earned her the nickname 'Iron Lady' from the *Krasnaya Zvezda* Soviet Army Journal. Apparently it stuck.

Inflation. An energy crisis. Crumbling cities. Bad fashion and crap cars. Nothing seemed to be working. British life was beige. But the future was arriving faster than anyone could predict. In the summer of 1977 Sebastian Coe broke the UK national record for 800m – outdoors, where it mattered. Coe was in contention for greatness. He ran hard. He ran from the front without fear. And he was relentlessly chasing fast times.

★

For Steve Ovett fast times meant nothing in 1977. It was all about winning. Being faster than all the other blokes on the day. His Olympic debut in Montreal a year earlier had been solid. Fifth in the 800m, but he hadn't qualified for the 1500m, getting his legs tangled over a faller on the last bend of the semi-final. Disappointment fuelled his winter training and launched him into the summer race season in excellent shape. Emboldened to be more physical, more savvy, and more imposing in races after the Olympic experience, Ovett set about mastering the art of being in the right place at the right time, then striking in ruthless fashion.

His progression in 1977 saw a sequence of impressive wins. The tactics were working well. Running in the slipstream of the leader – *relaxed* – then beating everyone with a sudden change of pace somewhere in the last two-hundred metres. His kick finish was so good he was also trademarking a victory wave halfway down the home straight, often unfurled while overtaking the leader. Such exuberance was unheard of and it nettled many observers: the stuffy traditionalists whose whole world was under attack from in-your-face punk rock. Others, especially the youngsters, revelled in Ovett's audacity and brazen showmanship. He was their guy and loads of them started going to stadiums to watch him run. Athletics was the sport of the masses. Ovett and his new legion of track fans celebrated win after win with unbridled joy. Such a meteoric star confused staid British society, but like him or not the sporting public couldn't fail to notice the new phenomenon. Ten straight wins over the mile and the 1500m. Ten straight victory waves. Ovett was not so much arriving on the scene as romping onto it.

In the summer of 1977 UK cinemas were packed to the rafters for *The Spy Who Loved Me.* Finally, culture which spoke to us! Audiences rejoiced at its preposterously cool British hero and his outrageous Union Jack arrogance. James Bond had the sleekest car, a dazzling array of tactical gadgets, and he left opponents for dead in devastating style. In September 1977 Steve Ovett borrowed the formula for his own middle-distance blockbuster of the season: *From Düsseldorf With Love.*

The IAAF World Cup 1500m.

The Ovett finishing tactics had not gone unnoticed by rivals on the international circuit. Neither had the relatively slow winning times of his races. The Brighton man was feared, but some thought he had yet to be properly tested in a fast race. The IAAF World Cup in Düsseldorf was the biggest meet of the season. As a championship-style event there were no pacemakers laid on. If you required a fast pace you would have to make it yourself. None of the main contenders wanted to sacrifice their own chances by leading out the pack. Even a breath of wind makes it suicidal to front-run a 1500m. If you had a sprint finish like Ovett there was certainly no need to do any work at the front. In Düsseldorf his rivals knew that a slow pace would hand Ovett an easy win, with the strong likelihood of a victory wave to rub salt into the wounds.

A plot was hatched. John Walker, Thomas Wessinghage, and Dave Hill of Canada all needed to run the kick out of the new British star. They agreed to share the front-running for one lap each in order to sabotage Ovett with a fast pace which he couldn't handle. The sprightly Wessinghage would take the first lap, then reigning Olympic 1500m champion Walker would take it on for the second 400. On the third lap Dave Hill of Canada would hit the front and take them through to the bell. From then on it would be every man for himself, hopefully with Ovett suffering. The perfect murder. Secrecy was vital. As they bounced up and down and shook off their legs on the start line, the gunpowder plotters did not exchange words. Ovett had no inkling that the sting was on.

On your marks. BANG!

Wessinghage goes immediately to the front in his white West Germany vest with a thick red hoop. The Düsseldorf crowd is animated by this ballsy early showing from their man. One of Europe's finest 1500m men Wessinghage has a powerful springy style, somehow both loping and compact, head angled slightly downward with determination. Today he is brimming with energy and speed. Already *Vollgas!*

Three metres back in second position is John Walker in the yellow singlet of Oceania. Walker is the established middle-distance rock megastar – the status quo. Already a legend in his own lifetime, there's an imperious air to his running and his flowing hairstyle. To commentators always Big John Walker, he has the physique you would genetically engineer for a 1500m runner: volcanic power in the legs, cavernous lungs, and thin arms like pipe-cleaners. Walker has the 1500m Olympic gold medal in his back pocket as well as the world mile record set in 1975.

An aggressive start. They're strung out into single file.
That's an incredible time for four-hundred metres.

Fifty-six seconds laid down by Wessinghage. On plan. Such a front-loaded race is exactly what Ovett doesn't want. The third conspirator Dave Hill knows the exact pace the first two laps will be run at. He can chill out at the back of the train and wait for his turn. The Canadian is wearing the blue kit of The Americas team and his signature *CHiPs* sunglasses. At the front John Walker takes the lead and picks the pace up. Wessinghage in second. Ovett three.

Steve Ovett has a new short haircut and is wearing the silky all-white strip of Europe. The athletes in the IAAF World Cup represented the five continents, and three national teams: the USA, West Germany and the DDR. Ovett's white Europe vest has a blue capital letter E on the front. He flows in third place, one metre behind Wessinghage for the whole second lap.

The big New Zealander. Full of running. Looking superbly fit.
1:54 – quick. Only two seconds off world record pace.

Walker hustles – efficient, compact, aggressive – keeping the pace high. He leads the pack into the third lap, but it's a lead he no longer wants. Where is Dave Hill of Canada? Down the back straight Walker senses movement and looks over his shoulder, but it's not the arrival of Hill. It's Ovett gliding past Wessinghage into second place. Ovett wants to be poised. Two metres back you might not feel a change of pace instantaneously. One metre is where you want to be. Ovett is now sitting on Walker's right shoulder half a stride back.

No plan survives battle and sure enough something in the gunpowder plot misfires. Dave Hill moves up from the back to take his turn, but he trips against Abderrahmane Morceli and stumbles badly. It costs Hill valuable strides and it takes him three hundred metres too long to get anywhere near the lead. John Walker looks cheesed off as he waits for Hill to come through and take his turn. The New Zealander runs almost two laps at the front, no doubt assuming he's been double-crossed.

DING! DING! DING!

Dave Hill finally arrives.
The injection of pace gaps Walker in second.
Ovett – comfortable! – brushes past Walker, chases the Canadian.

Hill puts in a strong bend then opens up into the back straight with an incremental surge. With 300 metres to go the plot is approaching its climax. The three conspirators look to have great legs for their final act, but Ovett also knows the moment is nigh. He draws onto Hill's right shoulder and matches him stride for stride. Poised. No sign yet of being in trouble but it has been very fast. Have they run the kick out of Ovett? All four runners are looking sensational here. Anyone's race this.

Hill leads.
Ovett second. Walker three. Wessinghage four.
Dave Hill of Canada having a real run at this.

Walker moves into strike position on Ovett up the short inside line. Hill is hammering it in front. Halfway down the back straight Wessinghage buzzes Ovett with a move onto his right shoulder. Threats everywhere, but who is preying upon whom? Ovett watches. Ovett waits. Any moment now. 240 metres to go. 230. 225. The last bend is approaching. Big John Walker edges further up the inside. Wessinghage attempts to get a shoulder ahead of Ovett on the outside just before the final bend. Then with 220 metres to go, in a blinding flash of all-white, 1977 became the future.

And Ovett goes!

The kick takes three metres out of the others into the bend. First it's a gap – then it's a chasm. Hill and Walker have no response. Wessinghage in second makes the best chase he can but this is an absolute massacre. Ovett runs the bend in 11.8 seconds, rocketing himself eight nine ten twelve metres clear. Eleven-point-eight! Oh, to even dream of such power, of discovering that wormhole across the space-time curvature around the top bend and appearing on the home straight before it's even happened. If only once to wonder.

With 100 metres to go the gap is still widening.
One man's blazing speed has torn this field asunder!

Ovett powers down the home straight. Head perfectly still. Flowing arms. *Relaxed*. What panache! Every stride pops off the track like a champagne cork. Ovett is so far ahead he can afford to showboat to the Düsseldorf crowd. The wave is there. The confidence is there. Ovett is tearing away to an incredibly fast time.

Ovett wins.
Wessinghage second. Jürgen Straub third.

Photographers surround Ovett for the first official shot of the new era. The victor with a beaming smile raises both arms aloft. Welcome to the show! A dejected John Walker walks down the infield scratching his sideburns; so stunned by the kick, he stepped off the track on the top bend. He will always be a New Zealand legend, a track icon universally beloved, but from Düsseldorf onwards Big John Walker is no longer the sport's reigning megastar. Ovett is congratulated by Thomas Wessinghage – already a good friend on the circuit – with an embrace, a shake of the head, and a laugh of disbelief. Wessinghage knows what just destroyed him is special.

Ovett milks the crowd. The new king in his all-white vest with the capital E on the front – *E for Easy*.

It was worth a try but the gunpowder plot fails. It only demonstrates who packs the highest-grade explosives. The Ovett kick is dramatic and sustained. Even with a victory wave he runs the last two hundred in twenty-five seconds, speeding away from danger like Roger Moore in an all-white Lotus Esprit. With such ice-cool race tactics and the biggest kick in town, Steve Ovett is now the middle-distance man everyone has to beat. Nobody does it better.

Anastasia de Lune

★

Babushkinskaya Park. Another nine seconds chipped off my 5k season's best. Afterwards I check the Parkrun website for the latest times of Spider-Man and Wolverine at the 50-Years-Of-October. They've been consistent each week. Good, yes very good. Taking them on around their hilly home patch will be a big ask, but not impossible. I've done three weeks of great training, following the exact sessions that Apollo has given the gang back home. 5k tempo runs. Long incline reps. Circuits. 12 x 400m off a minute. Steady runs. 6 x 800m off 90. Hills fartleks. Weights. Short incline reps. Core stability. Stretching. I'm 1.5kg lighter. So yeah – I'll run the flat 5k at Gorky next weekend to prime myself, then have an easier week building up to the 50-Years-Of-October rematch.

★

After significant progress in the 1977 summer season, the soon-to-be titans returned to their leafy British training idylls for the winter programme. In Sheffield Seb Coe floated his 800-metre reps on the Rivelin Valley Road. In Brighton Steve Ovett cruised his 12 x 400m at the Withdean Stadium. Coe knocked out mileage on the Yorkshire Moors. Ovett ran the South Downs. Coe powerlifted with the sprinters group at Loughborough University. Ovett went to Merthyr Mawr to run up the Big Dipper sand dune. Leg strength. They each built the domination of their era a long way from Central Lenin Stadium.

Spring 1978. A long way from Central Lenin Stadium. Kabul. A murderous internal coup takes place in the Afghan capital. The victors of the bloodshed are the PDPA, the People's Democratic Party of Afghanistan, pro-Soviet communists. Following the coup, the PDPA implements a brutal regime of land reforms which bring chaos and instability to the tribal structure of the country. The US government under new President Jimmy Carter begins to take a far greater interest in Afghanistan. No Soviet influence in the coup can be proven, but Washington speculates with concern upon Kremlin intentions for the region. Neither side of the Cold War knows the time bomb which has been set for the Moscow Olympics, still two years away. Halfway through their four-year Olympic preparation cycle, athletes around the world continue their training unaware of the coming storm. I run a beautiful evening steady around Cherkizovsky Park lake.

★

Östersund, Sweden. January 2016.
The European Biathlon Championships -- ongoing.

INT. A hotel room.

An attractive young couple enter in the throes of a passionate embrace. Both are sportily dressed. The man is tall and handsome, rugged-yet-boyish in the way only Swedish men can be. The woman only has to tip-toe slightly to engage in the extended kiss they are enjoying. The room door closes behind them. The young man disengages from the kiss and apologises.

Sitting on an armchair in the corner of the room is a second man. In a grey suit. An English man. Somewhat stocky. The woman looks to the Swede, with disappointment but not rage. He motions to her to sit down.

NEVIS: Thank you, Nils.

The Swedish man repeats his apology and leaves. The young woman sits down on the end of the bed. Within a few short months of delicate negotiation this woman will become known to a highly select few in the British Secret Service as APPLECROSS. She takes off her coat, a ski jacket with a Russian insignia on the front, and places it beside her.

NEVIS: Zdrastye.

APPLECROSS: [icily] Who are you?

NEVIS: A friend. Would you like to work for me?

APPLECROSS: I don't mix business with pleasure.

NEVIS: A very wise policy. Forgive me. Then please think of me only as a potential employer. [a beat --] You love your country, don't you?

APPLECROSS: Sometimes.

NEVIS: But you love your family more.

APPLECROSS: Fuck off.

NEVIS: Would you kill him? If you had the chance. [a pause for his bluntness to sink in] Not only you and your family are wishing this happens. The world would be a safer place. Russia could finally blossom.

To this Nevis does not expect an answer. He walks to leave the room, but before opening the door he says in Russian.

NEVIS: A pleasure to meet you. I'm very sorry for your loss. And forgive me for disturbing your evening. Nils I'm sure was genuine in his feelings as well as... My apologies for that. You can call me Nevis. I will endeavour to make contact again when you've had time to think about my proposal. If it's a no, I will respect your choice. Da svidanya -- and good luck tomorrow in the competition.

Nevis leaves the room, gently closing the door behind him.

Minutes later Applecross finds ten thousand roubles in new notes by her bathroom mirror. The process of denial, refusal, inner turmoil, a second and third meeting with this stranger, and the final crossing of the threshold has begun. She hated the offer, but somehow she had not hated the man. Nevis spoke directly to her soul. He understood. There was someone in the world who Applecross would do anything to kill. If it wasn't a trap, maybe this Nevis could make her wish come true.

Lubyanka. I've found a great gym just off Myasnitskaya Ulitsa. Only six metro stops away from home. CCCP Fitness – a new gym chain doing lots of effective promo. Strongly branded on Soviet nostalgia and strict Bolshevik dogma. I've signed up for their flexi-month membership. They have a twenty-five-metre pool, steam room, cold plunge pool, and a sauna with a plasma screen which shows *Wild Russia* nature documentaries on loop (through a window). It's open until midnight and they lend you a fresh towel each visit, which frees up crucial rucksack space.

To: Nevis. Applecross confirms new mission status. Available and willing regardless of the danger. But she has no access to target, nor any ideas yet how to achieve this. From: Station R

I love the comrade chic décor. Red and bold. Nods to austerity. Yet optimism. An arena of toil and progress. The weights room is fully set up for hardcore communist man-strength: squat rack, deadlift platform, Olympic bars, bumper plates, and a hamstring curl machine. All the essentials for my sprint conditioning *revolutsiya.*

Dossier Applecross: Height 175cm. Eyes hazel-grey. Body muscular and lean. Glamorous.

Today an extremely attractive personal trainer welcomes me. I spy her name badge. She has a twinkle in her eyes but I cynically assume these are rouble signs as she woos me as a potential client. I've currently got hardly any disposable income so I have to politely rebuff her advances, which I immediately regret doing upon closer inspection of her in the weights room mirrors. She seems exceptionally 'motivating'.

Dossier Applecross: Linguistic savante. Russian, English, Finnish, Byelorussian, Japanese and possibly others. Expert in identity transposition [polymorphism] and seduction. Bisexual.

So, Anastasia Lunovskaya. She has hazel-grey eyes, long fair hair and an athletic figure. It shimmers in a blue CCCP t-shirt and matching navy short shorts, which are short enough to expose a half inch preview of curved ass cheek. And legs. It's legs for miles. Lean but powerful.

Silky smooth. They get lovelier each time my eyes trespass on them. Their light bronze tan is accentuated against ice white Adidas Boost trainers which she wears sockless. Of course she does.

`Dossier Applecross: Smolensk Region Biathlon Champion 2015. Russian national squad 2016.`

Easy warm-up. Gradually building into it. On the incline bench I hold a 5-kilo plate across my chest for back raises. With each raise I get a testosterone-boosting eyeful of Anastasia in her shorty short shorts. She's late twenties. Or bang on thirty? Yeah, everything about it. Must have been into sport all her life. Possibly former elite at something. Now probably competes in fitness shows. *Miss Fyzicheskaya 2021*? Aah – Anastasia! I bloody love this gym. Twenty minutes into the session and I'm super-pumped to lift.

`Dossier Applecross: Fully weapons trained. Access at short notice to certain models of rifle, with watertight cover story to stock them briefly. Marksmanship in competition surpasses current maximum grade X-1 standard for military snipers.`

Light squats. Deadlifts with a set of burpees in between one of the sets. Enough already. Less is more in *Mr M45-Universe.* Am I a mystery to Anastasia? My skinny frame and puny weights (so far) suggest I'm new to the lifting platform. Yet my leg definition screams explosive performance. She'll have already guessed I'm a runner, obviously, but does she join the dots to 800m specialist and a personal best of 1:58.67?

Dossier Applecross: CONFIRMED kills. Nalchik 2017. Omsk 2018. Almaty 2019. St Petersburg 2020. UNCONFIRMED. Moscow 2021.

Afterwards in the changing rooms I check out my upper body in the mirror. Always lots of hench after deadlifts. Would my new Anastasia approve? I squeeze in some tension to simulate her gaze. Those prying hazel-grey eyes all over me – needing a hero.

Tense. Release. *Tense! Hnngh.* And release.

Starboard Glove Pylon

★

Gorky Park. The Moskva is a mill pond. You can't even tell which way is downstream. I sit on the embankment bench and change into my turquoise Sauconys. This morning is my last Saturday run-out before the Spider-Man 5k rematch at 50-Years-Of-October. Just a smooth one today. Strictly no fireworks. I eat a dried apricot for super-condensed energy.

Two Cannondales zoom past. Pan flat road and zero wind. The coffee kiosk lady opens up her hatch for the early walkers and rollerbladers. A black-headed gull swoops and soars in joyful shapes. I've researched him online; he's an Anguillan Laughing Gull. Such a beautiful blue sky for him today. I foam-rolled for ten minutes at home so my legs are already nicely awake. Foam-rolling is a painful process but it's worth every grimace for race-ready legs. Today I do my jog warm-up on the flat along the river.

Ate well yesterday. Slept well. The dried apricot. Relaxed.

Back at my bag as I start my stretching routine other runners begin to appear. Ignore them. Lying on my front in pigeon pose I lower my forehead onto my arms, closing my eyes, breathing, and sinking into a blissful glute stretch. All super-loose after the rest day. My zen is disturbed by a group placing their bags next to mine. They exchange banter and seem up for the race. One boisterous voice sounds familiar. Surely not – not here? I look up: the calf guards, those baggy shorts with too many zips, the long torso, the red-and-blue arm-warmers with the Marvel logo. Well well… Spider-Man!

That tears up the screenplay. I suppose it was inevitable he would ambush me with a foray outside his 50-Years-

Of-October Park. And look who he's brought with him for the party – his grinning sidekick Wolverine. Bring it on, baby.

Their group are right next to my spot. I nod to Spider-Man pretending to only half-remember him. Two of his groupies exchange whispers. So. This Gorky visit is no coincidence. Wolverine for his part looks gormless and naïve, as if the last four weeks of interval training never even happened.

On the jogging track by the river railings I savour my drills routine. All clean and aggressive. Fast-twitchy. Fifteen minutes until go time. Strides. There are runners everywhere now. I do one extended stride at race pace along the road for two hundred metres. My turnover is so good I have to hold myself back. Some days you just feel sensational. Warm-up nailed. Time to chill out in the call room.

In my rucksack I make an unexpected find – my red Puma race vest. Fresh and unused from midweek weights. Before the era of kit sponsors, Steve Ovett wore a red Soviet vest for most of his victories; a vest he had swapped with a Russian athlete at an international meet early in his career. It even had the hammer and sickle on the chest. The tabloid press speculated on its political significance, but Steve simply liked the way it fitted. Me? I love the fit of Puma: a low open cut around the shoulders. I peel off my t-shirt and slip on the red vest. It hangs slightly loose on my sparse torso. 72.8kg this morning. I look across at Spider-Man stretching his stodgy calves. Clever ambush – but be careful what you wish for.

Tactics. What's the plan for this unexpected showdown? I don't need to factor in Wolverine on a flat course. Unless he finds twenty-five seconds down the back of the sofa, he can't beat me. No, this is all about Spider-Man. At 50-Years-Of-October it would have been simple: sit on him, call his bluff, and surprise him in the last 500 metres. He would be over-confident on the familiar tarmac of the October hills. But here it's flat. Why play games with his confidence when I can just trash it?

```
To: Nevis. I have an option to meet mission
requirements. Creative logistics. Very
public - which might help. From: Pythagoras
```

I walk through the joggers towards the front, losing count of all the female runners who check out my sculpted 800-metre legs – oiled last night in front of the mirror and they still have a golden sheen. Wolverine ostentatiously resets his Suunto GPS gizmo watch. He exchanges light-hearted remarks with Spider-Man; casual stuff, jokey, almost as if this isn't a big deal. No young whippets today – maybe they've got an indoor track meet? The Gorky Park usual suspects are here in full force: Propaganda, Yellow Brick Road, Marathon Man. Spider-Man has pulled his arm-warmers up over his biceps. I wink at Clockwork Orange. He nods back and we clench a fist to each other.

The organiser invites us up to the start-line. I nudge myself into the front rank and toe the line of cones, finger poised on my Casio start button. Spider-Man is on my left. I look down at the turquoise of my 218-gram Saucony racers. We all crouch in start position. On my right is Wolverine, the tragic cunt in his 285-gram Asics.

Vnymanye. KLAXON!

And I take it out with a booming sprint and get a five-metre lead straight away. As I force myself to settle, Spider-Man works up to me and tags on, as expected. I keep my cadence high and my stride length compact, exploding off each foot-strike. But settle! Shoulders loose. *Relaxation* is the key to front-running – my pace, my rhythm… my supremacy.

```
To: Nevis. Request Kalashnikov SVD with all
the gubbins. PSO-1 sight if possible.
Delivery the usual way. From: Pythagoras
```

The metro bridge. Only 200 metres in and we already have daylight on the rest of the field. With no whippets today the overall win is up for grabs. Breathe. Spider-Man is right there on my tail – large, bustling away, pressurising me – but I'm absolutely Kool & The Gang. With all the fast interval reps in the bank I'm balanced and coordinated at this pace, although I still need to match my breathing tempo with my legs. *Relax*. Just let it happen.

Along the tree line. My spring off the tarmac feels good. Still no wind. The Anguillan gull is keeping a close eye on me from mid-stream. He knows it. We pass the elephant leg cable car pylon and Central Lenin Stadium across the river. The ether. I check my one-kilometre split. Quick.

Quicker pace than I've run for five years but it feels okay. I even wonder if I should speed up? Negative. Just stay in front and cruise. We enter the tunnel of trees, now just bark skeletons. The road has brush marks where a sweeper vehicle has cleared the leaves for us. I don't switch up to the dirt path. Need the full traction of the tarmac. This feels fucking good already. Spidey? Two strides behind me.

```
To: Pythagoras. No can do. Suggest an
Izhmash 7-4 biathlon standard. Takes .22
ammunition. Our armourer says it has plenty
enough stopping power for a head shot on a
seventy-year-old from 202 yards. Tested one
myself last night on the fox who's been
after my chickens. Bingo! Will send Izhmash.
Test it yourself. If you need more gusto let
me know. From: Nevis
```

The Vorobyovy Gory escarpment rises directly from the left kerb of the road; a reminder of all the work I've put in. A hills fartlek here every week, laying a rock solid foundation of leg strength. On my fartlek I would turn left off this road into the woods. Eighty metres of elevation up through the trees. My covert paths are only signposted by small openings between the branches and by Mizuno Wave Sky 3 tread marks in the mud. Secret gateways to the Ovett hills kingdom.

Molotov Ridge. The Lydiard Steps. Red November. Hairpinsky. Wottlegrad. Some of my rep sections are short eyeballs-out sprints, others are longer undulating efforts. Molotov Ridge is a trilogy of paths up to the same peak, thirty seconds blast each. My fastest time up the Lydiard Steps is now sixty-five seconds. Wottlegrad is five minutes up the full elevation of the escarpment, a winding path but an even gradient apart from the killer finish.

```
To: Applecross. We need an Izhmash 7-4
please. And .22 ammunition. Delivery via
```

florist according to Station R directions.
From: Nevis

In 1972 Dave Wottle of the USA won the 800m final at the Munich Olympics with a negative split in a positive split race. Most athletes need a positive split – two-seconds quicker over the first lap – to run their best time. Even pace or a negative split can be risky because you lag well behind and often lose a slipstream, but some 800m guys like it (see also: Yury Borzakovsky). In Munich the unfancied and unfashionable Wottle, running in a beige golf cap, lagged twenty strides behind the leaders after the first 200 metres. The American TV commentators even speculated sympathetically that their man might be carrying an injury. By the bell the pack had fractionally slowed its fierce pace and Wottle was back within ten metres of the leaders. Not in the mix but no longer an embarrassment to himself and his nation. A slower third bend from the leaders finally allowed Wottle to tag onto the pack. On the back straight the American worked up only two places, but race favourite Evgeni Arzhanov (USSR) powered hard from seventh place into the lead. On the top bend Wottle held back again, waiting for two runners to fade to give himself an easier overtake. By the slingshot Wottle was into fourth with only the two Kenyans, Robert Ouku and Mike Boit, and then Arzhanov to catch. The final sprint was on. But for fifty metres Wottle made no ground. Then Ouku cracked. Wottle was going to get a medal. Bronze? Forty metres to go. Boit was also coming backwards. It might be the silver for Wottle. With thirty metres to go Arzhanov still had five metres daylight. Gold for the USA was impossible but Wottle kept driving his arms – he still had the leg speed. With twenty metres to go Arzhanov finally reached his lactic event horizon and could barely make a forward stride. Dave Wottle maintained his sprint and won on the line by three-hundredths of a second.

Sometimes I deliberately get myself lost in Vorobyovy Gory and have to run up a new trail which I don't know how to pace. Up. Down. Around. Up again. Never get bored. Fifty-five minutes total. The run includes anywhere from twelve to twenty hill reps. Strength on the hills translates into greater ability to push hard off the top of the tarmac on the flat. It gives me an extra centimetre on my stride length and aerobic comfort at a higher cadence. Spider-Man is currently noticing this improvement with growing alarm. I raise my turnover a notch and relax my arms. He's still sitting on me. Maybe we're both wondering who's in charge?

```
To: Gyllyngvase. Pythagoras has cooked up
something ridiculous or brilliant. I can't
decide which. Best not to divulge [yet].
Suffice to say, high profile but potentially
'clean'. If PM can quietly nod [or not nod
if easier] we'll give it a whirl. From:
Nevis
```

The pitted section of tarmac. I move up onto the dirt track at the puddle in the road. The moving line of skyscrapers on the horizon are already close. That came quick. The white Hollywood sign: *SCHASTYE V PARKYE*. The waymarkers are all the same, only this time with Spider-Man's shadow all over me. Rhythm. We reach the halfway cones and the hi-viz marshall man. He shouts the split but I'm in a bubble of concentration. Yes, I hear the split but the number doesn't become an emotion. All I need is here inside my bubble: pace feel, composure, and today *yes* arrogance.

```
To: Nevis. Prime Minister nods. Asks
approximate timescale of the plan. From:
Gyllyngvase

To: Gyllyngvase. Why don't you come up my
way for a drink? We can discuss whatever
specifics are available. Or I can pop into
Vauxhall Cross? From: Nevis

To: Nevis. I'll come to you. A pint in the
Brown Horse?

To: Gyllyngvase. Negative. The snug has eyes
and ears. Better option is Pinewood Studios.
The Heatherden Hall bar has eleven varieties
of gin. Or good tonic if you're driving. The
only eyes and ears will be exhausted
cameramen and pissed off Hollywood actors.
We can cheer them up with the likelihood of
nuclear Armageddon. 8pm.
```

2.5km. We turn. Spider-Man is right on me. So close that even around the halfway cones I'd have to look back to see him. I can hear his breathing. He can hear mine. This is usually an indicator of who is working harder, but nothing yet says either of us are in greater or less distress. From the turn I start the race all over again – a big surge made to seem effortless, then settle. Spider-Man has to work to get back on. Am I in his head yet? The sum of all his fears. The never-ending gazelle. When David Moorcroft broke the 5000m world record in 1982 he stuck to his target splits all the way despite how little pain he was feeling. After breaking the world record by six seconds all Moorcroft felt was disappointment: *It never hurt. I wish I'd gone quicker.* I nudge it on for fifty metres. Spider-Man loses two strides.

We start passing the trailing runners the other side of the

tree line. Wolverine is leading the chasing pack but is already grimacing and rolling his head. Clockwork Orange is a stride behind him attached like a limpet, and Wolverine isn't liking it. Marathon Man, Yellow Brick Road, and Propaganda are also chilling out in the wolf-shaped slipstream, making it four runners all over Wolverine and no Mickey Mouse fifteen percent hills anywhere to get rid of them. Horrible.

The second half of the race is dangerous. From the U-turn the cable cars are already visible 1.5km in the distance. They approach slowly which psyches you out if you target them too much. I focus on the here and now. Where is the limit and can I drive any further into the fire? I loosen my shoulders and enjoy the Ovett ether. The aerobic escalation is under control. That day at 50-Years-Of-October must feel a lifetime ago to Spider-Man. A tuneful zephyr whistles along the river as we follow the Moskva down to Gorky Park, listening to the wind of change.

At the mid-point of Central Lenin Stadium I look at my 4km split. Crazy time if I can finish this off. All about *relaxation*. Technique wins this. We pass under the cable car. Shoulders loose. Empty face. Gliding over the top of the tarmac. Ovett waits. The moment to strike is near. The Anguillan seagull lands on the river railings beside us and squawks: *This is on, boy!* Today no one is below deck on the pleasure cruiser. They're all topside roaring on Ovett in the race. And listen to this crowd! Absolute sell-out. The dark woods of Vorobyovy Gory become a vast sloping terrace of baying athletics fans. The front row are banging on the advertising hoardings and chanting in time with my strides.

O-Vett! O-Vett! O-Vett!

I once came fifth in the British Masters 1500m. Lost touch just before the bell as three runners wound it up for a fast last lap. After the finish, as I peeled myself off the track, the winner was crowing loudly with the other two medallists about how epic their 59-second last lap had been. I hated not being good enough to join the party. Not being able to follow their attack. Not moving onto his shoulder on the slingshot. Not blitzing the fucker down the home straight. No need to rub it in by shouting about it, mate. I've never forgotten it. Everything. His Adizero Cadence spikes. That crowing voice. The accent. Just the whole fucking smugness of the cunt. Never even knew his name, but I resented him more than any other rival and visualised our rematch on a thousand training runs. But I never saw or heard him at any other champs. Until now. Now his voice echoes in the race ether. And this time deliverance is right there for the taking. Spider-Man, the fool, has walked himself right into it!

Cable car to metro bridge is always a tough section. I allow myself to admit this is fucking hurting. We have 750 metres to go. Spider-Man moves up alongside. His shoulder is closer than it needs to be. A message. He wants the win. Good. Whatever the pain factor I'm in complete control here just matching him stride-for-stride. Does Spider-Man know he's already lost? He can do whatever he likes now, it won't make a scrap of difference. I'm loose in the shoulders. *Relaxed.*

My glute missiles are twitching, waiting to fire. Bad boyz loaded either side. Sidewinders on starboard glove pylon. Sparrows on port. Ready to roar.

We pass the near side of the metro bridge. I'll wait for his move just to see what he's got. It comes the moment we hit the sunshine out of the shadow of the bridge. More than a surge. He throws everything at it. In fact, yeah nice one. But not big enough, pal. Willkommen in Düsseldorf.

And Ovett goes!

In ten strides I demolish him with outrageous speed. His puny shithouse kick is nothing compared to the O-bomb. The gap is already a chasm. Spider-Man sees the magi-white soles of my Saucony flicking up in his face. The more I *relax* the faster I go. Every stride pops off the road like an Ovett champagne cork. I can coast the last hundred metres on pure momentum. The wave is there. The arrogance is there. And he's tearing away to an incredibly fast time. Nothing hurts.

Ovett wins.
Spider-Man second. Clockwork Orange third.

Apollo will love that – my fastest 5k time in seven years. 249 days until the World Masters. We're taking care of business. Spider-Man is gracious. He accepts what just destroyed him is special. We fist bump. *Molodyetz*. Yeah thanks. Winning isn't even a thing.

★

CCCP Fitness. On the way to the gym there's a snow flurry. Not enough to settle but the deep Moscow winter is on its way. Cars now crackle with studded tyres on the road. Dogs wear thermal jackets for their walks. Blokes have switched from trainers to black leather shoes.

Heavy coats. Warm hats.

I stroll onto the gym floor in my workout Stan Smiths. And yes! Anastasia is here. She's in the weights area but off-duty, training in her own gym kit: a full-length black Lycra one-piece. Ffff! So motivational it's not even funny. She's doing the incline leg press machine. I move as close as possible to do oblique side raises on the back extension bench right next to her. The illicit proximity is thrilling. As is the waft of her *Obsession* by Calvin Klein.

The seat of the incline press is at floor level and her legs are straight, with her raised feet planted on the platform. Poised. Anastasia lowers the stack until her knees are at a right angle, then drives it from the glutes, smoothly, powerfully, back up to the top. Then completes her exhale. Five times. The load? One big plate, one medium, and one light disc each side. She is leg pressing 72.0 kilograms – my bodyweight.

★

Yes, I do have a job. Teaching English. For my sins. Today is a lesson observation; a compulsory thing but Phil Kimby and I always wangle it that we observe each other and don't bother with feedback. Phil Kimby is the only other maverick teacher so we've formed a secret alliance. I'll watch his teenager intermediates this afternoon. Later he'll watch my advanced CPE exam class, with seven attractive women for him to potentially lure into his Sugar Daddy realm. The alliance works well. My straighter bat reflects well off his toffish eccentricity. Today he's wearing two-toned brogues, claret chinos, and a double-cuffed white shirt with flamingo motifs. Phil is still handsome and badly-behaved well into his sixties. I introduced him to a student of mine in the spring – the *elegantnaya* Oksana. Blonde, forty-something and married. Phil Kimby was boning it all summer, as he would recount in appalling detail at our fortnightly trip to the Shakespeare Pub on Myasnitskaya. His filth can be a bit too tangy at times, but boring monk-like runners need friends with vices to live vicariously through. And lest it be forgotten, Phil Kimby has several high-quality adult students of his own and he knows my approximate spec. He'll reciprocate quite often with an offering, although I rarely get beyond a platonic coffee. That said, the last one did end up being my sports masseuse for seven weeks. Katya. Brunette. She liked Salsa but her Friday evening dance social clashed with my pre-5k-tempo early night. So I bought a foam roller instead.

EXT. Pinewood Film Studios, South Bucks.

Evening [8pm]. A black Aston Martin DB11 pulls into a parking spot. Gyllyngvase gets out. His clobber is stylish: blazer, a black roll-neck sweater, twill slacks, and suedes in elephant grey. The suave look suggests he is meeting a lady friend later. Which he is. At Pinewood the feline and good-looking Gyllyngvase could easily by mistaken for one of the Hollywood actors. He walks for two minutes then calls Nevis.

GYLLYNGVASE: No idea where I am, chum. This place is a maze. Where is this Heatherden Hall? I've parked and am now walking down... [looks up] Goldfinger Avenue.

NEVIS: Wrong way. Turn back and turn right. It's the old white building. I'll come out and look for you.

Nevis stands outside the entrance to Heatherden Hall holding a tall glass of Italian lager. He is wearing a crew-neck sweater with shoulder patches, corduroy trousers in potato-beige, and a comfortable pair of black Clarks. At Pinewood the sturdy and practical Nevis could easily be mistaken for an exhausted cameraman, but one nicely re-energised after a relaxing sip of lager.

Gyllyngvase appears. They walk into the Victorian splendour of Heatherden Hall.

INT. A long carpeted corridor with framed film stills [poster size] along each wall. Gyllyngvase stops to look at one of the photos -- then another. Nevis likes this.

NEVIS: Have a look at this one.

The two men stand in front of a large colour photo of a well-known British film from the late 1960s. Gyllyngvase smiles.

NEVIS: Now here's the thing. What do you see?

GYLLYNGVASE: Carry On Camping.

NEVIS: [pressing] And who do you see? Who are the characters?

GYLLYNGVASE: Sid James is a spiv type in a bad jacket. Up to no good. And Bernard Bresslaw is his mate, a dopey put-upon husband in a fawn cardigan. They're teaming up to pull a fast one on their wives. Been ages since I've seen it but probably younger crumpet involved.

NEVIS: Top marks. Now look at this one.

The next photo in the corridor is of George Lazenby playing James Bond. Classic square jaw. Immaculately groomed. In a royal blue ski suit with a modish jacket to it. He's about to ski down a mountain and escape from the evil villain's lair.

GYLLYNGVASE: On Her Majesty's Secret Service.

NEVIS: Who do you see?

GYLLYNGVASE: James Bond. Rocking the late-sixties style.

NEVIS: Handsome, isn't he? That Lazenby -- heroic. Now look back at Sid James. What do you see?

GYLLYNGVASE: Spiv. Bad jacket. Wrinkles on his face and hair.

NEVIS: [enjoying] Exactly. But look. It's the SAME jacket -- same blue, same collar here, same zip, same white roll-neck underneath. But on Sid James it makes him a spiv pulling a fast one. On George Lazenby it makes him the most dashing hero in the world. Gives him panache. Lazenby wears dopey Bresslaw's cardigan in one of the other scenes. Both films were made here in 1969 on next-door sound stages. Same costume department.

GYLLYNGVASE: Funny. What's your point?

NEVIS: It took fifty years for anyone to notice. Longer than the Official Secrets Act. No one saw it. Polymorphism.

GYLLYNGVASE: Which is?

NEVIS: Projecting yourself into and out from a different person. The skill of actors and spies. Using simple props like a jacket, or a cardigan, or new glasses, and somehow becoming a totally different character. Morphing into a persona the world sees. You don't hide anything -- but in your manner, your aura, you reflect back what other people expect. You inhabit their perceptions. It's the ultimate disguise because you don't wear it. Other people wear it in their minds.

GYLLYNGVASE: I don't get it. What about Sid James's face? Those wrinkles. He's never playing James Bond.

NEVIS: What about Lazenby's face? He took that jacket off and never worked again. Wasn't polymorphic. It's not about the face. Could be the same face. Think of this, chum. Marilyn Monroe walking along the beach with an old friend and guess what? Nobody notices her. Because with her friend she's just Norma Jean. The friend is surprised that they've attracted no attention at all. Nothing. So Monroe says: D'you wanna see her? -- see who? -- see 'her'... And she switches to Marilyn the film star: the walk, the mannerisms, the ditziness, with only sunglasses as a prop. And the people instantly see, suddenly surrounding her for autographs and photos. Gee, that Marilyn's swell. Polymorphism. It's not acting. It's being. Professional actors are good at it. Film stars and prostitutes are even better. And spies are the best. Natural selection. If you can't do it you get killed.

GYLLYNGVASE: Can you train your agents to do it?

NEVIS: To a degree. But only if you psychologically need to be someone else. In your mind you are that other person. That's why we use damaged subjects. Criminals. Victims. Orphans. People who have needed to be someone else just to survive. The earlier they were damaged the better. They become the spies we make them. A persona out of nothing. Danger barely exists for them. They can't die because they aren't real anyway. And they can kill in cold blood because they're psychopaths, which is what we often need them to do. Serial killers. But we dress them up in smart clothes and they look like James Bond -- or Marilyn Monroe.

GYLLYNGVASE: You should write a book.

NEVIS: Too busy, chum. Let's go gin tasting. Going to take us a while to go through this Moscow business. Winterfold - Natalya Shakalova. The Jackal! The best agent I ever had. A pure polymorph. We'll never know what gave her away. Maybe she wasn't damaged enough to hide who she really was. Or met someone even more damaged who detected her. Like Marilyn did.

The two men walk into the bar and sit in deep leather armchairs. They talk. Threeman is discussed. Winterfold is also discussed. Nevis avoids offering much information about Operation Plum, apart from that it will be very public, and now that Winterfold is dead it can't happen until next spring-summer. The month of May is suggested. Time passes. As it happens, no gin is drunk. Nevis talks at length about his role in the Pinewood Studios planning application and the preponderance of chalk streams in Buckinghamshire. Gyllyngvase asks about Applecross, at which point Nevis excuses himself and goes to the toilet.

Gyllyngvase receives a message on his phone. Nevis returns and is soon back into conversational flow. Gyllyngvase is now torn -- although keen to stay to know the specifics of Operation Plum he is late for a prior engagement. He makes his excuses and bids Nevis farewell.

One hour later Alec Gyllyngvase meets his secretary for dinner in a London restaurant. She is seventeen years younger than him and conspicuously attractive. Gyllyngvase does not return to his own house that evening. His wife and kids are away in Cornwall.

Nevis stays on his own at Pinewood for one more pint and, since his taste buds have been promised it, a double shot of Monkey 47 Distiller's Cut [on ice]. Ironically, two pissed off Hollywood actors do turn up, faces like thunder, but Nevis ignores them. He is thinking of the bigger fish to fry. After his gin he walks the half-mile home to Fulmer musing on a very successful evening.

Trippelganger

★

Sokolniki. The wooden swing door of the metro opens into an icy blast of wind down Ulitsa Stromynka. It snowed all night. A fleet of six diesel sweepers are working in half chevron formation brushing the unloved snow to the side of the road. Beauty was its only crime. The pavement is still inches deep. Winter boots and a happy functional stomp required. I pass the Old Fire Tower. A hundred years ago this mustard-brick lookout was one of the tallest buildings in Moscow. It's now dwarfed by the forty-storey Sokolniki Plaza and the Holiday Inn. Cranes and pile-drivers on the other side of Stromynka are laying foundations for an even bigger high-rise. I arrive at the track to lay foundations of my own. Speed endurance.

The Brothers Znamensky Olympic Centre in Sokolniki has an outdoor track and an indoor arena. It's only one metro stop from my apartment. Anticipating the snowbound winters I specifically rented a place nearby. The arena is rectangular and narrow, so the 200-metre track has longer straights than a normal indoors. This means the bends are tighter with steeper banking. The main track is traditional red. In the infield is a blue sixty-metre sprint track, a pole vault bed, a long jump pit, and the high jump area. On a lifting platform just behind the track banking a girl in a weights belt loads a bar on the squat rack. Two fifteens either side. 50-kilos.

I jog around the infield in lane minus one. Along the home straight there are seven rows of brown plastic seats. They might still be from the original fit-out, or at least the 1980 Olympic refurb. The centre was built in 1961 and the feel is heroically Soviet. Hanging over the glass sidewalls is a gallery of honour for legends of the Moscow Athletics Federation. The centre of this display is a black-and-white poster of Georgy and Seraphim Znamensky, two middle-distance titans from the 1930s after whom the track is named. The brothers are standing by a finish line. Each has ruffled hair and a beaming endorphin smile. Georgy's race top has wide flappy collars. Seraphim is in a cotton singlet. Both athletes have barrel-chested physiques and a glint in their eye suggesting it had been a terrific race. Seraphim killed himself aged thirty-six. Georgy died of cancer in his mid-forties. Run as fast as you can.

The arena is an epic facility of which the Znamenskys would be proud. With winter days dropping below minus twenty, the arena is a home from home for Moscow's elite. About thirty athletes are dotted around the arena doing drills, reps, lifts, exercises, stretches. Half of them are in national team kit: bright blue Lycra with 'RUSSIA' on the back or down the thigh. Nobody training looks much over twenty, apart from me and an M50 bloke in Nike Maxcats doing sprints.

This is a high-performance centre. On the banked track five skinny lads are doing 600-metre reps off short recoveries: the long-distance boys. In lane three a muscular girl in Russia kit is doing 150-metre sprints off four-minute recoveries. I get a stopwatch on one of her reps: twenty-three seconds... Not even close for a good 400m or 800m runner, but solid for a heptathlete with other events to practice that day. Later I see her doing shot put in the throws net at the far end. A guy with matinée idol looks is doing sled pulls off a three-point start. He has a powerful backside, wide lats, and he seems to have the run of the ladies: 100-metre sprinter.

Half a dozen of the elites are doing the same drills as

Apollo taught me all those years ago. On the sixty-metre straight we skip, flick, high-knee, lunge, hop, and bound to warm-up, to activate our fast-twitch muscles, to hone our coordination. I'm already fired up by the vibe.

A female coach glances down at a stopwatch as her athlete sprints: *Davay!* The coach is in her early forties with spikey peroxide blonde hair. From a distance she looks slender but closer-up her track trousers are bursting at the seams. Glutes like cannonballs: former Olympic sprinter. Anyone new who arrives says hello to Peroxide Blonde. Between each of my drills I walk back slowly and confidently. I'm not fazed being among really good athletes – because I *am* one. In training arrogance is simply being calm and knowing your routine. Being a perfect doppelganger for an Olympic Champion also helps.

`Dossier Threeman: Height 182cm. Weight 71-75kg depending. Slim and muscular physique. Balding/bald.`

On the sixty-metre track I gradually build up my leg turnover. Stride at sixty percent. Stride at seventy percent. Stride at seventy-five percent. No rush to get loose. Just keep striding until it comes. The arena encourages a long build-up to a session. It's warm, dry, and full of young people with physiques to aspire to. Their waists are the thing. If I could get down to that lean I would absolutely smash it.

A brunette in Russia leggings laces up her Saucony Spitfires and pads over to the start of the back straight. Rolling down the banking into a sprint she absolutely cruises a one-fifty in [*click*] sub-twenty seconds. Her ponytail flicks side-to-side with each foot-strike of her effortless flow. Incredible. By osmosis my own legs are now turning over well. I do two more fast strides to try and be as majestic as Spitfire Girl. And I'm ready to rock n roll. The whole warm-up takes forty-five minutes and is integral to the thrill of being an elite athlete.

Today is 12 x 300 metres off 60 second recoveries. Race flats today. No need for spikes in December. I'll start each rep on the home straight so that my 300s finish on the opposite side where Peroxide Blonde is now standing. Maybe she'll notice my form? The diagonal walk back across between reps will take exactly one minute. Twelve reps.

Work. But relax the mind – maybe even drift away.
The first 300 feels smooth.

Why I started running. Thirteen years ago – or fourteen? Time flies at sub-two race pace. I was thirty-three. The pseudo-handsome looks of my twenties heyday were deteriorating fast. In a full-length mirror I was horrified by the tubby stranger with thin formless legs. It could no longer be denied that my hair was receding. When did my smile become a lop-sided squint? Grotesque. There was no sparkle of youth left and no sheen of career success to trade on into my mid-thirties. I wasn't good at anything. The biggest failure of anyone I knew.

`Dossier: Threeman. Oxford University. Graduated 1996 in Modern Languages [French, German, Russian - dissertation on 'The science of the brain and the narrative of consciousness in Fyodor Dostoyevsky']. Academically weak. Badly-behaved and unpopular among peers and tutors. Handsome.`

My lifestyle revolved around weekends out and about for a few lagers – then a few more. Meeting loose women perhaps for mutually degrading encounters. Shagging was fun but at thirty-something the lager thing was becoming hard work: every hangover spiked with paranoia. Yet the weekends kept coming. Always a pub crawl into town via the backstreet boozers with the best jukeboxes. The Rolling Stones or some riffy Britpop. Lager top, please John. Sometimes I ordered it as a 'quarter-shandy' for maximum slide-down zing. Nibbles? Yep. Dry roasted peanuts. Usually two packets per first three ales. Always on my own. Friends hadn't really been happening for a while.

The weekend also meant curry. Lamb rogan josh or a solid chicken madras depending on my flavour du jour. Mondays might be a takeaway pizza. Tuesdays? The McDonald's drive-thru in Slough was open 24-hours so... Wednesdays maybe a visit to the Colonel and pile into a tower meal. Mayo dolloped on most things. Never enough chocolate for dessert.

Aware I was clocking up a hefty calorie intake I would jog in the evenings during the week. Forty minutes pounding the streets, fat and slow, occasionally stopping to urinate against a wall. And there went my sporting career – gone, all over, finished, *sayonara* mate. A blaze of mediocrity in a few team sports had fizzled out into nothing without me even noticing, no resistance, without me even firing a shot back. I was reduced to burning calories as a pitiful keep-fit jogger. An absolute fucking shit show.

I needed to find something different – a spark. But what?

The jogging helped, releasing endorphins, but only lethargic ones which chemically couldn't really be bothered. I enjoyed running on the grass up The Long Walk. From the castle gates to The Copper Horse it was 4km there and 4km back. Dead straight. The relentless monotony appealed to me. I did it more and more often. Even started to take splits: at the road, at the turnstile gate, and at The Copper Horse itself. Never looked at the stopwatch on the way back. Just focused on inflicting the punishment. Which I deserved. Because I was a cunt. Everyone by their absence said so.

HMP Wormwood Scrubs, London. 1998.
INT. B Wing. Cell 53 [second landing].

Daytime. DARIUS DARNELL, gangster, convicted murderer, the kingpin of social order and heroin distribution in HMP Wormwood Scrubs. Darnell is lying on his bed reading a car magazine. THREEMAN knocks on the open cell door. Threeman is only wearing a bath towel around his waist, and he has blood coming from an open wound on his face.

THREEMAN: Something to show you Shithead.

DARNELL: Fuck off Manslaughter. Only my friends call me Shithead.

THREEMAN: Follow me.

Darnell resents the impertinence but follows. The two men walk down from the second landing to the ground floor, past a scruffy pool table, watched by other inmates in silence. They enter the communal showers. A heavily tattooed man is lying dead with blood over his face and throat. His neck is at an unnatural angle. Beside him on the stone floor is a football sock with three pool balls inside it. One shower head is still running.

DARNELL: Useless cunt. I told him you'd be half-decent.

THREEMAN: No. I just got lucky.

DARNELL: [A beat. Then --] Why show me?

THREEMAN: I'm sorry for how you've had to live, Darius. I know you probably didn't have a choice.

After turning off the running shower, Threeman walks to the door and takes his clothes from a peg. He has his back to Darnell who picks up the football sock.

DARNELL: Hey --

Darnell empties the pool balls from the sock and throws one in a looping underarm towards Threeman, who catches it.

DARNELL: -- Rack em up.

My 8k on The Long Walk started to improve so I tested to see if fewer curries made me quicker. It did. Not sure I had weighed myself for a decade or so – eighty-seven kilos on the scales seemed a lot, and when did I go metric? A couple of soft-drink weekends gave an immediate payoff in my jogging. I bought a pair of Adidas trail shoes and entered some off-road events: long, hilly slogs through woods or over army training land. They were fun and my legs were holding up, but it made me angry who was ahead of me. Who the fuck are you anyway?

These fitness drives had not been uncommon over the years, but they usually dissipated, momentum depth-charged in nine or ten/eleven lagers, each with a party dash of R Whites. But this particular running phase aged thirty-three felt different. It felt more… crucial. As if it might be my last chance before a very slippery slope.

DING! DING! DING!

That summer I had an English teaching job at a local university. It was strange to enjoy work. It felt intellectual. Worthy? One day after classes I took my gear up to the campus track to run four times a mile. The track was deserted when I started, then one girl appeared and started warming up: a proper athlete. In my second rep recovery I said hello. She was competing in the Junior Commonwealths in Delhi the next week. Her coach was on his way to give her a speed session. By my third recovery the coach had arrived and said a cheery hello to me.

– What's your session? he asked.
– Four miles, I said as a sad apology of my session.
– Nice one. What event do you do?

I didn't have an answer but didn't want to sound like a joker either. Memories flashed up. Grainy half-forgotten images and commentary nuggets from back when, yes, when I used to be really into running.

And Ovett goes!
The world record exchange of 1981
Sprint races in the playground
Coe bounding along – maintaining good form
John Walker and Steve Scott in Sub-4 kit

Didn't I win that middle school cross-country?
BBC *Superstars* gym tests
Welcome to Oslo, the Dream Mile starring Steve Ovett
Beating my time around the block
Ovett against Moorcroft and Maree at Crystal Palace
David Coleman on commentary
Or Ron Pickering
Los Angeles 1984
Here's the real dangerman, Joaquim Cruz
My size 5 Nike Pegasus
New Balance
And Coe's going to defend his title!
Olympians Choice sports shop in Slough
Club Nike
Steve Cram
Kellogg's START made from three wholesome grains not one
Ovett in Edinburgh
Coe in Stuttgart
Seoul.

What event do I do? There seemed to be enough to justify an answer. It wasn't definitive but it was better than no answer at all. The coach's eyes were gleaming with such enthusiasm that it drew the words out of me.

– Eight hundred metres, I said.
– Who do you run with?
– Nobody. Just on my own.

I fast-jogged my last rep. It must have looked crap. Or maybe there was something? As I put my tracksuit top on to leave, the coach asked if I would be interested in joining in with his student middle-distance group. The university term would be starting on Monday and there would be lots of new athletes. Yes please, I'd like that.

Nice to meet you, Apollo.

HMP Wormwood Scrubs. 1998.
Vetting, Cross-Verification and Recruitment
Initial Interview

INT. An interview cell. Nevis in a plain grey suit, white shirt, and dark tie. A thick thatch of black hair [20+ years younger]. Of medium build with strong shoulders and quads. He is holding a manilla dossier. There is a single table in the middle of the cell at which a man is sitting, the man who in future would become known as Threeman but who is currently just any other miserable prison inmate. Threeman is wearing trainers, jeans [with no belt], and a regulation prison work shirt. Nevis sits down. The dialogue is measured and cold.

NEVIS: I'm Nevis.

THREEMAN: [cynical] Nice to meet you.

NEVIS: Why did you kill him?

THREEMAN: I didn't.

NEVIS: Let's see [checks file notes]. Your first punch broke his left eye socket. You immediately flipped him onto the floor where, while fending off his counter-attacks, you smashed your fists and elbow multiple times into his throat until his windpipe collapsed. Then you took a neck hold and applied a twist, sudden and forceful enough to sever the spinal cord at the C2 cervical vertebra.

THREEMAN: Says who?

NEVIS: That information is courtesy of the pathologist and the shower room CCTV.

THREEMAN: He attacked me first.

NEVIS: Only tamely.

THREEMAN: [matching Nevis's flat delivery] He's a convicted murderer. I'm naked. He comes at me from behind swinging a long sock with three pool balls inside it. Aiming for my head. His first strike narrowly misses my cranium and lands on my neck and shoulder. I'm on the floor face down as he takes his second swing. Tame?

NEVIS: You replied with superior force. To a jury that's murder.

THREEMAN: The jury can study the footage. A frenzied situation of extreme violence which he initiated. There were only two of us and death was inevitable. Heads it's him. Tails it's me. Wasn't me who flipped the coin.

NEVIS: Would you like to kill again?

THREEMAN: No.

NEVIS: For me. If I paid you.

They look into each other's eyes. An extended silence. Zero emotion or facial expressions. Nevis knows there won't be an answer -- and he never expected one. Both characters know the conversation is over. Nevis picks up the file and walks to the door of the interview cell -- looks back.

NEVIS: Think about it.

I walked away not really knowing.
But. *Athletics*. Something felt right.
The spark?

Monday. I was the first to arrive. On a sloping rugby field next to the track we did an insane shuttle run session. Runners everywhere trying to beat each other. I tried to keep up with as many of the young students as I could. This wasn't that many but I wasn't a shambles either. Running fast was fun. Running fast *against* people was intoxicating. The weapons-grade endorphins pinballed around my system for hours afterwards. I felt happy for the first time in a long while.

Tuesday. We ran a 20-minute fartlek around the track with Apollo's coaching whistles going off all over the place to signal a short surge or an explosive kick. Battered. Then we jogged to the indoor track and did three sets of bodyweight circuits. 30-second efforts. Counting our reps. Like the BBC *Superstars* gym tests but this was real, very real.

Wednesday. Reps on the track. 12 x 200m. In lanes. Fast.

Thursday. Indoor drills. High kneed skips. Heel flicks. Lunges. Bounding. Hopping. Four 100-metre fast strides. Then three rounds of *Superstars*. At home I did some extra press-ups to accelerate my rise up the pecking order.

Friday. Rest day. Not even a jog was allowed. I obeyed.

Saturday. We met in the Great Park and did cross-country hill reps. Blasting up and down slopes on grass, grit, and mud. The light 1500m lads were crazy quick around these loops. I lumbered around like a sack of spuds but loved it. In the afternoon I bought a running vest and a pair of track trousers with zips up the side. Dear diary, ate a salad for dinner.

Sunday. Apollo said to do a long run on our own, ideally on soft ground. I drove to Black Park and did thirty-five minutes on a new route, taking splits at the major turns.

Three weeks later. HMP Wormwood Scrubs.

INT. The interview cell. Nevis and Threeman are opposite each other across a small table, matching one another's calm body language. We don't hear the question. It might not even have been asked.

THREEMAN: No.

NEVIS: You seem skilled at it. Instinctive.

THREEMAN: I killed him in self-defence. He was a murderer and a heroin dealer. An addict himself. I did him a favour.

NEVIS: I agree. I'd only ask you to kill bad people. Scum who make the world a nastier place, who attack other people with pool balls in a sock, or with machetes, guns, or armies. The work needs to be done. I'd always explain to you why.

THREEMAN: I'll do my time here. Find yourself another fucked-up hero.

And on it went. I turned up for every session of the second week and got my forty-minute steady run in on Sunday. The third week couldn't come soon enough. By week four I had bought myself a cheap pair of Adidas

Arriba running spikes: ice white with three silver stripes. The difference they made was incredible. With each footstrike I exploded forwards off the track.

Four months later. HMP Wormwood Scrubs.

INT. The interview cell. Threeman is in a suit. Not yet changed back into his prison clothes after court. He sits with his hands on the interview table and says nothing.

NEVIS: Sorry to hear about the jury verdict.

With precision Nevis places a manilla dossier on the table. The front of the dossier is marked 'CONFIDENTIAL'. With equal precision Nevis places a thick wad of mint fifty-pound notes on top of the dossier.

NEVIS: Govority po-russky?

THREEMAN: Da, konyeshno.

The conversation continues in Russian. [with on-screen English subtitles]

NEVIS: There's a plane leaving for St Petersburg in an hour. The man we want dead has killed a waitress, a taxi driver and five policemen, as well as an eighth victim who I'm not at liberty to describe to you. That's just in Europe. Elsewhere his body count is considerably higher. He's a Russian national. An arms dealer whose principal customers are the Syrian Hezbollah, or at least a renegade offshoot of it. He has access to fake documentation and is known to have entered the UK three times in the last year, each time without being identified, each time leaving unscathed. We're still cleaning up his most recent mess which was not too long ago. By chance we picked him up on the grid on his way home -- to Russia via Stockholm. His ferry to St Petersburg arrives in seven hours. We need a Russian language specialist.

Threeman does not react. From the right side pocket of his suit Nevis takes a hand-gun and places it on the table. From his left pocket he places a silencer alongside it.

NEVIS: Glock-23. And a Banish Whispertech suppressor. You can test it here. Identicals will be given to you on arrival in St Petersburg. There's a small holdall of clothes ready for you, naturally. Flight tickets. Passport. When you come back you won't be living here anymore. If you agree, you'll be paid in instalments. The first will be --

Calmly, Threeman takes the money and throws it into the corner of the room. He takes the gun and screws in the silencer. He aims and fires one shot [only a heavy metallic click] into the thick wad of notes. This sends up a small cloud of paper confetti which then settles. Throughout this Nevis has looked straight ahead at Threeman -- who then opens the dossier.

THREEMAN: So.

I launched into the structure of it all. Each training session was planned for us. Apollo gave out printed copies of the schedule for the next three months. Finally my days had a meaning. Every track session was my Olympic final. The familiar red of the track. Rows of spectators rising up to the heavens. I stayed in on Fridays because the Saturday hills were so epic. Blockbuster reps up quad-killer slopes. The original Hamburger Hill. Hacksaw Ridge. Heartbreak Hotel. Cheeseburger Hill

The handsome swagger returned. I felt young again. As if the clock had been wound back twenty years to what should have happened: talent iD-ed and nurtured to greatness from the age of thirteen. I talked less. Each recovery between reps was too precious to waste talking. Deep breaths and savour the oxygen. Silence. Staying strong in the recoveries was huge. I became calmer during training and in the hours either side of a session.

`Dossier Threeman: Convicted of manslaughter March 1997. Sentenced to eight years. Vetting for the Service commenced inside HMP Wormwood Scrubs. Received additional seven-year sentence May 1998. Sentences rescinded. New identity assigned. Field training in Hereford and other locations followed his first mission [successful] in 1998.`

The more track sessions I completed the more people in the group accepted me. By turning up every time, by slugging out every rep, by never caving in, I was becoming one of the gang. All our daring adventures were to the same place: an oxygen-depleted floodlit world with pace whistles and a lactic cement mixer parked uncomfortably close by. Even if it was 24 x 200m (off 30 seconds) no rep was ever the same, and we ran them as fast as we could.

Each session chipped away at my physique. By Christmas I had already bought slimmer jeans. Twice. I was down to 75kg and looked sensational. Yeah. The programme left no stone unturned with an attention to detail which made me feel supremely important. The king was back from exile.

Dossier Threeman: Marksmanship grade X-1 [sniper class], hand-to-hand combat, ciphers, BARS performance driving A-licence, fluent in French, German, Serbo-Croat, Russian.

The *Superstars* circuits improved my strength. Drills polished up my running technique. Hurdle walkovers made my hips more flexible. Strides increased my coordination. Press-ups. Powerdrives. Plyos. Fast-twitch muscles were developing from all the sprint reps. Every day I was sending the same message to my body. *Speed!* The adaption was real and happening before my eyes. In the mirror suddenly an athlete was looking back… and a long-lost friend. My legs were now muscular works of art, definition sculpted to perfection. At Saturday hills the mud splattered abstract expressionism onto my calves – my beautiful calves. The svelte hips of bygone youth were back: 29-inches. My torso was ripped to shreds, knocking out thirty-six press-ups per set. Dips. Pull-ups. My lats rose out of my running vest like a giant spitting cobra.

Month on month my rep times on the track improved. I rose in the pecking order of my rivals – and now friends. Thanks to them I was tougher on the long reps, faster on the short sprints, and better on all the ones in between. We ran a multi-pace training system.

Dossier Threeman: history of substance excess, mild sexual predation, PTSD [see: manslaughter conviction], dissociative identity disorder.

In the 1960s the New Zealand athletes of Arthur Lydiard achieved prolific success on a programme of relentless endurance mileage. Lydiard was a distrusted maverick when he started coaching. His gruff, abrasive manner made him unpopular with the establishment who attempted to keep him in his place. However, the problem for the New Zealand selectors was that very soon Lydiard had an entire stable of local athletes dominating the national championships. The endurance mileage was working. The maverick could no longer be shunned. But Lydiard was aiming far higher than mere national domination, and his approach was vindicated when his athlete Peter Snell won the Olympic 800m in Rome in 1960, beating world record holder Roger Moens up the inside line. Nobody wins up the inside! This finishing power was built on a programme of 100-mile weeks, most of it run in the hills of Auckland. In 1964 Snell won the 800-1500m double in Tokyo. Along the way he set world records for the 800m and the mile. It was the swinging sixties and stamina ruled the middle-distance world. Peter Snell wore the crown and Arthur Lydiard was the master coach with the golden whistle.

Then in the 1970s British coach Frank Horwill re-considered the importance of speed in middle-distance events. He pioneered a structure to hone an athlete at different training speeds: from 5k tempos, through 3k pace, 1500m, 800m, and 400m race paces.

Both methodologies were entirely correct for their era. With Mr Lydiard's system Snell won the Commonwealth Games 800m on a grass track and three Olympic gold medals on heavy cinder tracks in leather spikes. When rubberized tracks were introduced in the late sixties the relative advantage of pure speed increased massively.

With metal spikes biting into the new grippy surface, each stride was launched off absolute traction. Spiked racing shoes also became lighter and had stiffer soles made from synthetic materials. By sacrificing some endurance miles, the Horwill multi-pace training system incorporated flat-out sprinting speed into 800m and 1500m training. Before long the British athletes whose coaches were adopting these principles started to win races. Frank Horwill became the guru of middle-distance running.

Among his acolytes was Steve Ovett's coach Harry Wilson who collaborated with Horwill on the training manual *The Complete Middle-Distance Runner* (1972). The new speed-based methodology made perfect sense when dealing with an animal as talented as Ovett. How do you train a panther? Run him fast.

Peter Coe was another disciple. With his engineering background he crunched his own numbers and applied nuances to Horwill's fundamentals, trimming down mileage and turbo-charging the programme with even more quality speedwork. Off the back of Seb Coe's career *Winning Running* (1996) by Peter Coe became the de facto bible of the 800m and 1500m events. It was followed to the letter by Hicham El Guerrouj et al.

As an aspiring coach Apollo made a pilgrimage to meet Peter Coe at his home. Warmly welcomed, he was invited into the study, the nerve centre of the operation, and was shown the leather briefcase containing the sacred training files: every rep time and recovery time from Hallamshire Harriers juniors through to LA84. The coaches drank tea and compared notes. Peter's notes on Seb's Olympic golds and Apollo's annotated dreams for his future

Olympians. Kindred spirits. As Peter bid his new protégé farewell he wished him luck, then paused and with melancholy in his voice said:

They've all come. El Guerrouj. The Kenyans. Ethiopians. Algerians. All of them. But you're the only person from this country who's ever asked how we did it.

The numbers were important, but what Peter Coe and Harry Wilson both understood was the art of coaching numbers out of people. The shared love of each stride your athlete takes. The individuality of an athlete. How to nurture a racing brain. The physicality of mentality. Quality. Honing. Focusing on the tiny margins. Peter and Harry (and Arthur Lydiard) lived lives obsessed by each hundredth of a second.

The athlete's job is simple: eat well, sleep well, turn up on time, and do what your coach tells you. The master coach cannot live so easily. She or he lies awake at night tortured by that hundredth of a second. Wondering how to find ten of them to make the next point-one. Every tenth of a second in the legs delegates more tactical decisions to the race synapses. While the athlete sleeps the coach goes out to the forest with an axe and chops wood – logs, branches, dry twigs, kindling – and constructs a bonfire for the athlete to light up in the next training session. The bonfire of arrogance.

A few weeks after their chat Apollo arranged for Peter Coe to give a presentation in the club room at the Windsor track. Though old and a little frail by this time, Peter's eyes still burned with the Olympic flame. From his leather briefcase he produced a succession of A4 transparencies one after another like a cabaret magician.

Each sheet of acetate was laid on the projector glass with surgical precision, illuminating on-screen yet another series of priceless coaching data from Seb Coe's career. For an hour he detailed every phase of his athlete's development from the age of fourteen up until breaking the 800m, the mile, the 1500m and 1000m world records. Apollo coached our group with the same multi-pace programme. All our training sessions came directly from Peter Coe's magic briefcase. We sipped our glucose drinks from the middle-distance Holy Grail.

After six months of the programme I weighed 71.0kg. Now I was specifically not looking sensational. Being a superb middle-distance runner meant being so lean that in casual clothes you looked scrawny and ill. A pencil-thin neck and an emaciated edge to the jawline. Non-running friends noticed this and softly body-shamed you, because your new lifestyle was a threat. Their empty lives meant nothing to you anymore.

I had new friends, track friends, with personalities based on their training traits. Some front-loaded sessions. Some had a fast last rep. Some were simply better and stamped on you if you even get close. Some had poor pace judgement, so you let them go on the first rep, but you were all over them by rep five, or rep eleven, or rep nineteen. Danny Hodge, like an Anguillan seagull patrolling for fish, would float and wait, slipstreaming, saving his best, then swoop and pick you off the moment he saw a chink, and cackle with laughter as he crossed the finish line one stride ahead. Over our thousands of reps they became protagonists in the story.

My running persona? I could not deny the physical likeness to Ovett. Same height. Similar physique.

Identical running style. The more people said it the smoother I ran. My head was the same egg shape with the exact same balding pattern time-stamped to Los Angeles 1984. Facially I wasn't a million miles off either, especially down at race weight with hollow shade beneath my cheek bones. In split-shorts my quads were long. In spikes my calves were beautiful. There was some degree of Ovett track arrogance, I hoped, and a definite tendency to showboat. A huge kick finish? Guilty.

Already within a few weeks Apollo had started calling me 'Steve' as a thing. It stuck. Within three months everyone in the group was calling me Steve. My real name faded from use down at the track. Naturally, I embraced the comparison. What middle-distance runner wouldn't? I wore a red vest for training sessions and bought myself retro Nike Pegasus flats. Bedtime reading was now *Ovett: An Autobiography* (1984). I ex-communicated the press, let my spikes do the talking, sat on the leader, and unleashed monstrous last rep kicks while waving to the mob-like crowd. I rewatched the YouTube clips of world records I had seen live on telly as a young Ovett fan. Races from the fantasy island of international athletics.

Oslo. Rieti. Crystal Palace. Koblenz.

The new alter ego only increased my motivation and my first summer season was arriving to prove my credentials. Races! I knew the training sessions like the back of my hand, but I had no race time on the board. No time no identity. Athletes have names and we have numbers.

Usain Bolt	*nine-five-eight*
Allyson Felix	*twenty-one-six-nine*
Joaquim Cruz	*one-forty-one*
Hicham El Guerrouj	*three-twenty-six-flat*

At middle-distance the convention is to drop the decimal places (if you have any) and always round down.

Eight months into my athletics career, aged thirty-four, I lined up for my first ever 800-metre race. A graded meet where everyone enters with the time they expect to run. I nailed my bollocks to the mast and put down 2:00 on my entry. Positive intent. Why not? If I got dragged along in a quick race I should deliver there or thereabouts. The Ovett red vest was chosen for the occasion, teamed with black split-shorts and my beloved Adidas Arriba spikes. Graded meant in theory the win was up for grabs. I drew lane eight, feeling a bit exposed but okay. Other than that, yes very confident.

On your marks. BANG!

I'm brave off the start. As fast as feels comfortable with my beginner's confidence. I'm definitely going fast, but shit, lanes seven and six are all over me here. We break from lanes and I have to speed up to tag onto the bunch. Now uncomfortably fast and already scary. I settle at the back. Timid. What the fuck is this pace? Way too fast down the back straight but at least I'm out of the wind. With each stride it gets harder to stay tagged onto the race. Tactics are now irrelevant. Pain is the only commodity. The frenzied pack is one stride ahead of me: a twenty-eight-limbed monster writhing with anger. I'm just relieved not to be in the middle of it. We round the second bend. Not nice already – not fucking nice at all.

No one in the pack is letting up. Shit did we just accelerate? The first home straight is already hurting. Badly. Everywhere. This pain has accumulated way faster than I was expecting or am cool with. Why were you confident you fucking idiot? Keep working! As I push to stay in the mix suddenly a horrible thought occurs, and recurs, each stride scarier, an utterly terrifying spectre – the second lap.

DING! DING! DING!
I glance to the left at the race clock on the infield. 1:01…

Sixty-one. I always look at the split. A race marshall usually shouts the time as you go through, but you can always see the split to be certain. All meets are electronically timed. At some meets the race timer stops to show the leader's split. Makes sense. Sometimes you see the rolling split. Also good. Some people never look, which I just don't get. The bigger picture is knowing exactly what you can and cannot finish off. I just learnt my first parameter: what through in sixty-one meant.

I'm with the pack at the bell, well-positioned for a slipstream down the soon-come back straight, but sixty-one has utterly ruined me. The moment the others get excited and step it up around the bend they drop me like a stone. I'm run out of it by 450 metres.

The back straight wind is gusty and the required slipstream is disappearing metre-by-metre into the distance. The lactic starts to drip, trickle, then fucking pour in, and within barely ten strides I have no concept of putting one leg in front of the other for another 290… 289… 288 metres. The sudden heaviness of my quads is horrendous. Gravity just tripled and it burns like hell. I know what excessive lactic feels like from training, but I've never run so far with such volumes of it filling my legs. Also I can't breathe. Totally fucked. Survival instinct tells me to keep pumping my arms. Work! Goodness knows how I even finish. I fall apart and run a soul-destroying 2:08. What the fuck was *that?*

That was the shock of how brutal racing is. A whole different gravy to training. Reps in training were hard but you carefully measured the pain into small economical portions. You diluted it as equally as possible over the number of reps. And all the fast reps were short – even an eyeballs-out 500 is not an 800. You backed off by three percent down the home straight in training knowing there were more reps to come. You paced the entire session to get the best average. In a race there was no average. Just one chance. You had to push every chip in your stack into the middle of the table. All-in.

Early pain. Sustained pain. Maximal pain. All-in means still running as fast as you possibly can long after it's unbearable. In an 800m you have to 'accelerate' on the second lap to maintain the same speed, and even then you will slow down. Most world records and personal bests are set off a two-second positive differential: the first lap is about two seconds quicker than the second lap.

David Rudisha	49.3	51.6	+2.3
Rick Wohlhuter	50.7	52.9	+2.2
Pamela Jelimo	55.8	58.2	+2.4
Sebastian Coe	49.7	52.0	+2.3
Wilson Kipketer	49.3	51.8	+2.5

This pacing matrix doesn't really change down from world record holders to club athletes. Two seconds is spot on. If you get your split wrong your time is screwed. A second too fast on the first lap can cost you five seconds on the second lap. Or more. Two seconds too cautious on the first 400m and you can never catch up the time after the bell. With fluctuations in form through a season you never know exactly what your ideal split is, and even if you did know you often have to sacrifice it for race position. My first-race splits of 61-67 were bad pacing even in the theoretical light of day, but to actually run it felt like Armageddon. That is the 800m. It is hard.

At least I was in the mix for a lap. Identity earned – 2:08. Now I could look other athletes in the eye. I was officially an 800m runner. Like Steve Ovett.

`Dossier Threeman: Operational 1998-present.`

One week later at Barnet Copthall I ran 2:07 and didn't come last. In my first three races the following summer I also ran 2:07. Frustrating. Then 2:04 happened. I was in the mix.

In the mix was more than just a race time, more than just being in a pack with a possible chance to win. In the mix was the graduation from being a runner to being an athlete. In the mix made the question not *if* you run, but *what event* you run. In the mix meant also racing a 1500m and being horrified all over again at the different pain signature of three-and-three-quarter laps. But then you had a second number to work on too – 4:28. Now you were a fully-fledged middle-distance runner.

Dossier Threeman: CONFIRMED kills. Saint Petersburg 1998. Marrakesh 2000. Antwerp 2003. International waters [Indian Ocean] 2007. Sacramento 2011. Porto Alegre 2013. Mogadishu 2017. Malaga 2018.

In the mix meant you ran in minimalist two-inch split shorts. Like Juantorena. Like Wilson Kipketer. Like Big John Walker. Long powerful quads psyche out the opposition. In the mix meant you trained in 'flats' or spikes. In the mix meant you ate salads, nuts, bananas, dried apricots. Or steak after weights. You weighed yourself to one decimal place every morning, after taking a shit.

Dossier Threeman: No next of kin.

In the mix was Olympic gold medallists in your everyday life. You said hello to Linford down at the track. Denise asked you about your last race. In the mix meant Sally Pearson doing sprint hurdle drills in lane four as you warm-up. You smirk and invite her to do 4 x 800m with you. She declines (obviously) and the joke soon backfires when you are impaled on the track in absolute pieces after the third rep. Sally stands over you: *That's why I never do four times eight-hundred.* She laughs at you. Her coach laughs. And you laugh too. Then you peel yourself off the track, take your eight-minute rest, and then you're fucking nails on the last rep too. One man's blazing speed has torn this field asunder. As you jog past Sally on your cool-down you quip that: *It's hard work making it look that easy.*

In the mix was everything I ever wanted to be. After a season of athletics it was becoming clear that not only was I keen and dedicated, I was also – whisper it – quite good. Then Apollo dropped the bombshell.

– Hey Steve, if you turn thirty-five next season you can compete in all the Masters stuff. The British Champs are usually in Birmingham. And every year you have either the Europeans or the Worlds. Next year is Sacramento.

The World Masters Athletics Championships.
You had me at hello.

Peroxide Blonde has her back to me when I pass her on my last 300-metre rep. The tight bends at Sokolniki suck your legs into the track with the centrifugal force. The faster you go the worse it is. But the straights felt good. I threw in a couple of big ones halfway through the set then just flowed. Has Peroxide Blonde been watching the show? I hope so.

Job done. I drink my flask of tea in the stands watching the other athletes. The recovery starts. Rehydration, eating, and sleeping are my only tasks until tomorrow's steady run. Apart from the real world where I have two English classes to teach this evening. This double life is required to make ends meet, to exist outside the athletic dimension. I do the hours and it pays for food, rent, and racing flats. Of course, I prepare lessons and have affection for all my students, but I can't let the classroom define me. When all is said and done – who am I?

`Dossier Threeman: Moscow sleeper asset: RED3`

I'm a good English teacher.
I'm a majestic 800-metre runner.

An Ingot for an Eye

★

By 1978 the meticulous science of Peter Coe was bearing fruit. Seb started the new season with his usual series of low-key races and was soon showing great form.

From day one when Sebastian was a twelve-year-old junior, Peter had factored in the high-quality opposition that would inevitably be met on the way to the top. He explained to his schoolboy athlete the maths of the competition as he progressed through the ranks. Being the fastest boy in the school was only the first goal. Then he had to be the best in Sheffield. Beyond that he must beat everyone in Yorkshire. And win the Inter-Counties. With each increase in geographical scope and each step up in age-group the number of good athletes would increase. Many of these lads would be equally as talented and be working equally as hard. The difference would be the development of quality in the Peter Coe programme: *Why pound the life out of a young runner when you can develop them with quality?*

In middle-distance running 'quality' is a synonym for speed: hitting target times in the key track sessions at fast paces. Peter limited the endurance mileage so Seb was fresh enough to blast every rep on the track. His athlete committed to the programme with such dedication that Peter's main task was actually to limit the total volume of training. Freshness and long-term enthusiasm were vital in the evolution from club junior into senior athlete, then international athlete, then Olympian.

The development was bang on schedule. In the summer of 1978 Coe lowered his own UK 800m record at the Van Damme Memorial meeting in Brussels. 1:44.3 with an extremely fast split of 50.5. This personal best was now less than a second off Alberto Juantorena's world record. The stopwatch was complying to the joint will of the Coe project. However, the stated mission was to win the 1980 Olympics. Nothing less. Only Moscow mattered. And even as early as 1978 the Coe analytics were having to factor in a *force majeure.*

An element of unforeseeable magnitude. Ovett.

While Coe was setting national records at 800m and finding his feet as a race tactician, Ovett was already beating world class fields in the 800m, and decimating them in the 1500m. Steve's results over 1500m and the mile in 1978 continued a satisfying trend. All wins. All dominant wins. The sheer panache of Ovett's performances were unnerving for his rivals. He seemed to do whatever he wanted, off any pace, against any opposition, and still win at a canter. Each victory wave a sign of how easy it was. The Moscow Olympics were only two race seasons away. Seb and Peter Coe acknowledged this clear and present danger to their plans and identified an opportunity accordingly.

The 1978 European Championships 800m. Prague.

Before the championships Ovett and Coe had avoided racing against each other. Mutual recognition of the threat? Both were in form and neither athlete wanted to give an iota of tactical insight as to how they might beat each other. Was the avoidance fifty-fifty? Maybe. Peter outlined Seb's race season well in advance. In contrast Ovett seemed to follow a random race schedule with a knack of being elsewhere whenever Coe was on the start-sheet. Ovett also had a penchant for European race venues a long way off the beaten track. However, as a classic 'feel' athlete Steve's schedule was often just a case of going with the flow of his body rhythm. *You looked fantastic today Steve, you need a race.* This approach wasn't necessarily a systematic strategy to avoid Coe. But yes, if you chose your races at the last minute, you did know where your rival would or wouldn't be racing. Either way, the Coes guessed this dance would continue right up until Moscow and played their own equal part in the quickstep.

Despite the close-knit European circuit, the two British stars always managed to dodge head-to-head races over the same distance. If Seb ran the 800m, Steve would run the mile. When Coe ran in Brussels, Ovett would be at Crystal Palace. The only race between 1978 and the 1980 Olympics where Steve Ovett would absolutely *have* to race Sebastian Coe was at the European Championships. And yet neither Coe nor Ovett won the European 800m in Prague. It was won by rank outsider Olaf Beyer of East Germany. How?

The Coes were obsessed with the threat Ovett posed for Moscow. They knew Prague would be the only chance to test Ovett's deadly finishing speed in the 800m. Peter's belief was that Seb was faster in a hypothetical time trial, or at least *would* be faster by 1980, but that Ovett's pet tactic of sitting on a front-runner always gave him an advantage in a race. Just as Walker, Wessinghage, and Hill had wondered in Düsseldorf, so Peter and Seb speculated upon in Prague. Where did this advantage end? At what pace could Ovett not kick? Numbers were crunched and the result was Coe committing himself to a 50-second first lap. Ideally 50-low and if he could 50-point. This would be a faster split than the world record but Coe believed he was capable of such a fast first lap and still finishing well.

50-54 splits? Maybe 50-53. His UK record of 1:44.3 made the question at least askable. Peter's coaching brief on the warm-up track made no bones about the aim:

Stick to what we planned. We've come here to find out something and we won't find it out from the back of the field. You'll probably blow it and set them up for a record – but if you don't try, I won't know; and we've spent a lot of time and money for this. We can't go back without knowing what we've come to find out. This is only a stepping stone on the way for what we're after.

By taking it out from the start Coe would, he hoped, make it a pure two-horse race and remove the pack and race position as a tactical variable. To get the slipstream he so enjoyed, Ovett would have to follow him. Pace distribution would thus be isolated as an experimental factor. Coe would force Ovett to show exactly what he was, or was not, capable of running. The race in Prague was a sacrifice in the name of empirical science. Win or lose, the data would set the tactical parameters for 1980 in Moscow.

50-low? The calculations were typically objective from Coe. However, the execution of the plan demanded a hot streak of madness. It's one thing nominating a crazy first lap but actually running one is another thing entirely. The second lap is always there in your head, the terrifying spectre screaming at you to back off. The recklessness required to put the plan into operation was also the inherent risk. It could backfire badly.

And it did. Coe went through in 49.3.

Fifty-point was very ambitious. Forty-nine-three was just suicidal. On the plus side, Coe had dragged Olaf Beyer and Steve Ovett along with him on this insane pace to the halfway bell, but the second lap became a Vietnam movie. The camouflaged sniper in the trees waited until 600 metres and then started to gun down Coe. Quads first. Ovett saw the chinks, waited around the top bend, and then picked him off with 100 metres to go. Beyer, who had gone through the bell in second, had let Ovett pass him down the back straight, the East German preferring to save something for the end of the race. Off the last bend Beyer had made it back up to the two GB vests. As the Brits battled each other for supremacy, both Ovett and Coe were targets for the invisible sniper. In the home straight both were taking direct hits. Legs. Body shots. Shoulders. Lactic acid splattered everywhere. Beyer found deep reserves of speed and took out Coe then a fading Ovett in the run for the line.

Beyer wins.
Ovett second. Coe third.

– Who the fuck was *that?* asked Steve Ovett ruefully to his teammate as the two Britons shook hands.

That was a talented athlete and a smart racer respecting the boundaries of the positive split: the two-second differential. Olaf Beyer had seen the forty-nine split and backed off Coe's push in the third quarter of the race. By doing so he timed his self-destruction the best. He was in radio contact with the lactic sniper in the trees. He may possibly-perhaps-allegedly-according-to-Stasi-files have been energised in accordance with the East German 'system' of the era, but even with your eyeballs on storks optimum pace distribution mattered.

Ovett considered he'd made a tactical mistake to ease off

on the last bend waiting for Coe to crack. This let Beyer back in the race. You only have limited ability to accelerate or re-accelerate in an 800m. Momentum is important. Tactics are only tactics within the context of running virtually flat out the whole way. Ovett learnt more than Coe did in Prague. Keep running hard and expect the unexpected – an Olaf in a blue moon. The consolation for Steve was beating his personal best for the silver medal.

1:44.1. Ovett was now the 800m UK record holder.

Three days later he was also European Champion. Unlike Coe he was doubling up, and in a rough and tumble 1500m final Ovett dominated. Kicking at 200 then purring down the home straight to cheers from his Czech fans. Bohemia roaring on the ultimate running Bohemian. Rhapsody in spikes. Gold meant a successful championships.

Not so for Coe. Yes, he did indeed find out where Ovett's breaking point was, but he had paid an exorbitant price to do so. An ingot for an eye. Coe had thrown away a golden chance to race Ovett at a sensible pace and, quite possibly, to beat him. By offering himself up as nothing more than a lamb to the slaughter, the Coe pacing experiment had ignored a far more significant race factor. Fear. The debilitating hollow-legged fear which Steve Ovett was instilling in everyone he raced. A pyrrhic 49.3 split from Coe in Prague had not deconstructed Ovett's weaknesses to any great degree. Not being able to finish strongly off a 49-second split was as obvious as the red colour of the track. What the race did instead was to confirm a psychological stranglehold. There was an unspeakable truth in the ether that only one person knew, and even that person was denying to himself. Coe was scared of Ovett.

Warspite

★

EXT. Stoke Park, South Bucks.

Evening. A sweeping leisure estate with an eighteenth-century Palladian mansion painted in clotted cream, and a 1908 Harry Colt championship golf course. The opulence is matched with an appropriate musical score [orchestral reworking of the Threeman theme].

The parking area outside the mansion is populated with luxury car marques [Porsche, Maybach, Lamborghini]. Guests in dinner jackets and fabulous dresses are entering the mansion. Nevis pulls up in his Renault Twingo and squeezes out of the driver-side door into the arena of wealth.

Two weeks after winning 1500m gold in Prague, Ovett lined up for his last race of the 1978 season in front of an eager home crowd in South London. Having taken care of business in the European 1500m this two-mile race was a perfect way to round off the year. A capacity crowd crammed into Crystal Palace to watch the show. Steve Ovett was now box-office gold. Truth be told, some of the seventeen thousand fans may also have been there to watch the 800m race one hour before, starring Sebastian Coe. And Coe had delivered, breaking the UK national record. Ovett's best mark from Prague had lasted only seventeen days.

Steve Ovett 1:44.1
Sebastian Coe 1:44.0 – an eye for an eye

Nevis admires the array of cars, although some are not necessarily to his taste. He writes the occasional piece [under pseudonym] for a sports car association magazine, and he attends performance driving tours in the rare periods when not consumed by his work. Seeing a tangerine Lamborghini at Stoke Park raises a definite smirk. The whiff of new money always amused him. This place would never change.

Could Ovett steal back the psychological ascendancy? If not, tomorrow's back page headlines would be all about the other fella.

The two-mile field pitted him against the Lion King of long-distance running, the great Henry Rono of Kenya. Rono had dominated the 1978 track season breaking *four* world records. The 10k, 5000m, 3000m steeplechase, and most significantly the 3000m flat. Over two miles, 3218m, Rono would be formidable. Ovett had barely trained in the fortnight since Prague and wasn't sure how his legs would react to a step-up in distance and a hard race. Refreshed or rusty? He suspected he might only be in shape to roll round, but nice to turn up and give something back to the fans.

Nevis is wearing black tie. He appears to have owned his dinner jacket for several years. It has large lapels and shoulders. The cut and Nevis's thick build make it unclear whether the jacket is slightly too large or slightly too small for him. The trousers are almost certainly newer replacements. He is wearing glasses [as usual] and a polka dot bow tie. The central dot on the knot of the tie is a pin-hole camera which he can activate with a button in its wing tip. He is also wearing a smartwatch and carrying his phone in his pocket. He walks to the mansion entrance where he is greeted politely by a muscular official [also in black tie]. Nevis presents his belongings for a security screening -- walks through the body scanner -- then his watch, phone, car key, and glasses are returned to him.

INT. The mansion. Plush and decadent. Throngs of rich guests. Nevis passes through the entrance hall, bidding hellos and good evenings as he goes -- enters the ballroom [art deco]. A hundred or so people are mingling and drinking from champagne flutes. Eclectic guests still sizing each other up. On a gaudy stage a jazz band gently massages the atmosphere. The polite early stages of an extravagant soirée. Shunning the proffered champagne, Nevis heads purposefully towards the bar.

The race was stacked with talent to keep Rono and Ovett honest. Mike McLeod the latest distance star off the north-east production line. Scotland's John Robson and Ireland's Eamonn Coghlan who had both featured strongly in the Prague 1500m final. Bronislaw Malinowski of Poland newly crowned as the European 3000m steeplechase champion. It was a cocktail of middle-distance speedsters and distance hardmen. If Henry Rono shook it up as they all expected, it would be an explosive mix. Eight laps. Everyone was in form. Would speed or endurance triumph?

On your marks. BANG!

Two assigned pacemakers hit the front to control the first three laps. If the pacing is right a world record is an outside possibility. Rono's 3000m world record of 7:32 would crunch out at 8:04 pro rata for 3218 metres – nine seconds faster than Brendan Foster's current two-mile world record. With the two pacers in front Ovett is happy to sit in third place. Rono sits in fourth, sometimes fifth. Everyone in a race is told what the pacemakers have been instructed to do. Ovett and Rono know it's going to be world record schedule until the pacemakers drop out, which ran evenly is laps of 61.3 seconds. Despite some wind on the back straight, lap 1 is 61.0. Their second lap is a solid 61.5.

```
Nevis circulates alone holding a tall glass
of Italian lager.
```

After two laps only one pacemaker is left with Henry Rono poised on his shoulder. The second pacer can only help for half a lap more and Rono, we suspect, might not want the race controlled with even pacing. The Kenyan, in white vest and black shorts, duly takes it on with a surge off the front. Ovett follows in his lucky Soviet vest.

Totally unafraid, Rono. He'll be trying to burn off Steve Ovett.
Rono – Ovett – Malinowski – McLeod – Coghlan.

Lap 3 is 62.0. Quick so far, but after livening it up on the back straight Rono drops it right back down again. The first big yoyo in pace. Only Rono wants to lead and he's now forcing everyone to dance to his fast-slow-fast tune, so lap 4 is slower. 64.5 seconds. At the halfway mark they are three seconds outside world record schedule.

Not ideal weather conditions either. The flags at the end of the stadium are starting to billow and flap. But just as it looks as if the middle of the race will get tactical… Kaboom! Malinowski detonates it again. The fearless Pole with the stuntman looks hits the front. Silky blue vest. Red Adidas shorts. *Magnum PI* moustache. He puts in an almighty surge and shuffles the pack.

Malinowski – Ovett – McLeod – Rono – Robson.
With his great tactical sense Malinowski knew it was dropping and piled on the pace and still makes this record attempt a possible one.

After one lap from Malinowski the lead is seized again by Rono marauding through from fourth place. Ovett passes Malinowski to maintain second place. Now Mike McLeod in fourth has to gamble, and his synapses take him past Malinowski. Unless McLeod tags onto Rono and Ovett he loses the connection. It's a horrendous risk to have to take so early, so deep into the red, but one which Rono is forcing upon everyone behind him. The next few strides are the entire race for McLeod. He knows it and commits. Pure pedigree from the Elswick Harrier. The ability to hurt yourself is a talent. McLeod has to go beyond his pain threshold to get in the Ovett slipstream which he hopes will then help. Is the slipstream a mental construct? Yes. Clicking into the Ovett stride pattern will negate some of the pain and force McLeod to make every single stride count to stay on him – a massive help. Then the mental converts to physical when it becomes a gravity pulling you along. It's you not working because he's doing all the work in front. If you're on someone you're attacking him, and running form is better in attack mode. So the slipstream is ninety percent mental and once you're there the other half is physical. McLeod's gamble is that Rono will not use any more gears this far out from the finish. He guessed wrong. Rono nails it again and McLeod is out of the race.

`Stealthily, a vol-au-vent here and there between sips of Peroni.`

Steve Ovett follows. Rono has launched a sustained attack all the way down the back straight. He can't afford to gift the 1500m specialist an easy pace or an even pace. With three laps to go, Rono has to put Ovett through the mincer and either get rid of him or negate his finishing speed.

Rono's got to go! And this is the test. Can Ovett live with it? The gauntlet is thrown down from the Nandi Hills.

Rono rips the field apart. The back straight grandstand goes wild at such a huge move from Rono, and at the sight of their local hero accelerating to stay on him. Ovett is hypnotically smooth even in the teeth of the Kenyan hurricane: a 61-second lap. Now it looks like a straight duel between the big two. Malinowski in third has lost ten metres. Mike McLeod is resigned to racing a different race.

`An attractive woman stumbles backwards into Nevis. He deftly prevents her falling and assists her back upright -- a relatively easy task for him due to his wide base and low centre of gravity. He smiles. She laughs and thanks him. The wife of a Russian oligarch he has on file. Nevis continues his sweep.`

Two laps to go. Rono spins the yoyo pace low and slow. Malinowski tags onto the front pair again, for three seconds, only for Rono to kick hard again around the bend. Yoyo up. Ovett is on it. Malinowski is dropped once more, broken now surely? Each Rono surge is followed with cavalier ease by Ovett, making a mockery of the destruction behind.

Assessing it's time to mingle, Nevis approaches a small cluster of guests and intrudes into their circle -- their conversation dies down awkwardly. Nevis scans his audience. High-powered foreign men, probably dangerous. Their slim attractive wives, probably mistresses. A woman on the opposite side of the circle is wearing a fabulous pink ball gown. Nevis offers 'cheers' to everyone then addresses the woman in pink.

NEVIS: I love your dress. You look like a pig. [sips lager]

After a shocked pause the entire group collapse in laughter at the remark. A round of agreement is directed affectionately to the woman in pink, who swoons with pleasure at the wave of attention she is now receiving. Nevis moves onto his next group.

650m to go. Rono messes around with the pace again. It drops so low Ovett even has to check a stride on the back straight. Relentless variety from Rono, targeting the weak point of the even-paced European running style. Infuriating to run against and Rono is the master at it. A tenacious Malinowski tags on once again tucking in behind Ovett on the top bend.

Into the home straight for the penultimate time.
Rono slows it again. Ovett waits – supremely cool.

In a magical piece of theatre, Rono moves wide on the last section of the bend to have a look inside. As if to signpost the imminent burn-up for the main grandstand. He also wants to know for sure who is behind him – the footsteps don't always have a name. Today the crowd hysteria should be the giveaway. Is it him? Yes. The red Soviet vest, those relaxed shoulders, that cold empty face. Rono knows the danger. Knows he only has one option. The long finish! With 450m to go Rono puts the hammer down for the final time. Finally Malinowski cracks. Ovett clicks his rhythm onto the latest surge, but this must be hurting now.

DING! DING! DING!
Down to two. Kenya versus Britain.

The time at the bell is irrelevant. This is gladiatorial now: the world's greatest distance runner versus the world's greatest miler. One for the ages. And Rono has gone all-in. His yoyo is of no more use. Now it's all about who has the biggest gun. The long finish needs to get rid of the biggest gunslinger in town. Ovett is just one metre back. He holds on down the back straight with smooth calculated speed.

And listen to this crowd! Absolute sell-out.

Seventeen thousand Ovett fans rise for the grandstand finish. What can he have left after seven-and-a-half laps of such crazily uneven pace? His breaking point must be very close. Into the last bend.

200 to go.
Rono doing everything he can to shake the tail off.
But the shadow is still there!

Stalking the Kenyan all the way. Off the slingshot and into the home straight Ovett moves onto Rono's shoulder. Looking immaculate. The roars multiply. Here it comes. The crowd are ready. Can he? Will he? 100

metres to go. Ovett moves wider and kicks majestically past Rono. Effortless. Making the sprint finish look like a training spin. Only one stride into the lead and Ovett is already waving to the Crystal Palace crowd.

And he's making it look ridiculous.

Ovett wins.
Rono second. Malinowski third.

With his sweep complete, Nevis stands by a fake palm tree near the stage and speculates on when the band will start to ginger it up a bit. A wink from the double bass player suggests it will be a while. Nevis acknowledges the intel with a chuckle and a glass raise -- still good music. A WAITER approaches with a tray of vol-au-vents.

WAITER: Would sir care for any nibbles?

NEVIS: You must be a mind reader. Do you have any Twiglets?

WAITER: I prefer Scampi Fries myself.

NEVIS: Precisely.

The waiter and Nevis walk out of the ballroom and surreptitiously head upstairs away from the party. After several corridors the men arrive at a double door with a body scanner in front of it. Nevis has his smartwatch and phone politely confiscated and placed in a padded tray for safe-keeping. The waiter gestures to Nevis's glasses.

WAITER: I'm sorry, sir.

NEVIS: Of course. [places glasses in tray -- adjusts bow tie.]

The double door is opened. An expansive room with a crystal chandelier hanging over a huge oak table around which are a dozen seating places. Eleven people. Everyone at the table is in black tie. Eyes follow Nevis as he enters. It's a who's who of Russian business tycoons, an array of gold watches and gnarled faces. The type of men you never ask how they made their first million. Nevis sits down in the one vacant seat. One of the Russians stands up to initiate proceedings.

TYCOON #1: So gentlemen...

Ovett raises his arms in triumph. 8:13.51. The world record has gone! A brilliant run superbly co-authored by Rono, with a vital contribution from Malinowski who saved the pace with his strong lap at the front. The Crystal Palace ovation is for all three warriors.

Some minutes later.

A different Russian [ADMIRAL MYOD] is now upstanding having just finished a lengthy and detailed address to the group. He places his hands together to express gratitude and respect. Nods. Then sits down.

TYCOON #1: Thank you Admiral Myod for these most inspiring words. We consider the proposal ambitious but entirely suitable to the agenda. We will proceed.

There are no dissenting voices from the group. Nevis nods.

In athletics the winner doesn't take it all. Such epic races only happen with aggressive protagonists such as Rono and Malinowski. Due to the controversial boycott era, Henry Rono would never grace an Olympic track, but the Lion King's world records were chased by a generation of distance runners, many of whom also grew up in the Nandi Hills. The fearless Bronislaw Malinowski would go on to win the 3000m steeplechase at the Moscow Olympics, where he did it Ovett-style – sitting in third place until the bell then unleashing a majestic finish. The glorious two-mile night at Crystal Palace, even without a single medal at stake, can be cherished for the pure drama of the race. A hero won, a hero came second, and another hero came third. Run as fast as you can. One late summer night in 1981 Bronislaw Malinowski was driving over the Vistula River in the medieval town of Grudziadz. A truck was approaching the same bridge from the opposite direction. Every year on the 27th of September flowers are laid on the Bronislaw Malinowski Bridge.

He was thirty years young.

```
EXT. The ornamental garden of Stoke Park
mansion. Night.

ADMIRAL MYOD stands by a stone balustrade
overlooking the moonlit eighteenth fairway.
As a French window of the mansion opens and
closes the sound of the party is briefly
audible. Myod takes a pensive look at his
gold watch. The stout silhouette of a man
approaches -- arrives -- they stand side by
side. An owl hoots.
```

MYOD: Mister Nevis. Do you have the particulars?

NEVIS: Everything we agreed, Admiral.

With a look around Nevis passes a dossier to Myod who briefly opens it to view the file in the moonlight. He seems satisfied with the contents.

MYOD: Inspiration class and Destroyer class?

NEVIS: Yes both. And the Dreadnought class. Our new ballistic submarine. Trident delivery. Seven under construction. One already launched. HMS Warspite.

Myod closes the dossier. From a distance of about 150 yards in the shadow of the trees, an infrared lens has the two men in its sights -- the camera has recorded the entire exchange including clear images of both men's faces. It records Admiral Myod and Nevis shaking hands and Myod sliding the dossier into his dinner jacket. In the shadows the camera and lens are pocketed in a black tactical jacket. As the figure turns to leave, we see the handsome chiselled profile. The slick heroic hair. Gyllyngvase. He smiles. A very successful evening.

Espionaut

★

The sporting press got the taste for the Coe-Ovett rivalry in 1978. The British record was exchanging hands every race. Now Ovett also had a world record. The drama was obvious despite the disappointment of Olaf Beyer having stolen their Prague 800m showdown. At least Ovett had won the 1500m. There was huge scope in the narrative, especially with 800m specialist Seb Coe now starting to do well in 1500m races. The trajectory of both athletes was skyward. The European athletics circuit was booming. The BBC and ITV were now showing races from exotic continental cities. Floodlights illuminated the players on the stage. Steve Ovett had been a central character since defeating John Walker in Düsseldorf the previous year. Ovett was now the European champion. His exploits always made a back page splash despite his refusal to give press interviews. The victory wave could be successfully angled two ways within the same sentence: irresistible charisma or un-British arrogance. Both angles sold newspapers. Sebastian Coe had also arrived, impressing with his fast times and daring front-running. Moscow 1980 was already on the horizon. Prague in 1978 was merely an hors d'oeuvre for the column inches which could be filled if the rivalry escalated over the next two years.

The tabloid playwrights got to work.

And it did require work because Coe and Ovett were very much alike. Athletes tend to be very similar within the same event. Middle-distance running requires a certain physique at elite level and you also need a curious psychology; a definite screw loose somewhere to enjoy both the punishing endurance work and the stinging sprint sessions. 800m running is fast, thrilling, and horrible, and that's just the training. In races there is triple the lactic and everyone wants to kill you. The sacrifices needed off the track affect your life. If you signed up you've done the same multiple 300m, 400m, 500m reps at eyeballs-out pace, you've lived the short recoveries, suffered the lactic inferno, been on all-fours retching on the infield or in a bush outside lane eight. This is your idea of fun. Or salvation. Some athletes are faster, some are younger or older, some enjoy the short stuff while others smash the long reps, but we all live by the same stopwatch. So did Steve Ovett and Sebastian Coe.

They were both intelligent young men, born only eleven months apart, who both grew up in provincial British towns. Both had a strong supportive family. Steven and Sebastian both attended state schools, coping well with their education and, obviously, excelling on the sports field. They shared the same hobby of training hard with their mates down at the track four or five days a week. Yet they also had a streak of independence resulting from the relentless solo efforts required for their level of sport. As athletes they both started out favouring the 800m. With maturity both evolved into phenomenal 1500m runners and milers. By 1978 their personal best times were within tenths of each other, indeed within hundredths as electronic timing systems were gradually introduced across the sport.

Coe and Ovett took the same joy in running fast.

They were both beautiful runners. Athletic and aesthetic perfection. Compact, smooth, graceful, always noticeable in a race pack as the most fluid and floating shape. The only visible asymmetry was Ovett's right hand which gave a very slight flick during the backswing – perhaps what freed up his arm for the victory waves? Of course there were nuances in their styles. Ovett had the more muscular physique, while Coe had the more gazelle-like spring, but both athletes made running *and winning* look effortlessly easy. Watching either run live was to witness other-worldly greatness. The scenario was barely plausible: two once-in-a-lifetime talents had turned up in the same country, in all but the same year, running the same two events in almost identical record times. The two Brits, if you wanted them to be, were peas in a pod.

The press sought a more Shakespearian narrative.

The manipulation started in Prague and snowballed over the subsequent seasons. The two characters were split, twisted, contrasted, and realigned in direct opposition to one another. Rivals? No. They would be arch enemies. A race? No. A clash. The new script came with an assigned role to play. Ovett and Coe were no longer in control of their new personae. For all its faults and degrees of unfairness towards both runners, it was the story which had to be written. As greedy punters we fed at the trough of hyperbole as the legends evolved. Ovett fans revelled in his exuberance, the predatory finishing tactics, such overflowing panache, and the constant air of rebellion. He was roared on. His racing style created a mob-like atmosphere, intoxicating and visceral, thousands baying for the demolition. Meanwhile, Coe fans loved Seb's eloquent modesty, the innate politeness, his clean-cut effervescence on the track, and such devil-may-care front-running. In reality Steve Ovett was far more humble, sensitive, and sympathetic than he was ever portrayed. If anything these were his greatest qualities. And Seb Coe, while impeccable on-camera, was a shade more raffish behind the scenes, and thereby far more interesting. But reality was not the currency. What sold newspapers were their archetypes. Both were household names who transcended the sport. Athletics reached into every living room in the country through their record-breaking exploits. Crucially, most of the hype was based on facts provided regularly by the two antagonists.

Ovett won in Helsinki.
Coe won in Brussels

Coe broke the British record.
Ovett smashed the world record.

Who was better? No one really knew. It oscillated week by week depending on who had the more impressive win. Their contrasting tactics made it impossible to match them up from separate races. The tease was infuriating for the press who could only postulate, but did so with fervour as the newspapers flew off the stands each time either athlete featured. The more Coe and Ovett avoided racing each other the more incendiary the speculation became. It seemed that after Prague they might carry on avoiding each other all the way to the Olympics two years hence. The laser of intrigue had only one target. Central Lenin Stadium.

The pressmen were loading barrels of dynamite either side of the barricades. Whatever happened in the Olympics there would be a terrific story: a definitive winner with a golden smile next to the broken loser with a worthless silver. It was the harshest narrative, and more so that it was already written. Only the names needed to be filled into the blanks either side. Yet beneath the hype the story was based on an inescapable truth, one which neither athlete wished to deny: they both wanted the same two gold medals in Moscow.

With two years still to go until the Olympics, the whole of the country was being sucked into the battle. From club runner to keep-fit jogger. From kids racing in the playground to grandparents watching in their armchairs. Everyone had their favourite and everyone knew that you couldn't cheer for both. You were Coe. Or you were Ovett. It was on. The Clash of the Titans.

★

Arbat. I get there early. Barely a soul around. This is the most famous street in Moscow. In fact there are two streets: the old Arbat and its 1960s concrete rival Novy Arbat. They are both one kilometre running west-to-east converging towards each other and meeting at Arbatskaya metro and the Praga Hotel. Here in the city centre they clear the snow and grit the pavements. Runnable even today. Arbat is flat apart from a slight downhill start. I get into a great early rhythm but soon feel a strong wind funnelling between the buildings.

Work to keep the flow.

Arbat is imperial Russia. It's lined with classical buildings all immaculately refurbished in tasteful pastel tones. White pillars and stucco arches frame the entrances and windows. The street-lamps are in the style of old-fashioned lanterns. In the nineteenth century this is where the nobility lived. Arbat is the place for romantic walks and poetry. It's where Aleksandr Pushkin charmed his most elegant lovers. Tatyana. Elizaveta. Natalya. There are stone plaques commemorating famous residents: artists, poets and musicians from both sides of the revolution. Soviet beat poet Bulat Okudzhava has a statue in his own mini-square in a side street. Just past the New Balance shop a mural celebrates music pioneer Viktor Tsoi. Quaint souvenir shops sell *matryoshka* dolls and *ushanka* hats. Cafés and museums hint at the velvet ambiance of yesteryear. I often drink tea at the Starbucks at number 19. All the restaurants have outdoor seating in the summer when buskers, clowns, and jugglers perform in the street. Or you can watch contemporary dance and operettas at the palatial Vakhtangov Theatre whose online schedule proclaims itself to be: *A harmony of perfect form and profound psychological content.*

Arbat is pure Coe.

At the corner of Novinsky Bulvar I allow myself five breaths with my hands on my knees before starting the jog recovery. Four minutes across the short-side of the triangle to Novy Arbat. Quick hamstring stretch. Then restart my watch and accelerate into the rep.

Stay loose in the shoulders. Cadence.

Novy Arbat is a six-lane strip of bright lights and high-rise Soviet design. It slashed through the historical Arbat district in the 1960s, a swathe of demolition to bulldoze in modernism. This was the statement of a boundless society conceptualized in concrete. The utopianism of Le Corbusier fused with the bold futurism of Vladmir Tatlin. The street is vast and stark yet somehow seethes with energy. The tower blocks either side of Novy Arbat have lights bottom-to-top which flash in different colours at night. The pavement is a thirty-metre-wide promenade with a VIP parking lane. This morning only three cars are left over from the night before: a Porsche 911 in matte green, a black-and-cream Maybach, and a tango Lamborghini. There are designer clothes stores, diamond boutiques, and lounge bars with pink neon signs. This was the centre of the 1990s casino boom which the government had to break up because the mob-run system was too volatile. Coffee Mania pumps out expensive caffeine 24-hours a day. The restaurants are brash and in-your-face. Burger Heroes. Ketch Up. Steak-It-Easy. Ovo. Culture? The Oktyabrisky 11 Cinema hosts all the blockbuster movie premieres. There's action and excitement everywhere. I love this street and all its glitzy modern arrogance.

Novy Arbat is 24-carat Ovett.

I nail the last rep but my flow is so good downwind it doesn't even hurt. That's six kilometres of endurance in the bank. The indoor mile race is in two weeks.

★

```
To: Nevis. The plan requires an extra
person. Am not as young as I once was. Can
no longer manage the physical logistics of
what I've had in place for quite some time.
Is there an asset available? Requirements:
nimble, and accurate at 202 yards [with the
Izhmash 7-4]. From: Pythagoras
```

Pushkinskaya. Another pro-Navalny protest in Pushkin Square. He's been sentenced again on yet more falsified charges. Democracy is firmly behind bars. I'm walking to the metro after classes with Phil Kimby and we nearly get caught up in it. We divert into McDonald's to avoid the commotion, a better option than doubling back, reckons

Phil. We're older, the politzia won't be bothered about us. We eat nuggets with ketchup, guiltily ignoring the excessive aggression towards the young protesters outside the window. Phil Kimby asks me how many of my current female students I'm 'courting' and gives me a rundown of the 'available' married women in his upper-intermediate class. Though not exclusive in his tastes, Phil has a strong preference for Asian women. He reckons his demarcation point is Tashkent. Anything east of that is his tipple. He describes an Uzbek mountain enclave in Kyrgyrstan which he insists I simply must visit. You've gotta put a sock on it these days, he says, but you'll never know anything like it. He gives me the name of the hotel he stays at. Tell Karl you're mates with me and he'll sort you out. The crowd eventually disperses and after an hour we can leave and take the backstreets to the metro.

On the way home I pop into CCCP Fitness and knock out some deadlifts, to suck that excess McDonald's protein into my posterior drive chain. Anastasia isn't there, which is soul-wrenching, and her bland colleague Polina checks me out twice in the weights room mirrors. The taste of ashes.

```
To: Pythagoras. I have an appropriate asset.
Just your sort of fellow too. 800m runner.
Slightly mad. Codename is Threeman. Ophelia
is making the arrangements. Have not
mentioned details. Suggest you do the
briefing since it's your baby. If he's not
what you need, let me know. Did the florist
deliver? From: Nevis
```

★

Losiny Ostrov. Minus ten. I'm in winter tracksuit with track leggings underneath and a coat on top. I take the metro to the last stop on the red line, Bulvar Rokossovskovo, then jog slowly east for a mile to the edge of the forest. Snow everywhere. Q branch have winterised my Mizuno Wave Sky 3s with hex studs from a local hardware store. Twelve studs screwed into the rubber of each sole for grip. The stud configuration is carefully spaced around the perimeter of the sole so that none of them come through and stab me. The studs and a screwdriver only cost five-hundred roubles (a fiver – get in!) and they give me just enough traction in the snow to complete an effective steady run.

```
To: Nevis. Izhmash bouquet arrived from a
rather beautiful florist. Excellent. Tested
it at the dacha. Stopping power seems
enough. But will source dum-dum bullets in
case our asset thinks a conventional .22
might not get it done in one shot. From:
Pythagoras
```

Elk Island aka Losiny Ostrov is a national forest on the outskirts of Moscow, a protected natural environment for wildlife, especially elks. It starts in Sokolniki Park from where the woodland spreads out away from the city into a giant semi-wilderness where the elks live. The island of birch forest is large enough to get dangerously lost in. Thankfully it has a sixty-metre-wide swathe cut through it for electricity pylons which today I'll stick to. In my gadget snowshoes I can jog along the service road down the centre of Pylon Alley. It undulates gently to give me and several cross-country skiers something to focus on. The swathe is only grass, low brush, and reeds, which fully exposes us to the wind. My coat was a great call. After one mile Pylon Alley takes a ninety-degree left turn. The pylons then disappear into the snowbound distance for miles of dead straight path. Nothing but forest either side. Relentless monotony. Great. It's snowing heavily, eighty percent white-out. Each steel pylon rising from the snow adds a science fiction nuance. Lost in a post-apocalyptic blizzard but alive, he runs in search of civilisation and aerobic capacity. A lone elk who also survived the asteroid strike is standing close to the snowy path chewing happily on a shrub. He looks up at me. I stop to admire him. Who is this powerful untamed creature? He must be wondering.

Now then. Elk Island? My knowledge of the boreal fauna of Eurasia is improving rapidly thanks to the superb *Wild Russia* documentaries every sauna visit at CCCP Fitness. I'm pretty certain this fine fellow is not an elk at all. He's a fully-fledged moose! The bulging proboscis gives him a gentle and friendly demeanour despite being such an imposing unit: a handsome four-legged Juantorena with muscular humped shoulders. No antlers at this time of year but he's definitely a big healthy boy. That power-packed 800-metre rump. He can probably smash the back straight if riled. Today he's chilled out and accepts a kindred middle-distance spirit. Although when he makes a move forward to say hello I do back off, without an apple or sugar lump to offer in Olympic friendship. We're both sad when I run off towards the next pylon. *Da svidanya, Alberto.*

Where the snow is deep it's skiddy. I lose traction even with my hex studs. A semi-trodden line is disappearing as fresh snow lands, so I run on the skiers' tracks, compacted and much better for push off. I have to run squinting because the snowflakes sting when they hit my eyeballs. After three dead-straight miles there's a Tjunction in the path. The pylon swathe continues straight on but the path only goes left or right. A skier and a dog-walker take the eastward route into the forest. That could go on until Siberia, so I turn back and retrace my footprints through the bleak tundra of Pylon Alley. The snowfall increases.

```
To: Ophelia. Is it time for a banya? Suggest
we invite the newcomer. No mention of scheme
yet. We'll provide some of our usual friends
to welcome him into the fold. What's his
penchant? From: Pythagoras
```

Into the white wall of the blizzard. First pylon. Ten burpees. Flicking up snow behind me, driving from my glutes to jump as high as I can, and then continue running on heavier legs. Second pylon. Press-up pyramid. Heavier arms. One carat of World Masters 800m gold might be won or lost right here in the middle of a Russian birch forest.

```
To: Pythagoras. No penchant as such. The
filthy devil likes it all. Probably veers
towards tall and athletic. Can't imagine
he'd turn down curvaceous either. Suggest
our usual sparkling array. Blonde. Brunette.
Red. Far East definitely up his strasse too.
Let's sort him out with one or two of each.
Ideally enough so there are leftovers für
mich. Looking forward to it. From: Ophelia
```

Visibility is only one pylon-distance into the future. That wind in my face is now a howling interstellar gale. The only survivor, alone on this forsaken planet, Omega Ovett prays for home, knowing that home only exists in his memory. Was it really an asteroid or…? All humankind has been wiped out in this galaxy. Our hero's only friend is his faithful moose Alberto 1-2RNa. Ovett ploughs on through the blizzard, the *metelitsa*, fending off swarms of murderous robo-skiers. The galvanized feet of the pylons are a stark reminder every eighty metres of why the machines won. Could he have prevented it? Negative. Onwards, never look back. A secret agent beyond duty. *Stiv Ovyett: Espionaut #279.* He survives stride by stride thanks to the titanium hex studs in his Wave Sky 3s. But if he could locate his spacecraft in the desolation, he could repair it and escape to another galaxy. Maybe he could even find Anastasia. If only she knew that together they were the only chance to repopulate the species. Ovett drives on in hope.

To: Threeman. Operation Plum.
Follow to meeting in banya.

RECOGNITION CODE:
<<Don't cry. We have one more night left together.>>

RESPONSE CODE:
<<One more time I'll whisper: you're mine.>>

Contact codename is Pythagoras. From: Station R

Those burpees were overly bold. I'm battered. Alberto 1-2RNa has demobbed into the woods to snaffle some bark. I'd have done the same if I was a moose. After the right-angle turn I fartlek the last half-mile of pylons. My phone GPS says eight miles run. More than enough. I don't fancy the jog back, and right on the edge of Losiny Ostrov there's a tram stop with a tram already waiting. Lucozade Sport! I hop on and ride in the warmth back to the metro.

The Pink Ophelia
★

Got my session in early. 12 x 200m but no zip at all. Hate running track reps in flats. Leggy. Too much training volume. Phil Kimby has invited me to his 'traditional' New Year banya party. Am trying hard to think of an excuse to get out of it. Phil mentions a masseuse.

```
To: Ophelia. Banya selection all set. Two
blondes. One brunette. A sensational
redhead. And a dinky Asian [who you might
remember well]. He can absolutely fill his
boots. Circa 15:00 onwards. Bring your
speakers and Neil. From: Pythagoras
```

Scrambled eggs for lunch to try and refill my hollow legs. All my energy systems are low. You know what, actually, with my legs so battered a long sociable banya might be just the thing. Phil Kimby confirms via message that it 'could be' a sports masseuse.

```
To: Pythagoras. He's in. We'll see you
there. From: Ophelia
```

I take the brown line to Prospekt Mira. Exit the train. Look left. Look right. People get on or disappear up the escalators. The train leaves. Platform clear. Phil Kimby appears from behind a pillar wearing bright pink jeans and a brown duffel coat. It would be odd, even rude, not to say anything so I compliment him on the snazzy jeans. Hugo Boss from *TSUM*, he says. I'm merely in denim Wranglers and a black Montane puffer.

We walk along Prospekt Mira itself, then a side street, then a botanical garden. Not far, says Phil as we crunch through the snow. He launches into a riff about the half-Korean in his IELTS preparation class. Mid-thirties. Couple of weeks ago he set her extra homework on the lyrics of a Neil Young song. She 'responded' so he's been giving her one-to-ones at his place. Last lesson they listened to the whole *LIVE Rust* album. Naked, he adds unnecessarily, an assumption I was already trying to unsee. I admit to him that I'm jealous of his abandon, which elicits a strange wink.

The banya is in a basement on a tiny *peryulok* backstreet. The reception is unstaffed. Phil Kimby's mate Vadim hires the whole place and gets the key. Phil ushers me into the male changing rooms where he merrily greets two Russian friends who are undressing. I'm introduced and say hello. *Zdrastye.*

As I take off my socks I casually ask Phil what the er… protocol is. Do people wear trunks or a towel or is it, you know, nuts out? However you feel comfortable, says Phil Kimby as he drops his pink jeans and gives his donger a comfort shake. I hedge my bets, going without trunks, but from a pile of linen sheets I improvise a modesty sarong.

You're in cracking shape, says Phil. And that's the thing. Fully-clothed I look worryingly thin at 71.2kg. But in running gear or semi-naked I'm an absolute machine. A grenade of muscle packed onto each shoulder. It's why I'm better at the 800m than the 1500m. That extra edge of power. The sarong sits securely on my bony hips. Phil Kimby has a pot belly and is bollock naked except for his flip-flops and a gold St Christopher. We step through into the main banya area.

The interior décor is Scandinavian-style pine walls and ceiling. Underfoot it's green Astroturf carpet. My flip-flops squeak as we stroll in. On the right is an alcove with seating around a table upon which there are a dozen shot glasses and a carafe of water. Adjacent to the dining zone is a small plunge pool about four-metres-square in which one of the Russian blokes I just met is frolicking close to – no, touching – a brunette girl. Neither appear to have swimwear on. Hullo Valeria, you look very pretty today, says Phil. Some torque stirs in my sarong. Pretty? She's fucking stunning.

In this section it's room temperature but humid. From the plunge pool a short corridor with open showers leads to the banya. Let's introduce you, says Phil, and we head into the banya itself. Well it's really just a regular finnish sauna but in Russian 'banya' refers more to the social experience, it's a culturally ingrained… oh, er three naked women. Hello. I mean *zdrastye*. Where do I look? I style out the shock and assess the new landscape. Jesus, this is ridiculous. A platinum blonde is lying on her back on the top shelf of a four-tiered bank of seating. She is lean and long with slim-but-defined arms, quads, and a... it's all on display. Her breasts are shapely and pert even while lying horizontally. Sweat droplets glint all over her smooth bronze skin. Her nipples are perpendicular, reaching for and very nearly touching the pine ceiling. Me? I'm already sweating bullets. On the second tier of seating is a redhead of fractionally fuller physique. She is massaging the shoulders of a bloke on the tier below. This bloke, while receiving his massage, is talking to a petite Asian girl sat next to him. Kimby beams. Kiko!

On seeing Phil, the Asian rocket emits a squeal of delight, stands up and greets him with a mutually naked hug. As the newcomer I'm introduced. Am I also going to get a Kiko hug? Yes I am. She presses her play-size breasts against my chest and wraps both arms around me, her palms moving softly over my back in an affectionate stroking motion for several seconds more than I was expecting. No one here seems to be shy apart from Muggins Ovett wrapped in this shameful linen sheet. But I'm determined to go with the flow – so relax, just inhale, exhale, immerse and let myself enjoy it. Phil Kimby already has a semi.

Meet Vadim our leader, says Phil with mock grandeur. Vadim blushes at the reference as he shakes my hand. He's about Phil's age with a wild Karl Marx beard. I see with relief that Vadim is also sporting a modesty sarong. Welcome, he says. Big mix of demographics here. A strange set-up. Awkward? I'm more confused than uncomfortable, really. What the heck is this? Vadim proffers a space on the wooden slats of seating tier one, next to a second blonde with long frizzy curls who has appeared and joined the front rank. With relief I sit down, meaning I can finally hitch up my sarong a bit to temporarily conceal my erection. *Zdrastye*, I say to the naked frizzy blonde. Warmly reciprocated.

Focus. Okay names.

Leonid was the lucky bastard in the pool. Vadim is Karl Marx. Valeria is the brunette from the pool who is now on tier three of the banya. Anzhelika is the frizzy blonde next to me with her hand on my thigh. Kiko is the pocket dynamo who just left for the plunge pool with Phil Kimby. The mysterious platinum on tier four? Unknown. The voluptuous redhead who has just started massaging my shoulders? Don't know either.

Do you read Dostoyevsky? Asks Vadim. The icebreaker is extremely welcome respite. *Crime and Punishment. The*

Double. White Nights. The Brothers Karamazov. Keep thinking here. *Notes from the Underground. House of the Dead.* My cock subsides by point-nought-one percentile. Thanks Vadim. We discuss *The Double.* It's Vadim's favourite. Freedom of self-expression and the self-destructive impulse seem to interest him. He asks which English translation I've read. Can't say I know. But it's important, he says. The original translation of Dostoyevksy in the nineteenth century was done by Constance Garrett who also translated everything by Tolstoy, an author with a far less psychological slant. If you read the Garrett version you don't get the true Dostoyevsky. Stylistics are important, says Vadim. The redhead's hands are now stylistically exploring down my pectorals and obliques. I promise Vadim I'll buy the Russian version from Biblio Globus tomorrow. He laughs. Redhead also laughs and pulls me back further into her thighs. Meanwhile to note: frizzy Anzhelika hasn't stopped smiling at me the whole time. The ambient steam and her perspiration has now saturated those tight blonde curls which I absolutely love. She has beautiful teeth, lips, jawline, neck, breasts. I would ask permission to bury my face in them if this wasn't all so grotesquely public.

Have I jizzed yet? Might be the best option.
Then stash the soiled sarong somewhere.

Vadim is some sort of shaman type. Possibly how he gets all these stunning women. Their so-called leader? His aura says religion and the girls are deferential towards him. No one is currently massaging his shoulders, possibly because they are obscenely hairy. Wonder what the plunge pool is like?

– Can I try the plunge pool? I ask Vadim. What a fucking inane question.
– Freedom is the greatest thing you possess, says Vadim.
– The best way to keep a prisoner from escaping is to make sure he never knows he's in prison, I fire back from my latent A-Level Fyodor.
– Bravo!

Big laughs from Vadim there. My redhead appreciates it too and voluntarily follows me to the plunge pool while tugging at my sarong.

Phil Kimby and his faithful Kiko are sitting next to each other in the alcove. Their legs are overlapping and they're both giggling as Phil pours from the carafe of water which, yes okay now I see, it's vodka. Should have realised that at the start, shouldn't I. It must go straight to your head in this humidity. Kiko is presented with a huge measure by Phil. They clink glasses. Phil swallows his in one slug but Kiko can only half swallow hers. The other half she spills down herself.

– Don't waste any! exclaims Phil.

Oh for fuck's sake. I look away, unleash myself from the sarong and jump into the plunge pool. Splash.

Only a short diagonal to swim out of sight, out of mind, from the Kimbys. The water is cool but not icy cold; very much a mixed blessing. Pleasant enough to wallow in but not cold enough to make inroads into my boner. Especially not when a redhead whose name, thrillingly, I still don't know, swims up and presses herself against it. Too late for Dostoyevksy now. We wallow, our limbs gradually entwining, then a full embrace. Unsolicited, she moves playfully around to feel my chap press against her thighs, then her inner thighs. Thank God this is all underwater. My coyness is rapidly dissipating. I'm *way* out of my league here but fuck me I'm enjoying this. Redhead has me completely cornered and uses the rails at the edge of the pool to support herself as she rubs gently against me. Incredible. Such filth. With apparently zero expectation of conversation. Feels like small talk is actually verboten. And we now have an audience. Anzhelika, my erstwhile frizzy blonde, is sitting at the side of the pool watching, legs happily kicking in the water. I want to fuck her too, as well as this one I'm very-nearly-but-not fucking here in the pool.

And all the while a nagging thought just won't go away.
The platinum blonde on tier four!

Is this some sort of religious sect? Or just the local Dostoyevsky Appreciation Society? It's definitely not a swingers' club, far too philosophical for that, but is penetration frowned upon or de rigueur? And if so, how much cash am I going to owe Vadim? Yet they're not prostitutes. It's not that vibe, just not at all, which leaves me with no idea. Just bewildering accessibility.

All I know for sure is I'm in way too deep to stop. I want to go back to the banya. As if reading my mind, the redhead kisses me on the cheek and swims athletically to the pool ladder, then exits with a hop and a skip to the ladies changing room.

In a millisecond I'm back in that banya.
The second highest seating tier is entirely free – bingo!

Vadim is sitting on tier one with the brunette whose name I've already forgotten. They're whispering, possibly about Dostoyevsky's later works. Behind me is the platinum blonde, refreshingly older I now notice. The oldest of the group. Late thirties. Or even forty. Christ! Or am I just imagining such 'experience'? I've barely studied her face. Now I have. She's thirties somewhere. Her eyes are closed, her palms are facing down. The pine slats on the third tier creak beneath my buttocks. She rotates her hands so they are palms up. A message? I stroke the centre of her palm. Without opening her eyes, she lifts her arm and strokes down my shoulder, my arm, and back, then some torso. I have no idea where my modesty sarong has disappeared to.

– Do you know what it is? asks Vadim.
I shake my head blankly. My purple boner hasn't allowed rational thought for thirty-five minutes.
– Nobody competes, he says.

What does that even mean? But with that thought he leaves the banya, also minus sarong. We hear the clinking of glasses and Phil Kimby's laughter before the door closes. Only the brunette on the second row and the platinum blondinka are left. And Little Ol' me.

Yes, says the blonde. I didn't even ask a question. So do I? She takes and guides my hand but keeps her eyes shut – still! The brunette joins my tier and keeps hers open. Gulp. This is so good I'm crying. Don't think I've ever felt so happy, so free, yet so confusingly and dangerously intertwined. Each one of us is caressing something very nearby, gently, only tenderness, no crude mounting of any sort. After several minutes we hear singing through the banya door. Somebody has connected up a speaker.

Neil Young. Oh, let's go and sing, says the blonde, removing my hand from whence it had been. The brunette likewise removes her hand from my whence, and we go via a soapy shower with the brunette to the vodka singing party. By an absolute fucking miracle, or tragedy, I still haven't jizzed. In defiance of all the known and unknown laws of particle physics.

The singalong is in full swing. *Keep on Rockin' in the Free World.* Vadim loves this one. Phil Kimby is refilling the carafe and I have located my sarong. At the next break in the playlist I'm told to choose a song by the redhead. Not an expert on Neil Young but I do know one Russian song – *Ne Plach* – which I mention hoping it's too old for them. Wrong. In fact it's a popular choice. My opening line gets a round of applause and then everyone joins in.

Don't cry
We have one more night together
One more time I'll whisper: you're mine
One last time your eyes

The ultimate '90s ballad by Tatyana Bulanova. We sing all the verses. The girls know every line. Vadim knows the main bits and is a solid Marxist baritone. Phil Kimby air guitars the solo, mercifully in a modesty sarong. I don't touch the vodka but I'm drunk on happy naked women. More songs follow. All genres but favouring guitar-based ballads to which Phil Kimby can perform. On and on. Then. Eventually the eternal flame of karaoke dies down as people realise they're too pissed. Phil invites everyone to the Shakespeare 'for a couple of pints to sober up'. This is my window of opportunity to leave paradise. At last. I thank Vadim and discreetly extricate myself without too much fanfare or goodbye tears. It's a stagger home in a haze of illicit 'non-competition' or whatever the heck Vadim reckons it was. Who would have thought I'd be so lame and prudish? It doesn't officially count as an orgy, thankfully, nor as breaking my prostitution duck if they even were. Strictly speaking I didn't nob any of them, but as close as makes no difference with the redhead. And with. And.

I get home just as the New Year celebrations are starting. 10pm maybe? No idea. Bedtime. With a heavily soiled sarong beside me I fall asleep instantly. If there were midnight fireworks they didn't wake me.

★

```
To: Nevis. Asset seems suitable. If he's
accurate from 202 yards he's perfect. I
didn't get the chance to brief him though.
Others were in attendance. And wasn't the
right vibe for it. So we'll sort that asap
next week. From: Pythagoras
```

Tverskaya. My advanced English class. The lovely Natasha & Veronika et al. Age range circa 25-29. All-female. I'm wearing my favourite sweater. Their favourite sweater? We're doing essay sentence structure. The lesson aim is to reduce and vary their sentence word count. The Russian literary tradition values long, meandering, overly complex sentences, with extended noun phrases, multiple consecutive adjectives, and relative clause after relative clause. Therefore, I get incoherent spaghetti paragraphs from my group. Especially Natasha. Variety is a must, I say. You can have some long lyrical drifty sentences, but they risk the connection with your reader. You should mix in shorter punchier ones to make your point. Clarity trumps complexity. An article in our current chapter of the textbook proves my point. We are deconstructing it as Phil Kimby pokes his head around the door and smirks at Veronika. She does have a hint of the East.

– Is he behaving himself, ladies? I hope not, quips Phil.

The girls all laugh. They're bored with my writing skills bit. Too academic by far. Keep it simple, stupid.

– Fancy a drinky after class? I'm meeting up with Vadim in Red Square, says Phil.
– I can't tonight, I say.
– Oh, forgot to mention. You know your Ovett and Coe thing... Vadim was there.
– What?

– For the eight-hundred. In the stadium. Vadim saw it live. And the fifteen. We'll walk from here at nine.

Phil Kimby disappears from the doorway. Where was I? Distracted by this bombshell, I let the lesson descend into chit chat. Vadim at the 1980 Olympics! It's an effort to reboot and focus back on the class. Shall we do some… er conversation practice? I put the students into pairs (and a three) and spend time with each group listening, occasionally correcting, half-concentrating, but half-thinking whether Vadim could really have been there. The 800m live. Must be a wind-up. Central Lenin Stadium? Surely not. Very confusing. Why? Eventually I manage to re-engage with the students but in the wrong way. My professionalism is shot to pieces. Now it's about them all being so attractive and twenty-something. Should I invite one of them out? A simple coffee apropos of nothing. Then throw all that overrated professionalism out of the window like Phil Kimby does. The lesson ends and the students leave without paying any attention to me whatsoever. There's your answer.

Vadim is waiting for us at Resurrection Gate. We stroll along the cobbles. Red Square is lit up spectacularly as always. The colours of the domes of St Basil's are even more vibrant at night. As we walk diagonally towards the Lenin Mausoleum I raise the Coe-Ovett-1980-Olympics subject with Vadim, assuming Phil has been pulling my leg, but no it seems he hasn't.

Before the pot belly and the *Communist Manifesto* beard Vadim Ryazanov was a member of the CCCP track squad. From his wallet he produces a photo of himself, clean-shaven, hollow shade beneath each cheek bone, his eyes sparkling with youth, wearing a navy blue CCCP tracksuit. The Moscow Olympics. Vadim!

Quite matter-of-factly he backs up this astonishing reveal. He was twenty-five. Was in line for the third spot on the Soviet team but had run poorly for a couple of weeks. Tried to force it with some races and burnt himself out before selection. A dip at the wrong time. Had the Games been a month later he might have worked it out and got the last spot. He was never quite talented enough, so always had to be in perfect shape. That season he just couldn't there, not even within two seconds of the qualifying time. He settled for being warm-up buddy for his friends Anatoly Reshetnyak and Nikolay Kirov. Only Kirov made the final.

– We wondered what Busse would do, says Vadim.

You can't fake being an 800m runner. You either know it or you don't. It's as much about what you don't say as what you do. Vadim would have been the right age. Physique? He's older and tubbier now but he walks with his shoulders back, balanced, softly treading over the cobbles. Understated confidence. Arrogance back in the day? As we approach the Lenin Mausoleum I press him for details. I want details details details.

– What about Busse? I ask.
– We knew Coe or Ovett would win, but Busse could have really mixed it up. The only real chance for Nikolay was for someone else to take it out hard and hope that one or both of your Brits got in a muddle somewhere. Which they did, especially Ovett. But it was too slow and they had the finish to recover. Busse had run 1:44 already that summer and was the one we hoped would have a crack at Coe. He tracked Coe too closely though, stride

for stride, and realised too late that Coe wasn't going to blast the first lap. That's when Busse should have reacted and pressed hard on his own. Busse was talented but he didn't have the pure speed for a second lap burn-up. He didn't have demolition speed. Ovett ran the second 400 metres in 50.5 – brutal! Busse needed the perfect differential, and he needed to be right up at the front, going through in 51-high with a half-second cushion on both Coe and Ovett somewhere in the pack. Then bring it home in 52-something and hope one of them got blocked or got it badly wrong. Busse was the one with the class for a really aggressive option and it would have helped Nikolay's chances too. You always hope. We loved Ovett and Coe, obviously, but you tend to cheer for your own.

Vadim was at the 1980 Olympic final. In the stadium. I look up at the stars. My lucky ones. This was incredible. Maybe he could put me in touch with Nikolay Kirov. An interview. The whole thing snowballs. My Coe-Ovett thing. Phil Kimby is off chatting to some tourists. I need to pump Vadim for more right now while he's on a roll.

– So, you think Busse or Kirov could have won?
– No. But a lucky silver was an outside possibility. Busse was too passive. Nikolay was the opposite. He gave it a great go but would have had a better chance if he had tempered his surge and kept Ovett trapped. Dear Kolya! He got too excited and went too hard from too far out. But Ovett tended to hypnotise people like that. It was just scary how good he was. I only raced him once myself, way back before the Olympics. We swapped vests. I suspected Ovett would win. Coe didn't look right even on the warm-up track. I spoke to his coach.
– You spoke to Peter Coe?!

– We had been kind of put in touch earlier that year, so I knew him to chat to.
– What did he say on the warm-up track?
– Nothing much, but I could tell he was worried about his athlete. That was it really. The 800m unravels very quickly if you're not in form on the day. Sebastian lost. The sun still rose again the next day. Peter and I met again in between the eight and the fifteen. Here in fact. I walked him around Red Square. Fascinating man. He was particularly interested in the dimensions of the square. He even paced it out. Maybe he thought a training session on the cobbles would be fun. Typical coach. Everything is a potential session.
– Where did he pace out?
– For some reason he wanted to know the distance from the Lenin Mausoleum to St Basil's. Funny. On the day we were here there was a concert and things on, so he couldn't walk directly to the cathedral. Instead, he walked from here to the centre of the square. Then turned right to the cathedral. He worked out the distance from the mausoleum to the cathedral there by Pythagoras. It was his hypotenuse. Very proud he was. We kept in touch over the years. I miss him. Would you like to see inside the cathedral?

Vadim points to the nine colourful St. Basil's onion domes clustered together on their individual brick towers.

– It will be closed Vadim. It's nearly ten o'clock.
– I've got the keys. Didn't Phil tell you? I'm the priest.

Metelitsa

★

I exit Dinamo metro into a full-blown *metelitsa*, a swirling blizzard. Minus twelve. Plus windchill. New snow falling on compacted ice makes the footpath through Petrovsky Park treacherous. I have to half-stomp half-skate even in my grip matrix winter boots. There's a quarter inch of back-slip every step. Does this put me off or will it make me 'feel the benefit' when I have absolute traction in my race spikes? In the winter outdoor tracks are out of action from December until March. Fortunately the Moscow athletics circuit has a programme of indoor races to keep racers honest. I have pre-race dread in the pit of my stomach.

It's *CSKA* Arena.
It's Ovett.
It's the Sri Chinmoy 1-mile open meet.

I arrive an hour and five minutes before my race. Two event organisers are distributing race numbers from a table in the foyer. I pick up my number 279 and four safety pins. I'm in race seven and listed second last on the race start-sheet. I think they list races in order of the predicted times which athletes register with. This means I've put the second quickest time down. The last guy on the list with the fastest predicted time? Ruslan, the Green Goblin. I thrashed him last time in a mile here. That makes me favourite, oppressive expectation which I don't need.

```
To: Nevis. Briefing done. Complicated.
Threeman says it's not for him. He thought
plan was outrageous, although on reflection
possibly do-able. Accuracy possible at 202
yards but from such concealment the only
gauge of wind direction and speed would be
the Kremlin flag. He has minimal climbing
```

```
experience to reach the firing point, but I
showed him the hand holds. Also, he deemed
escape highly unlikely. Please advise. From:
Pythagoras
```

Along one side of the arena a bank of spectator seating rises to the ceiling. Twenty-three rows of seats with capacity for two thousand athletics fans. Around the other sides there are two rows of concrete balconies draped in army regalia. In 1980 this staged the Olympic wrestling. It's a jog around the perimeter to warm-up. During my drills I can feel the dry arena air rasping my throat already; always the worst thing about indoor racing. It fazes me. I nip to the foyer and buy a water. Two gargled sips and then I restart my drills routine again at the beginning. High-kneed skips. Sweat blooms in the centre of my warm-up t-shirt.

```
To: Pythagoras. Understandable. Advise you
work on better escape options to make the
plan seem rosier. He usually needs
persuasion. I will mobilize Applecross.
From: Nevis
```

Strides. Spikes on. Another sip of water. A final stride out. Nerves. The haunting of imminent pain. Vest on. The race before mine has just started. I cross the track at the back straight onto the infield. The first track race of the season is always bad – horrible, in fact – but there's no going back now. Loads of white vests around. Bit unusual. Our numbers are called out by the marshall with the clipboard. *Dvesty syemdisyat dyevit.* 279. I raise my hand and strut forward. Now shitting myself. There are fourteen in my race and most of them could be something. They all deserve their place at the Ovett dining table. Lean or muscular. Or both. Most look in their thirties apart from Rinat. Am I the favourite? Not really. Never means much in a graded meet. Neither do my GB race shorts.

Rinat says hello. We wish each other a good race. Rinat beat me over 800m in the summer (note: in my first outdoor race of the season). He's in a Russia team vest and matching blue Lycra shorts. Stylish Nike gear. Rinat is M50 but in terrific shape. Super-wiry. Really good at the 800m but I suspect his *spezialnost* could be the mile. He'll be there or thereabouts.

The Green Goblin is in his trademark green Brooks vest. He's a really nice guy, Goblin. We say hello and openly exchange our target times. It won't really affect the race. Just as Coe and Ovett knew each other's world records. In the first race each season you genuinely don't know anyway. He reckons he'll run 5:02. I say anything from 5:00 to 5:05. I'd really like it if we run alongside each other. He's a known pace quantity and I know he likes a long finish. Last time he smashed it from 600 out and it killed me to beat him.

5:00 pace is 37.5 seconds per 200m indoor lap.
75 on lap two.
I won't split lap three.
Then the crucial one – 2:30 at halfway.

We're all standing back from the start line. Lots of impressive hamstrings here and specialist middle-distance spikes on show. This won't be a picnic. A mile never is. We are beckoned forward to the start line: nine metres back from the finish line itself. 1609 metres. Eight and a bit indoor laps. The starter raises his electronic pistol.

Vnymanye. KRRR!

Shit. I'm slow to react but anyway we're off. Slight jostling for lane one into the first bend but nothing messy. I ignore the shape of the race on the first lap. Big bunch. Fast. I'm in lane two. All the usual so far. Kool. I'm a few metres off whatever is happening at the front which is fine because my split of 36 is spot on. The first split is always quick, especially indoors when it's a 200-metre split and includes the frenetic start.

On the second lap the race implodes. Five lads (or maybe six?) tear off the front for a big lead. It's three (or four) of the white vests, one blue vest, and the Green Goblin away into the distance. It's a huge move so early. They vanish from whatever race I'm in altogether. Crazy move if they're going to run 5:00. But what if that race list was alphabetical? They may have put down 4:55 or less. Fuck. It leaves me suddenly in limbo, both a long way behind and ahead of the rest, with no real race around me. Marooned in sixth at the front of a strung-out secondary pack. The win has gone already. I'm doing all my own work with very few footsteps behind me to transmit any of this pain onto.

I run for my splits. 74 – nailed.

Third lap and nothing. No structure anywhere to tag my pace to and no visible rivals. They're ahead somewhere. Twenty or thirty metres. Technically I could see them if I wanted to be in their race, but I'm not remotely interested in that pace. The footsteps behind me are benign. The threat is the nightmare early burn inside me: already the sandpaper throat of indoor racing, already lungs, already ominously heavy strides around the banked bends. Haven't calculated my third lap split but I look for it anyway. Maybe the number will mean something and spur me on? But the LEDs on the race clock aren't all working properly. If you know what you're looking for you'll see it, but I don't. Something 52? Means nothing. Fuck off. I'll just work and target the halfway split.

The fourth lap is identical to the third lap. As I come round to the finish line I check the lap counter to see if I've fallen into a time warp and repeated an extra lap for no reason. The white vest group are still miles ahead. Green Goblin. Shit he's nailing it. 5:02? That's damage later unless he's in incredible shape, which he might be.

Halfway. No race. Just empty chaos around me.
I hit my halfway split. 2:29.

The splits on a mile get easier, don't they? With each lap the extra nine metres at the start get spread over more distance, so your splits at the timer (on the finish line) make out you're faster, when you aren't. Shit. But I manage to flip this back and use it. Yes, I'm up and getting stronger, at least think it, believe it for one lap. My legs are wilting on the fifth lap so I accelerate to maintain the same pace. Accelerate into nothing. Onto no one. What the fuck is this?

All these laps are completely interchangeable. There's no plot whatsoever. No rivals. Not even much escalation of pain which was already disgusting after the first lap. In the novel *Hopscotch* by Julio Cortázar there are 155 chapters to the story. At the start of the book the author provides instructions. He suggests to either read only chapters 1 56 in the order they appear, or to follow a second 'hopscotch' order which is out of sequence but includes all 155 chapters. The hopscotch order which he gives misses out chapter 55 altogether and 'ends' on a recursive loop back and forth between chapters 58 and 131. A third option is also available says Cortázar: to read the chapters in any random order. Whichever approach is taken the narrative is likely to make equal sense, or equal *non*-sense of the characters and events. Julio Cortázar appears to have written my *CSKA* mile race:

Lap 1 – lap 5 – lap 2 – lap 4? – lap 3…

No lap has any meaning relating to the previous lap or to the lap to come. On each lap I'm in equal agony, equally adrift in sixth position, or seventh, each lap I'm in lane one, running tight to the inside line which isn't fucking helping as much as it should be. I have to push myself with no one and nothing around, apart from one set of annoying footsteps lurking in my slipstream. Or is it now two sets? The laps are endlessly recursive despite the instructions provided by the lap counter board. I'm a racer with no race.

I can't even target my splits anymore. In this much pain I can't add up 2:30 and 37.5 and then try to confirm my arithmetic on a timer with a dodgy display. I think I'm maintaining my pace. Or that I'm fading. So I think I kick again. This is hurting. The lap counter is my only lifeline. If it says '3' next time and I still haven't walked off the track in misery then I might do another lap. Then another. Where is the panache? My spikes detonating off the track are only underwater explosions, deadened leagues deep, barely a ripple reaches the surface from my ocean trench. The centrifugal vortex of the bends increases each time, and I've already run ten of them. Agony. And… '3' laps to go. Phew!

But fuck. Still 600 metres to go. Six hundred. I can't break that down in any way that helps. Three indoor laps. Which feels like three outdoor laps. Focus. Hang on until 400 to go then I might be able to build a finish. Until then it's only digging and survival: 590... 580... 575…

Whoosh!

A flash of Russian blue. Rinat passes me around the bend. In the same moment a white vest from the lead group appears ahead of me, ahead of us, in lane one. The white vest has caved in and we've caught him without even trying. He's running backwards but it still takes tungsten willpower to force myself to follow Rinat on the overtake.

I've lost and gained a place in the race that never was.

Commit now. I'm going with Rinat. This has already happened before I tell myself to do it. Good sign. It requires a definite gear change, which doesn't hurt initially but within a lap it might ruin me. Fuck it – within a lap I'll only have two laps to go. Okay now I've got something! Rinat doesn't get rid of me with his move. But he's aggressive. He has impressive power despite, no, *because of* his wiry upper body. His Lycra sprint shorts are a warning of his 800-metre speed. This guy is serious. Fucking get on him and pressurise.

Once I've settled in Rinat's slipstream I start to feel better. Relatively. Good enough to embrace the agony. With each burning quad drive and with each sandpaper breath I'm nearer 400 metres to go. The flow? Rinat's cadence is very similar to the Ovett wavelength. With each foot-strike nearer the lap counter it's a better and better match. Yes, rhythm! Suddenly I'm running on the top of the track. Smooth. Loose shoulders. Oh, I'm loving his stride here. Whatever the fuck he can do I can follow.

Two laps to go. Right, let's rock n roll!

Rinat ahead is having a real run at this but I'm all over him. *Ovett – comfortable!* There are footsteps close behind me now too, but no cunt is coming past this, we're flying. I edge half a lane out into the boss position. On the back straight I count down strides to the pole vault bed when it will be 300 metres to go. Three hundred is *very* close to home. The outskirts of Düsseldorf.

I'm fucking in this.

At the pole vault I'm still within a metre. Yes! This faster gear feels way more comfortable. Better mechanics. Now lots is happening. On the top bend we move out to pass the Green Goblin who is utterly ruined. Rinat and I both feed off the kill. On our toes. *Relaxed*. Majestic. Coming up to the bell which at *CSKA* is a small gong and a xylophone stick. It's Russia and Britain stride for stride. 200 metres to go. I sense Rinat is loving this too.

BONG! BONG! BONG!

At the gong over the line the lap-counter lady calls our numbers on a speaker to confirm it's our last lap. Her flat delivery contrasts with Big Ron Pickering up in the commentary box, now booming into his microphone as the battle reaches its climax.

Ovett closing in – and the crowd beginning to sense it.

On the penultimate bend we're going to pass another fading leader who went too big. The dark blue vest is it? Who cares. We pass him so fast it barely registers. Just more destruction in our wake. Those footsteps behind have fucked off too. Wanker!

150 metres to go. This is where it happens.

I unleash a fearsome *metelitsa* which engulfs Rinat. He has no answer to the snowstorm down the back straight. But it's a measured overtake rather than annihilating him in one go. This is partly my choice, tactical and artistic, and partly because Rinat is still so quick. I make it relaxed and controlled, saving something even bigger just in case. If I go into the last bend ahead in lane one then Rinat's chances decrease massively. The pole vault bed flashes past on my inside. I lean into the curve one metre in front. Decisive? It fucking has to be. Maintaining my speed around the top bend in the lead, dominating. I've got this in the bag. But have I?

Fifty to go.

Out of the final bend I kick for a nice time... but Rinat kicks to beat me. Big difference. And he's all over me again. This is a fucking race and he's got missile lock on me. He's beaten me once before and his synapses are telling him he can do it again. I don't look – never look – but I can hear his incredible sprint cadence reeling me in. Need to do something about this. And. Boom! This time a proper racing kick. Unleashed with full Ovett panache. At the finish line it's close. I only get it with full sprint arm drive, but frankly it was never in doubt.

And it's Ovett's day today!

Ovett wins (third).
Rinat second (fourth). Third (fifth)? Didn't see.

I'm sprawled on the track in agony. All fours. Gasping for air face down long enough to notice the tiny grains of rubber which spikes have dug out from the surface of the track. Pain. Eventually it will subside. And does. Finally, I can stand up.

What a race! From out of nowhere. Rinat and I shake hands. *Otlichno.* He thinks we were second and third in the end. I'll take it. So much for the white vests. All but one of them slain. What was the time? asks Rinat. Wait yes, I did stop my watch at the line. 4:57. *Molodyetz.* We chat in Russian about the race. I don't understand a word he says but yes racing each other massively helped.

I eat a banana and the two most succulent dried apricots in athletics history, and then sip from my flask of tea, an elixir for my scarred throat. Today I didn't swallow. Just ignored the sandpaper and suffered. Jog. Stretch. More tea.

A mile in 4:57 pro rata is 4:37 pace for 1500m. It's not remotely competitive at the World Masters but it's still only January. And I'm really an 800m man. Shitloads more training sessions to do. Race toughness gives you several seconds and that only comes from lots of horrible races. Then there's spring-summer speedwork to sharpen me up. I'm not a million miles away. A pleasing result…

… except truthfully I'm still one kilogram too heavy. I can get away with that here against local M50 guys but not against the M45 crème in Finland. Those guys will be monsters. My skinny summer race vests still don't fit.

Need to be super-wiry. Like Rinat. This is business to be taken care of.

So in the evening I go to CCCP Fitness. To weigh myself before and after a lite session. Anastasia isn't on shift. Bah! But she's updated her profile photo in the gym. While I'm on the exercise bike there is something on the NTV news channel about NATO. Putin doesn't like how cosy the Ukraine are getting with the West. That old chestnut again. I check BBC news online. Same thing. Probably just posturing. Putin does it all the time to cultivate his popularity at home. He's totally paranoid like that.

After some cardio I hit the sauna. Today it's stifling. One of the regulars thinks he's clever and pours scented water on the coals. On the second tier of seats we get scalded by a wave of steam, while he sits on the easy front row. The rude fucker. I focus on the plasma telly through the full-length window. *Wild Russia.* It's a new episode about a giant sinkhole on the Yamal Peninsula. A mysterious smouldering crater in the tundra. Nobody knows what caused it. The selfish twat pours on more of his scented water. It's way too hot. Fuck this for a game of soldiers. I leave.

`To: Nevis. Extent of R troop build-up on U border being disseminated as of tomorrow via news channels. Hoping gradual dissemination prevents market shock. No doubt that he's going through with it. Welcome back to 1939, chum. God help Ukraine. From: Gyllyngvase`

Seventy-Nine Steps

★

To: Ingot. Must meet soonest. I hear Starbucks down your way are doing a new alpaca milk latte. Am keen to try one. Size tall. With a cardboard holder. From: Nevis

March 1979. In the Herat Province of Afghanistan an army mutiny took place. Only a minor uprising at first. Attacks from mosque strongholds were launched on state buildings and other symbols of the communist PDPA rulers. A response battalion was sent to quell the revolt, but the soldiers of this battalion were ethnically aligned with the mutineers themselves. Instead of defeating the revolt they joined it. Their hold of Herat lasted one week. Armoured brigades then arrived from Kabul and massacred the entire city. Similar uprisings blazed throughout the country with the provincial resistance, the Mujahideen, now coordinating their efforts. This was a full-scale crisis for the communist regime. PDPA President Nur Muhammed Taraki pleaded with the Soviet Union to send military help to support the communist cause. The Politburo declined. Three months later Taraki was murdered by his own party. It was becoming increasingly difficult for Moscow to look the other way.

★

To: Nevis. Tomorrow. 07:15. What syrup do you want? From: Ingot

At the start of the 1979 track season Steve Ovett's unbeaten record over 1500m and the mile stood at twenty-four consecutive races. Winning big races was fun, but in the season before the Olympics Ovett's plans were structured specifically around lower-key races, and clusters of races which would simulate the gruelling championship schedule he would face in Moscow.

`To: Ingot. Surprise me. From: Nevis`

For championships it's crucial to know what your legs can do on consecutive race days. You need to experiment and see if there's anything that works particularly well, or badly, for recovery. You have to learn to reset the mind overnight and be ready to go again. It's impossible to simulate Olympic tension but physiologically Ovett wanted to put himself in equivalent situations. His season started with four 1500m wins. Crystal Palace. Enfield. Bremen. Nijmegen. Winning was still the Ovett modus but fast times were not on the radar.

The opposite was true for Sebastian Coe. Still perceived as being only second best – even at the back of his own mind? – Coe needed to even up the psychological stakes. Peter Coe knew his athlete was close to tip-top shape for a fast 800m. Training and warm-up races had gone well. Seb had been testing out his legs relative to the world record with either huge first laps or a super-fast second lap. He was ready to put the whole race together for a big one. On July 5, 1979, it happened at the Bislett Stadium in Oslo. Running relaxed and carefree, Coe obliterated Alberto Juantorena's 800m world record by a whole second. The headline typefaces couldn't get any bolder.

FANTASTIC RUN BY SEB COE… 1:42.33.
A new era for the 800m opens as world record is smashed in Oslo.

Coe had entered the big time. One-forty-two was the ultimate statement. It was two seconds quicker than virtually anyone else was running, with the Olympics only twelve months away. In the press scrum after the race everyone wanted a piece of the new superstar. The Nike rep, who had blanked Coe only the day before, sidled up with a business card and re-introduced himself. The message from Coe was cordial but clear: *Yesterday you could have had me for a pair of spikes. Now it's going to cost you.* The sporting media drooled. As much at the phenomenal time as with the style of the run. Down the Oslo back straight the gazelle barely looked to be working, bounding over the Serengeti without a worry in the world. If this happened in Moscow the result was a foregone conclusion. Even his rivals were stunned. John Walker:

The way he ran was just unbelievable. Looked like he could run under 1:40. He never tied up at all. Seb could win the 800 in Moscow and the 1500 in 1984. But he's got nothing to lose by going for the 800 and 1500 in Moscow. The 800 comes first so the 1500 is just a bonus.

No one knew the middle-distance contenders better than Walker, himself still very much one of them. From such a respected peer this was the highest praise one could receive. Or was it? *Nothing to lose. The 1500 is just a bonus.* The subtext from Big John Walker was crystal clear – Ovett would win the 1500m.

`Traffic cameras pick up a red Renault Twingo on the M40, the M25, and then the M4 [eastbound]. The car is travelling at normal speed. When it reaches the A4 the early morning traffic is a little heavier, but the driver has left plenty of contingency time. This drop would be a matter of life and death.`

Ovett's low-key season was already causing unintended issues. His off-beat race choices were ruffling feathers in the media and in GB selection rooms. Steve wanted to avoid major events, being potentially vulnerable as he clustered his races. Giving himself a break from the spotlight was also a wise move. However, this did not sit well with officialdom. A pressurised late decision to run in Birmingham in the AAA Championships in mid-July caused a spat between Ovett and the administrators. The tension was gleefully stirred by the press who were now coming down heavily on every Ovett foible, even his playful showboating. After his easy 1500m qualifying heat Athletics Weekly reported that:

Steve's popularity with the fans is as great as ever, but he will have fallen further in the estimation of his fellow competitors by his conduct in the heats. Did he need to demean the efforts of those mere mortals scrapping behind him for places in the final by running the last thirty metres diagonally into lane seven and eight?

A curious opinion given the attention and bums-on-seats that a qualifying heat of a AAAs race would otherwise have received. Also it hugely misrepresented Ovett's relationship with his fellow middle-distance runners. He was universally popular. The runners' runner in all ways, both at home and at international meets. A harmless victory gesture meant nothing to his competitors compared to the stardust he sprinkled on their races. But this likeability was ignored by the media to fit his designated trope. The knives were out after the AAAs final too:

Instead of having a go, Steve Ovett contented himself with a fairly unadventurous tactical victory.

Unless he left blood on the track it seemed Ovett was unable to please everyone all of the time. Drawing in thousands of athletics fans to Alexander Stadium, winning his race, and sharpening his tactical instincts was not deemed enough for the greedy scribes. Where on earth were they getting 'unadventurous' from? There had to be something else to such comments, between the lines, and it didn't take a master code-breaker to decipher the message. *Instead of having a go.* Again the subtext was clear – *having a go* like Coe would.

Within days the comparisons mutated further. On July 17, only twelve days after his 800m world record Sebastian Coe lined up at the Bislett Stadium track once again, this time for the Dream Mile. Ovett had declined the invitation to race in Oslo and made an off-hand remark that the race wouldn't mean as much without him in it. Technically not wrong. However, with a field including Coe himself and the likes of John Walker, Eamonn Coghlan, Thomas Wessinghage, Steve Scott, and Dave Moorcroft, the 1979 Dream Mile was the greatest mile field ever assembled. Pundits predicted a tough race in which the endurance of Coe, still only seen as an 800m specialist, might be found out on the demanding third lap. It took less than four minutes for Seb Coe to not only prove his third lap endurance, but to finish in style and re-write the annals of athletics history once again. Another world record. In the words of the adoring press:

Sebastian Coe ran the mile of the century… with that effortless floating style he stormed over the last 200m. The rest were nowhere. The Sun.

A field of exceptional talent was left shell shocked by the power, grace and speed of his running. Daily Mail.

Our new world record-holder is capable of under 3:47. But future times matter little today, after the incredible sight of Coe running further and further away from his mesmerised rivals until he took his last, unfaltering step. Evening Standard.

What a run! Steve Ovett must be eating his words about the victory in the race he missed being hollow. The Guardian.

Records are important, but the real contribution Seb Coe is making to our sport is the living proof that it's still possible for nice guys to win. Long may he thrive. Athletics Weekly.

Coe established himself as indisputably the world's greatest middle-distance runner – how does that feel Steve Ovett? Daily Mirror

Neither the Coe fireworks in Oslo nor these subsequent digs in the press goaded Ovett out of hiding. He stuck to his plans. Just another routine 1500m win in Hendon. Then a solid victory in Gothenburg over the same distance. His winning streak continued, but was anyone now even counting? On back pages everywhere it was all Coe Coe Coe and the whole country had world record fever. Also, Sebastian Coe was no longer just an 800m specialist, so the prospect of both races in Moscow now being up for grabs was sending the sporting media into spasms of excitement.

★

`Brompton Road, London. Early morning.`

`INT. The store of a well-known coffee chain`

[pending product placement negotiations].

06:55 Commuters in and out for their takeaways. The harsh sound of the coffee grinder. The hissing of milk being heated. The first customer of the morning, a man in a mid-range business suit, already has his drink and is installed at a window seat facing outwards onto the street. His coffee cup is in front of him and slightly to his left. The window seat is a breakfast bar which stretches the length of the shop frontage. His Renault Twingo is illegally parked in some mews half a mile away, but his number plate means he won't get clamped. Nevis motions to sip his coffee but there is no audible slurp.

In July 1979 the United States provided half a million dollars to the Mujahideen in their fight against the ruling PDPA communists. Officially 'non-lethal aid' for radios and medical supplies, this was effectively cash to buy weapons. With Afghanistan now in the midst of a full civil war US President Jimmy Carter was making a symbolic gesture of support towards the anti-communist insurgents. With the situation deteriorating, America had bought a stake in the outcome.

07:12. A new customer enters. Female. Tall and conspicuously well-dressed. She turns heads, specifically those of the barista lads and all the male customers in the queue. But not Nevis. The woman's face is hidden. We see only a grey power suit, white blouse, and long platinum blonde hair. She orders an alpaca latte and a croissant. Just before paying she decides to have a shot of syrup. The barista writes the spec on the cup in black marker and asks for her name, then writes 'Inge'. The woman's real name would be Jemima or Charlotte. Possibly Henrietta. We never see her face.

★

Switzerland. The Weltklasse in Zurich is one of the crown jewels of the European athletics circuit. The meet has been run at the Letzigrund Stadium since 1928. History was on the agenda again for Sebastian Coe. Just twenty-nine days after his world mile record in Oslo, Seb laced up his spikes in Zurich for a 1500m. This time there was no element of surprise. An emphatic Coe victory was taken for granted. To ramp up the psychological test for his athlete Peter Coe decided to announce it as a world record attempt: *Go on, you've got two, so let's make it three.* Music to the meet promoters' ears. The Letzigrund was buzzing with expectant track fans. Ten million viewers watched back in the UK where the BBC, unprecedentedly, interrupted the nine o'clock news to broadcast the entire race live.

The woman 'Inge' sits down at the window breakfast bar. There are a few bar chairs free, but strangely she chooses one right next to another customer. On her right is a man. She puts her coffee cup in front of her and slightly to the right so it is close to the man's drink.

Three and three-quarter laps and 3:32.1 later…

Then she puts the bag with her croissant against the window. From outside it is now unlikely any potential observer could see the two coffee cups clearly. The cups are the same size. Both have a cardboard holder

```
and virtually the same spec written on them,
which both customers have rotated to be
facing towards them. From outside the
woman's face is now hidden behind the decal
logo of the coffee chain [prominent for X
seconds on screen].
```

WELTREKORD flashed on the giant scoreboard in dot matrix lights as photographers jostled around the exhausted athlete. This one hurt. The early pacing had been way too fast, yet somehow he had regrouped and held on for the record. Mission accomplished. In forty-one days Sebastian Coe had gone from not being able to cadge a free pair of Nike spikes, into being the biggest name in the sport. Stardom for the boy next door. Three world records at three different distances. The talk about the Moscow Olympics now changed from the outside possibility of one Coe gold medal to the strong likelihood of the double. The eight *and* the fifteen? It was now on the table and only one man could stop him.

```
She gets out a compact and assesses her
make-up, carefully noticing whether any of
the customers or baristas behind her are
paying any attention to her, which they're
not. She places the mirror back in her Louis
Vuitton and takes a sip from her coffee,
which is not her coffee, and there is no
audible slurp. Nobody has seen the switch.
```

★

Two weeks later Ovett beat a class field in a mile at Crystal Palace. He won in the time of 3:49.6. Only six tenths off Coe's world record from the Bislett in Oslo. This intensified the speculation about what might transpire on the Olympic track when they finally met.

Was this fast Ovett run a coincidence? It had to be quick to beat an in-form Thomas Wessinghage, but it didn't tally with Ovett's previously-stated plans for the 1979 season. Had the Coe pyrotechnics in Oslo and Zurich got into his psyche? Was the gushing press coverage over their new darling starting to rankle Ovett? His next race left little doubt.

```
After the switch, the man next to her also
takes a sip from his coffee. This time there
is a slurp, and an approving 'aah'.
```

NEVIS: `Pecan. Are you a mind reader?`

Brussels. The 1979 Van Damme Memorial 1500m. Top class pacemakers were laid on for an unofficial world record attempt. Ovett would be in the armchair until the big finish, but how much work would he then have to do on his own? Could the pure racer, the ultimate gladiator, also race against the clock?

The pacemakers did a perfect job.
On schedule at the bell. But only just.

Ovett needs a sub-57 second last lap. With 200 metres to go he is on his own and winding it up for the record, lactic acid accumulating with every stride. Nasty. But it doesn't show. Ovett's form is perfect even on the last killer bend before he can truly unleash. Beauty with brutality in an exhilarating quasi-mystical flow, the athletic *je ne sais quoi.* Some just have it. Allyson Felix all day long. Hicham El Guerrouj. Usain Bolt. Pamela Jelimo. Carl Lewis for sure. Ovett. Of course Coe. No power appears in the visible dimension, only smoothness. If you're lucky enough you can see such athletes in real life at the track. Olivia Borlée at warm-weather training in Tenerife. The Saucony Spitfire Girl at Sokolniki. Ed Whitlock in the M80 1500m final in Sacramento. I want to be like you. Ovett runs beautifully down the home straight, hurting, but relaxing so he can accelerate further into the flames. He wins comfortably but misses the world record by one tenth of a second. In the build up to the Clash of the Titans in Moscow it was now that close: one tenth over 1500 metres.

Sebastian Coe 3:32.1
Steve Ovett 3:32.2

Only nought-point-one. The thickness of a red vest in Brussels, or a white Great Britain vest in Moscow. With the 1980 Olympics less than a year away the rivalry couldn't have been more tantalisingly poised, and yet the clash to end all clashes very nearly didn't happen at all. The convergence of the two racing careers was mirrored by the collision course in Afghanistan. Before the end of the year the Soviet Union finally got lured into Kabul.

No other words are exchanged. The platinum blonde leaves with the coffee cup and croissant. Back to her Henrietta or Jemima world. She will later read in detail the contents of that Starbucks coffee cup and then destroy the message as instructed.

Storm-333
★

KGB Archives - Lubyanka
SOVERSHENNO SEKRETNO
File-10778: The Coe and Ovyett File.
Dokument-10778.1a

<u>Operation Ace</u>
Submitted for consideration to the Committee.

The upcoming Olympics are important for the perception of Communism in non-aligned areas of the world. A successful medal haul for Soviet comrades is required to demonstrate our society to be of superior physical and moral value to the weak-fibred West. Despite our undoubted supremacy there are outliers of athletic performance under sub-optimal capitalist conditions. The secrets of such anomalies must be investigated and converted for the benefit of Soviet athletes and the global Communist cause. Proposed targets for surveillance:

OVYETT Stiven Mikhail James
COE Sebastiyan Newbold

The training methodology of Coe and Ovyett should be monitored and recorded for application to the CCCP track team.

<u>Committee decision:</u>

Of minor importance, but agree use of disposable assets may provide useful intel on fieldcraft with such a projekt. Suggest give the work to the otherwise useless Leningrad branch.

Signed: Y. V. Andropov - Chairman
November 3. 1979

December 1979. The KGB air-dropped 700 commandos into Kabul in Operation Storm-333. The objective was to depose one leader and install another. The new leader of the PDPA Hafizullah Amin had lost control. His interpretation of communism also veered too closely towards Islamic nationalism and the Kremlin feared such an extreme Islamist regime would destabilise their neighbouring Soviet Republics. Worse was the suspicion that Amin had been courting support from the Americans. Storm-333 was conceived as a short intervention to replace Hafizullah Amin with a hand-picked leader and an alternative Communist government. However, within days the Spetznaz commando units were backed up by ground troops entering the country from the north. When Soviet tanks crossed the Afghan borders the operation could only be viewed one way by the West. Invasion. Of a sovereign state. Invasion for the territorial expansion of the Soviet Union.

The Cold War had taken a significant turn. In the diplomatic stand-off over Afghanistan, the Moscow Olympics were immediately under threat, and with it the medal hopes of a generation of athletes, including Steve Ovett and Sebastian Coe.

From a military perspective, there was an advantageous element to the Russians being dragged into a messy and unwinnable situation, a lesson America itself had learned the hard way in Vietnam. Such strategic thinking did not stop the outcry within the political corridors of Washington and at the speaking lecterns. President Carter was suffering on the economic front and faced an election the following year. A strong American response would bolster his presidency, but what else could he do? The USSR had started a war. Afghanistan bordered Iran and Pakistan. If the Soviets went for them as well, Communist territory would open up onto the Arabian Sea, dangerously close to a lot of oil. The 1980 Olympics became a pinball in the geopolitical game. The White House was unequivocal: under no circumstances would American athletes take part in Moscow while Soviet troops remained in Afghanistan. It was six months and counting until the opening ceremony in Central Lenin Stadium. The sporting world descended into chaos.

The National Archives
MI6 Documents Database

Search terms:
Ryazanov, Vadim, KGB, Coe, Ovett, Olympics
Year: 1980
Declassified Matches: 1

Personal Files: Chief of MI6.

14 January 1980.
Monday.

In Sheffield a man unconnected to the Service was contacted three days ago by a Soviet agent at the IEEE Instrumentation and Measurement Conference. This foreign national initially claimed to be an East German called TORSTEN DASSLER from Leipzig, and his passport stated as such.

However, at a second meeting the next day at a local athletics stadium he revealed his identity as Major VADIM RYAZANOV of the KGB, and offered himself as an agent for MI6. He agreed to meet with an MI6 handler on condition that his Sheffield contact was present.

```
Major Ryazanov [identity confirmed] presents
an opportunity for unthinkable access to
high-level Soviet intelligence, or as a
priceless sleeper agent for times of crisis.
He is not strongly opposed to Communism per
se but is an idealist with oppressed
religious beliefs. He did not mention
monetary gain [though this will have to be
considered].

Ryazanov is 25 years old and was recently
promoted to Major to carry out a
surveillance mission on UK territory. He
could only make contact nine days after his
arrival due to the presence on his mission
of a KGB colleague [a distrustful zealot,
subsequently identified by unrelated
events].

Instead of assigning a handler I went up to
Sheffield myself and was impressed both by
Ryazanov and the Sheffield man whose
understated skill arranging and mediating
the meeting was exceptional. Both subjects
are recommended to the Vetting, Cross-
Verification, and Recruitment Committee.

Major Ryazanov identified this summer in
Moscow as the next feasible meeting, during
the Olympic Games at which [potentially] he
may even be competing. The Sheffield man has
a strong connection to that event himself
which makes this a highly viable prospect.

Note to file:
Maybe SHEFFIELD should be handler?
```

Plans were considered to switch the Olympic Games away from Moscow. The practicality was assessed of Montreal and Los Angeles as alternative venues. In the UK newly elected Prime Minister Margaret Thatcher was as appalled as the Americans by the invasion. Her first thought was also to hold events in different cities around the world. London's Crystal Palace was suggested for the swimming. These ideas were quickly proven unrealistic. The political clamour to strip Moscow of the Games was ignored by the International Olympic Committee. The IOC knew the years of planning and construction which had gone into the Moscow infrastructure to host the Games. The IOC understood the strength of passion for the Olympics behind the iron curtain and valued the deep levels of organisation and coaching which supported sport within the Soviet system. The whole point of choosing Moscow for the 1980 Games had been friendship and dialogue across the ideological divide. Athletes were supposed to unify through the Olympic spirit. Elite sport would not be exploited by Kremlin warmongers. Would it?

When the option of changing venues was rejected, the United States and its Western allies worked on a painful but more feasible alternative: to withdraw their athletes from the Games. The Olympic associations of all countries are deemed to be independent bodies. The US President could not order any American athlete to boycott. Constitutionally the decision rested with the United States Olympic Committee who were pressed to hold a vote. With considerable political leverage in play behind the scenes, the result of the vote was a 2:1 majority in favour of a boycott. And that was that. American athletes lost their dreams. 1980 would not happen. Tears were shed at running tracks across America. The nominal US Olympic Trials took place at Hayward Field in Eugene, with athletes knowing they would not be travelling to Moscow to compete. West Germany reluctantly followed America's lead and withdrew their athletes, as did Canada, China, Japan and a total of sixty-five countries, including most African nations, and much of South America.

The United Kingdom? Home of the two biggest stars in the sport. Would British athletics take a stand against the Soviet invasion? The Thatcher government pressured the British Olympic Association to follow the American decision. However, a delegation of athletes from across all sports made it clear to the BOA and the government that they wished to compete, and that they intended to travel to Moscow regardless of what the politicians said. There was no easy answer when a nation armed with thousands of nuclear warheads decided to invade.

In pursuit of a boycott the UK Government targeted the individual athletes themselves. Politicians claimed that medals won in Moscow would be of lesser sporting value with so few competing nations. Peter Coe was invited to confidentially 'discuss' the matter with cabinet minister Douglas Hurd. The discussion failed to coerce Coe. Politicians, the coach argued, simply could not comprehend the sacrifice they were expecting of young athletes. Peter was adamant that he and his athlete should go to Moscow and take care of business.

```
        Secret and Strictly Personal
    EYES ONLY: PM and Minister of Defence

From: MI6
Date: 25 January 1980
Dear Prime Minister

May I bring some information to your
attention, with utmost respect for our
government's strong response to the terrible
```

```
developments in Afghanistan. Last week our
department made first contact with a serving
KGB Major with a stated wish to operate as
an MI6 double agent. We have met with this
asset on UK soil, but only once. His
identity and rank have been cross-verified.
The credibility of his offer is considered
high enough to proceed should we have the
means. The next proposed rendezvous is in
Moscow itself during the Olympics. The asset
insists he will only deal with one contact:
an ancillary member of the Great Britain
Olympic Team. Might a major intelligence
coup make our participation in the Games
palatable?

Faithfully: [signature]
```

While some UK sports bowed to the political pressure and withdrew, many were resolute in their wish to compete. The British Olympic Association agreed they would do so under the BOA banner rather than under the national flag. The politicians were fuming. British athletes had triumphed, but was it the right outcome? Who knows.

How would we react today if Russia invaded someone? Or is that simply unthinkable nowadays? They would become a global pariah. Vladimir Putin, however grubby and vile, is surely too intelligent not to foresee the disaster for Russia in the world. Isn't he?

The boycott era of Montreal 1976, Moscow 1980, and Los Angeles 1984 nearly caused the downfall of the Olympic movement. Hindsight may well say that the non-participation contributed little as a sanction against the Soviet-Afghan war. It may also suggest that US interaction with the Mujahadeen was not without future ramifications. However, history also tells us there was no escalation into a European or nuclear war. Does hindsight from January 2022 make it easier or more complicated to pass judgement? Simpler to narrate is the sadness that in 1980 the middle-distance events lost out on many worthy sporting heroes, racing spirits who deserved their place in the Moscow ether. A toast to absent friends.

Steve Scott
Wilson Waigwa
Steve Lacey
Todd Harbour
John Walker
Willi Wülbeck
Don Paige
Thomas Wessinghagc
Dave Hill
Mike Boit
and many others

Could any of them have taken gold? Maybe. Maybe not. The Olympic final is like any other race – anything can happen. On form it was unlikely any of them would have actually won. Both Coe and Ovett had been demolishing all of the above for three whole seasons. But would such talented absentees have altered the dynamics of a race? Absolutely yes. They would have multiplied the threats around the two favourites. The mindset of Coe and Ovett may have been more stressed, or more relaxed, as a result. Race pacing and the shape of the pack in the 1500m would have been totally different with a Scott or a Wessinghage smashing it at the front, with wildcard Dave Hill in the pack, and with Big John Walker pressing up his favoured inside line. The Ovett and Coe positions change, their synapses trigger different moves. Finishing tactics would be unrecognisable in the parallel universe where Walker-Wessinghage-Scott all run in the 1980 Olympic 1500m final. Even one runner different in an

800m race can alter how the pack forms. Would Don Paige have made the final? Does Mike Boit run the first lap as fast as he did against Dave Wottle in Munich? Willi Wülbeck was a major player over two laps and at six-foot-two is another large body in a pack. Although so would the now 400m specialist Alberto Juantorena have been and so would Ivo van Damme... Alas, these brilliant athletes are only footnotes that didn't happen in the story that did.

```
                 10 DOWNING STREET
                  PRIME MINISTER

                                     27 Jan. 1980
MI6:
Dear N - The athletes will go.
Proceed with recruitment. Keep me informed.

                                    [signed] M.T.
```

After all the machinations the outcome was that Seb Coe and Steve Ovett would be running at the Moscow Olympics. The middle-distance Clash of the Titans survived the intense months of political threat. It would take place as foretold in Central Lenin Stadium in the white vests of Great Britain, with one red hoop and one blue hoop around their torso, and a race number sewn on across the chest: Coe #254 and Ovett #279.

★

Race day. Except I don't race. I picked up a cold on Friday. Temperature. Achy tiredness. It's still there Saturday morning. Over-training? Hopefully only a minor burn-out. At the race start-time I'm sat in my local Starbucks. As I sip my miserable citrus tea I see

Anastasia walk past the window in a white ski-jacket with a furry hood. At least that makes it worth it.

```
Dossier Applecross: Sleeper agent since
March 2016. Recruited at the European
Biathlon Championships, Östersund, Sweden.
Handled by Nevis. Payments made via Ophelia.
```

Diagnosis: Covid-19. Which means isolation and no running for how many days? Feel absolutely rank. No way I could train even if I was allowed out of my flat. I order some food from the Delivery Club: two bag-loads of ready meals from Vkussville and one chocolate treat to cheer me up.

```
Dossier Applecross: European bank accounts
held under false names. Recent deposits made
in Estonia [Tallinn] and Finland [Helsinki].
```

Sleep the day. Then a night of insomnia in bed. At dawn the sofa. Stagnating. Regressing. The lemon paracetamol tastes sweet but not in the right way. Another triple-chocolate cookie helps, today's third. Phil Kimby pops by with two bags of food. He must have got my address off the school. We say hello at a distance on the doorstep but don't chat for long. He is covering one of my classes. Says the students say hello. Thanks.

```
To: Nevis. Is Applecross ready? Important
phase. From: Pythagoras
```

Quarantine day 12. Fed up. I open the fridge at 4am and scoff the last packet of chocolate buttons with a chaser of full fat milk, then microwave myself a ready-meal. Eating has won. I'm so heavy now I'll just be a keep-fit jogger again. M45? You're 47 you fat cunt. No more running. That whole World Masters thing was just a fucking pipedream. I officially give up. The End.

`To: Pythagoras. Yes Applecross in situ and fully briefed. From: Nevis`

The Applecross Anomaly

★

The Journal of International Friendship
Vol. 279 February 2022

Physical Culture, Handsomeness and Identity: Using Middle-Distance Running to (re)Connect Russian Women and the English Gentleman – a case study

Анастасия Луновская
and the man known to her as Стив Оветт

Abstract

In the common ground of CCCP Fitness it is suspected that Anastasia and Stiv Ovyett are destined to meet and become friends. Maybe more. Preeminent sociologists were invited to round-table this Anastasia-Ovyett friendship in its early stages. The discussion presented herein suggests that, contrary to mainstream thinking, an international friendship can indeed co-exist with elite middle-distance training. A suite of the required pre-conditions and catalysts is presented. Ovyett's initial gambit is described and the reasons for Anastasia half-liking him are identified. The potential of a future relatio-friendship is then analysed from both sides of the 'romantic coin'. The discussion concludes with a new paradigm of the English Gentleman and his likelihood of success when operating within the highest echelons of the macro-feminine framework.

Introduction

Anastasia Lunovskaya (30) is an employee of CCCP Fitness, the Lubyanka branch. She works there as a personal trainer. Her current client base of Moscow wives aged 35-50 pays well but does not fully satisfy her professional interest. Her hobbies are motorcycling and photography. Last year she attended the pro-Navalny demonstrations (but was not detained).

Stiv Ovyett (47) is an English language teacher by profession but touts himself primarily as an athlete, an 800m specialist, and pseudo-Olympic reincarnation. He also dabbles in novel-writing and cinema. Ovyett is halfway through a six-month membership at CCCP Fitness in Lubyanka, where he enjoys squats, deadlifts, and nature documentaries on the sauna TV.

The situation under analysis takes place primarily in the weights room and cardio zone of CCCP Fitness. It is February 2022 not long after Ovyett's convalescence from a short but depressing illness.

Findings: Round Table Discussion [Transcript]

If I may begin?
Please do, professor.

The first thing to state is that, in principle, there are no obstacles to Ovyett establishing Anastasia as an acquaintance. But this applies only if he keeps his egotism in check and can build a robust conversational bridgehead.
I agree.

However, it must be stated here for the academic record that further progression towards or beyond friendship presents greater difficulty and significantly more unknowns.
Yes, a lot more.

My initial concern is that we have no concrete proof that Stiv Ovyett is as handsome as he regularly claims to be. None at all. Let's for argument's sake say he's overplaying his looks. If this is true then all his eggs are de facto in the personality basket.
A traditionally weak position.

Exactly. Especially in his case because… well, he's not loaded, is he? Far from it. Therefore, he would be making a mistake to base his approach on a strict looks-personality paradigm. And so would we in our analysis.
Precisely. So where do you propose to start?

As I see it, his biggest asset is not personality but proximity.
I like where you're going.

The face time he gets several times a week at CCCP Fitness, as a paying member, could accumulate into warmth and even early-stage friendship. Although he will have to play his hand well – cautiously and mindfully.
Which he so far appears to be doing.

But again… his tactical awareness might be nowhere near what he leads us to believe. So far he's been totally ineffectual. He hasn't even spoken to her, despite the proximity. If we give him the benefit of the doubt then, yes, playing it cool works in his favour. But he's hanging his hat on this English Gentleman thing. Unique selling point? Not in modern Moscow. There are loads of other expats knocking around as well as plenty of Russian men with good manners and a 'gentle' demeanour. And frankly, hasn't the English Gentleman theorem already been debunked? It's an outdated myth left over from trashy British spy novels. Even if he could resurrect the archetype, no Anastasia gym-scenario is currently presenting itself for Ovyett to appear in black tie or driving a Lotus Esprit. Hence, CCCP is as much a limiting factor for him as it is a source of encouragement. So overall, it's a slim hope to foresee friendship. And categorically, the pre-conditions for romance do not and will not exist. Do you agree?

To an extent. I don't *dis*-agree. You give an excellent summary of the issues, professor, but I think you undervalue his fieldcraft and, if I may, the literary weight of British spy fiction.

Fieldcraft you say?

Indeed. My observations of Ovyett start with this aspect. Also, let's return 800m running to the forefront of our analysis. Now we have a framework in which his immediate problem is also a significant opportunity – namely, morale. If you'll permit me to project forward with this angle?

Yes, of course. How was his morale after two weeks with Covid?

Low. Rock bottom in fact. He had no energy to train. No motivation. Chocolate in any form was his solace. We know this. He hadn't dared weigh himself since the illness had struck. Had he done so he would have seen that he was right back to square one. His October weight: 75+ kilograms. All the hard work up in smoke. The 2022 World Masters dream was over.

So what did Ovyett do?

The only thing he could do. He made a cry for help.

A cry to whom?

To Anastasia. The most attractive employee at CCCP and by far Ovyett's favourite muse in Moscow. Anastasia

Lunovskaya had worked for two-and-a-half years at CCCP. The Lubyanka branch was only seven metro stops on the red line from her apartment opposite Cherkizovsky Park. Anastasia was thirty years old: happy, healthy, and very beautiful as we know. A former biathlete, she had represented her region (Smolensk Oblast) in the Russian championships and had been in the national squad for two seasons, although Stiv Ovyett did not know this. He was mostly pre-occupied with her looks. Anastasia had honey-coloured hair, long and silky, au naturelle. Her figure was lithe and strong: *sportivnaya*. She weighed exactly 60 kilograms on the scales. She had size 39 feet (Russian sizing) which were narrow, hence she usually favoured Adidas. With her sunny demeanour Anastasia enriched the weekly lives of her CCCP clients, most of whom were women. She enjoyed her job although it sometimes made her feet achy by the end of the day. She would bathe them in an ice footbath when she got home before preparing her dinner (either salad or soup). Anastasia had lived in Moscow for several years. She was originally from Smolensk and visited her parents there once a month for the weekend. She gazed out into the Russian countryside during these long train journeys and reflected on how content she was in her life – a life she deliberately kept simple. She had one semi-regular lover but did not consider it a binding relationship. It was more a friendship (from the biathlon days) which had evolved into beneficial arrangements. Though outwardly demure, Anastasia had strong sexual desires and Aleksandr fulfilled them on days (and nights) whenever she requested. It worked because Aleksandr understood her independent streak and never pushed for a more formal bond. Naturally, she had many male admirers and occasionally enjoyed them in discreet scenarios, when she trusted them not to pursue her for commitment. One day she would fall in love and marry (she knew) but she left this for the irony of fate to decide. Anastasia had a degree in Applied Sports Pedagogy from *SGU*, Smolensk State University, an achievement which made her parents extremely proud. Her father Yury was a doctor. He loved music and was also a talented sportsman. He enjoyed basketball in his youth and was a handy brown belt in karate. Nowadays, he only played table tennis (once a week in a local veterans league). Yury Lunovsky was tall and distinguished, a gentle man who drew innate respect from peers, especially with his topspin forehand smash. Oksana, Anastasia's mother, was a psychologist (Kleinian). In her free time she did yoga and enjoyed literature. Every fortnight she chaired a book club at the Klara Kafé. Last week they read *Breakfast at Tiffany's* (the Popova translation). Also, she had a cat and she played the guitar. Oksana Lunovskaya retained all the beauty of her youth and re-blossomed with each new decade, especially now in her elegant late-50s. Her honey-brown hair had yet to grey. Her figure was still the same as in her twenties, thanks to good diet and three-mile walks along the Dnieper. She had a small wardrobe of Italian couture (expensive, but never more items than she needed) and she wore the latest Adidas sneakers for her power walks. Oksana dearly loved her husband, and Yury was as enraptured with Oksana as the first day they had met. Spring 1990 – a time of political tumult which was making Yury edgy and more impulsive than usual. He had noticed Oksana on Bolshaya Sovetskaya, bought a bouquet of flowers (eleven lilies) from a street vendor, ran after her, and sheepishly presented them to her, wordlessly, before running off again, smitten but too terrified to talk. They met again by chance two months later (on the same street) and were married by the end of the year. Their beautiful baby daughter was born at three minutes to midnight on the last day of the Soviet Union, the 25th of December 1991, twenty-five minutes before her twin brother.

When (and how) did Stiv Ovyett make full conversational contact with Anastasia?
In mid-February. In the CCCP cardio zone. The jaded post-Covid Ovyett was cooling down on the cross-trainer after a short miserable session. Anastasia was walking past towards the changing rooms, breezily as she always did. Ovyett waved. She waved back but didn't break stride, so he changed his wave to a beckoning motion to flag her to a stop, so he could start an actual conversation. Their first.

– I have a question for you, he said in Russian.
– *Da*, said Anastasia with a smile so radiant it nearly scuttled his bravery.

Ovyett then delivered a short, semi-scripted monologue in Russian about having been ill with Covid for two-and-a-half weeks, about having lost his training mojo, about getting it back and could she, would she, help him?

Was Anastasia friendly?
Yes. Her smile was sincere as she listened to Stiv Ovyett, who had a surprisingly soft voice, she thought. His Russian was basic but oddly creative, even lyrical. The *anglisky* accent was thick on a couple of phonemes but his intonation was pitch-perfect Muscovite. There were grammar mistakes but these made him cute. She was actually relieved that Ovyett had finally broken the ice. For some weeks now there had been frissons of curiosity (and proto-sexual tension) in their hellos. They often passed on the stairs, or at reception, or in the corridors.

He had once held a door open for her. Ovyett remembered that circa seven months previously he had run past her in Cherkizovsky Park. It had been a hot day. Anastasia was wearing a white fast-wicking top and peachy (coloured) shorts with a floral motif. She had seemed sad, Ovyett thought. Also, weeks ago he had seen her in the metro at Preobrazhenskaya so he knew she lived nearby. As for Anastasia, well… she had once seen him running in Cherky Park by the lake. She noticed how fast but *relaxed* he looked. It was the day after she had had an unnecessary argument with Aleksandr. Ovyett had not recognised her. Why would he? She had also seen him once in the metro on the opposite banquette reading a thick novel. Ulysses. He hadn't looked up and seen her. She found Ovyett attractive, especially for his age – probably late-thirties? But she put the attraction down to his foreignness. Ordinarily he was too skinny to be her type, although from a professional perspective… *those* muscular legs, she thought.

So, Ovyett got off the cross-trainer and Anastasia trained him?
Nyet. He proposed a session the next week. He asked her if he could send her a message in order to arrange this. She agreed and gave him her number. In fact, she entered it into his phone personally with her delicate, smooth, long-fingered hands. Her nails were painted mauve. None of the fingers had a ring on. Interesting.

Did Ovyett maintain his cool at this point?
Yes and no.

How so?
Yes, because technically he had had access to her number for several weeks. Her business cards were displayed for potential clients next to her profile photo in the gym.

Ovyett had taken one such card several weeks ago and kept it for good luck in his rucksack. But no, because the official permission to message her was something he had long craved. The fantasy-turned-reality sent him aquiver. He stopped his legs on the cross-trainer to maintain composure.

What was Anastasia wearing at this initial encounter?
Great question. And that was the thing. He hardly noticed. It was his debut gazing into her hazel-grey eyes so he didn't absorb the minutiae of her gym gear. He was focusing on her facial configurations which seemed different somehow. Up until this moment he had only looked at her from stealthy oblique angles, from behind (or through) gym equipment, usually in mirror image. His database was mostly rear views which were strategically safer (yet rewarding on their own merits). Talking to her face-to-face in a non-imaginary conversation was new and confusing.

Often the way.
The new configurations were also extremely pleasant, just different. He recalibrated and soon started to notice all her other stuff again. She wore a silver necklace (with no pendant) and her neck was perfumed with *Obsession* by Calvin Klein: a fragrance Ovyett was absolutely all over.

Not one you easily forget.
As she walked away after their chat he noticed once again her shapely sockless ankles.

How did Anastasia feel about this first encounter?
An important point. She felt happy. Despite Ovyett being a CCCP regular, he had never said more than hello. This had seemed strange. She knew he was English (the

girls on reception never stopped talking about him) and maybe this was just what English guys were like. Was it shyness or unfriendliness? She just couldn't tell. It was a silly thing, but she even questioned her attractiveness. Then one day she had seen him staring at her in the mirrors from behind the lat-pull-down machine. Ovyett styled it out by doing three sets of lats and some wide-arm pull-ups, but from then on she knew the curiosity was mutual. The day of that first conversation, coincidentally, Anastasia had thought about him on the way to work. To train him appealed to her from a professional viewpoint. What would he be like? She had so many female clients who drained her energy with their constant whining and negative body image. The possibility of training an athletic male was fresh and interesting, variety which she needed. Anastasia also liked that Ovyett wasn't a beefcake muscleman type or a wannabe MMA fiend (all trapezoids and attitude). She was surrounded by these twats all day and they bored her. This new English gentleman was different. He had shown vulnerability by admitting he needed some help. Who was this balding semi-handsome enigma? He seemed calm, intelligent, even *kulturny*. The Englishness was a lure in itself. Gentleman. She repeated the word to herself. Yes, he would be kind and gentle, but she also sensed a cold brutality which excited her. Those blue eyes, she thought, somehow like chips of ice. She denied it to herself but this man stimulated her womanhood. Something deep inside her yearned to know more. And yes to *feel* more.

How was the first training session arranged?
He messaged her.

In Russian?

Correct. When he had asked her if she spoke English, she had blushed and said no. So he ploughed on in his basic spoken Russian. Written Russian was different though. For that he had resources: a translation app, a Collins pocket dictionary, and some Pushkin poetry books (ultimately not used).

What was the message exchange?
Ovyett wrote in professional register. Majestically polite.

Naturally.
He suggested Thursday and two times of the day he was available. Anastasia replied that she could train him at 14:00. Stiv Ovyett accepted the gift immediately. He also asked how much a sixty-minute session would cost and, to show that cost would not be a problem, he asked how best to do a transfer. Sberbank online, she replied. Yeah easy.

How much information did he give her about his training?
Yep. So in a follow-up message (he couldn't resist) he gave her some background, mainly to make her feel comfortable and so she wouldn't plan too much. He wanted to be the client she most looked forward to spending an hour with. Her athlete. A physical specimen. Serious, but if he also entertained her between deadlift sets, so be it.

Yes, a follow-up message works. Establishing dialogue as a thing. An extra inroad into her thoughts. Smart ploy. What were his actual words in the second message, translated back from the Russian, please?
Hi Anastasia
Information for the training session. I'm a sprinter. So I need strong legs [runner emoji]. In the gym I like

everything, especially squats and deadlifts. I don't need any cardio because I run most days at the track. As we chatted about earlier today, I just need motivation to make it interesting and fun.
See you on Thursday

Why did he tell her he was a sprinter? He isn't. Or is he?
Well. Firstly, he does race 400 metres occasionally. He can justifiably claim to be a sprinter on this basis. All his summer speed reps are sprints. Eight one-fifties. Apollo's classic six twos (off six minutes). The three threes. For this speedwork he wears Adidas Sprintstar. Also don't forget that as an M35 Ovyett won the 4 x 400m silver medal in his first World Masters in Sacramento 2011, holding off the American on the third leg. No 5k boys or half-marathon tortoises can say that.

Fair.
And secondly, to the layperson middle-distance doesn't really mean anything. They just don't get it. Oh you're a runner, do you run marathons? The question fucked Ovyett off. As if marathons (next to a bloke fancy-dressed as an emu) are the only running that exists. He didn't know Anastasia's sporting background. Would middle-distance – *sredny distanz* – mean anything to her? So to emphasise his credentials he told her he was a sprinter. He hoped this would steer her away from giving him any sets in the cardio zone. No... Ovyett only wanted to lift weights. Heavy weights on an Olympic bar. While Anastasia watched him. And *smelt* him. Nailing squats. Smashing deadlifts. Bulldozing his way into her psyche.

What did she think of this background information?
She read it at home while making her camomile tea. It read as expected. She had seen Ovyett doing his stuff in

the gym and could list his programme off by heart. Lots of hamstrings curls and loads on the deadlift platform. Squats. Press-up sets to failure. Apparently, he swam in the pool too. She knew it would be easy choosing set combinations he'd enjoy. After his illness the key would be to manage the intensity, building his energy levels back up gradually in a steady progression. She would do this over the several weeks (or months, she hoped) that she would be training him.

For the first session on Thursday was Ovyett on time?
Fifteen minutes early.

Did Anastasia arrive on time?
Five minutes early. But they started as per schedule.

Okay, this time let's analyse what Stiv Ovyett was wearing.
Academic rigour as ever, professor. Right. It took him three goes in the mirror to decide, as was often the case with so many options in his (superb) sports wardrobe. He eventually went for his navy Adidas rugby shorts with white three-stripes down the side. Mid-length. Their hem corresponded to the maximum circumference of his thighs – strategic, because his legs really were skinny until the definition appeared after a few squats. He teamed the shorts with a plain maroon t-shirt, the tightest one he could wear without making it too obvious. Footwear? His white Stan Smiths, which had sturdy soles for the lifting platform and for (if required) moonwalking.

[Note: although he preferred marquee brands, Ovyett had bought the maroon t-shirt on the cheap from a Decathlon store two metro stops from his flat. He was impressed by the material of the tee – soft, lite, stretchy – and by the reasonable price tag, so he bought the same t-shirt in three different colours: maroon, navy, and Soviet chocolate.]

Did Ovyett behave himself during the first training session?
Would you care to qualify the question?

I'm thinking of his own stated guidelines of gentlemanliness.
Yes indeed. He flew the flag. An absolute a paragon of good manners, of respect, and of playful cordiality. Did he check her out? Yes, her physique was all in order, but he kept his focus very much on her personality. The lovely legs were right there anyway and he'd seen them before, albeit at greater distance. Only once (under deep cover of following her to the squat rack) did he allow himself to notice her exquisite bum… spectacular glutes which, again, he was already aware of. No, the biggest take-home from getting much closer in was how broad and *sportivny* Anastasia's shoulders were. His penchant! They were a tantalising clue to an athletic hinterland Ovyett was extremely keen to explore. He also got several incidental sniffs of her perfume and Christ that *Obsession* smelt good!

Did Ovyett work hard during the training session?
Mostly yes, although he was a shambles during the abs set. Overall, Anastasia pitched the effort level perfectly. He knew she would. If truth be told, Ovyett was already feeling quite energised again. Merely asking her for help (and exchanging messages) had made him feel much better about himself. It had tickled his testosterone system back into play. The weights she gave him weren't too heavy, which was exactly the point. And he noted the scope to impress her with rapid improvement over the subsequent weeks. The focus on Ovyett's posterior drive chain was also noteworthy. He could have gone heavier

on the deadlifts at the start, but there was lots of legs which soon built up. No need to play the hero. She also gave him longish rests. The low effort level was appreciated by Ovyett post-illness. Also, he wanted those long recoveries to develop his Russian small talk.

The conversational bridgehead!
Yes. Anastasia was thinking the same. She knew rapport was an important human factor. It was only Ovyett's first session and she never battered a new client, especially not one who so clearly understood the principles of training periodization (Horwill & Wilson, 1972).

How did Stiv Ovyett cope with the language?
His Russian held up remarkably well. Not grammatically, obviously, but that's tough and he did okay. He was better at vocabulary, and considering the pressure this was solid and functional, with several trademark flourishes. His only major lexical mistake was that he mixed up the Russian words for muscle and mouse.

How often did Ovyett attempt to use the word muscle?
Three times.

1. What's this mouse called?
2. This mouse is always a bit stiff. [his groin]
3. I don't need big mice… I need *fast* mice.

In the conversation did he play it cool about his running?
This had been his gameplan, but as it went on modesty proved near impossible due to Anastasia's inquisitive nature. She asked him, how long have you been running?

And?
Ovyett completed his Bulgarian squats before replying. He gave her an abridged Russian version of the story.

Just the main bullet points. Mid-thirties guy. Handsome. Discovers he's an elite level 800-metre runner, and so on. Did he play it cool? Well, a degree of detail was required to recreate some scenes, so the modesty lapsed at times, but after telling the story Ovyett deflected the focus back onto her.

– What's your sport?
– Biathlon, said Anastasia with the hint of a blush.
– Great. I love watching that on TV. Is that the one with skiing and…? [Ovyett didn't know the Russian for 'rifle shooting' so he mimed it – successfully.]
– Yes.

Did he get her to elaborate?
She was sheepish at first, but then yes. She described the cardio element of cross-country skiing and the principal muscle groups involved. Glutes and quads. The lats when you're double-poling. She had to demonstrate a little because Ovyett didn't understand much of the Russian. This glimpse of her agility accelerated the drip-feed of testosterone.

– What rifle do you use in competitions?
– The Russian team mostly use the Izhmash, which is good, but I prefer the Anschütz Fortner.
– Why?
– Different pull action. You get more rounds in quicker. And the cheek rest is comfortable.
– What's the best sniper's rifle?
– Depends. For ballistics or stopping power?
– Let's say for an approximately equal measure of both, said Ovyett leaning in closer to smell her perfume.
– Well… the McMillan TAC-338. Or the Remington 700. The Spetznaz use the Kalashnikov SVD.

Excellent! This is exactly what conversations with girls should be like. It feels like this re-balanced the attention between the two of them. His egotism appears in check and he has shown he is (also) a good listener. This is great fieldcraft, I have to admit.
Yes, but then she fired back more questions about his athletics which he was obliged to field. Politeness and all. Her next one: Do you run in competitions?

A doozy. The absolute sweet spot. He couldn't not reply there.
Yes, she was lasering in. Ovyett felt less guilty elaborating in the second instalment of the story. He only used the phrase 'World Masters Final' three times. Possibly four. His grammar was problematic again. He mangled the Russian for 'fifth in Porto Alegre in 2013' but she got the meaning. Ovyett didn't mention his 4 x 400m relay silver medal in Sacramento 2011.

Strange omission. Why didn't Ovyett mention his relay medal?
He wanted to save the ace for a later round. Also, his Russian vocabulary was too limited for the task. A quick mental scan of the English language version revealed too many gaps in translation.

[Ovyett later translated the following key phrases.]

The baton. One metre in the lead. Huge American dude is all over me. 400m specialist. So I take it out. First bend. And then annihilate the back straight. I mean, just absolutely fucking killed it. Where he's probably expecting my relaxed phase. But he has to come with me – he can't risk that I'm really that good. Into the top bend. Driving out of the slingshot. Home straight. And listen to this crowd! Absolute sell-out. Tying up with lactic but drove my arms and techniqued it in. Great Britain still have daylight at the handover. 53.2 split.

[The American shook Ovyett's hand: *Yo crazy fool!*]

Did the session include any upper-body exercises?
No. All legs and core. The last ten minutes was stretching and great chit chat on the mats. He made jokes about his poor flexibility, which she enjoyed. Then Ovyett went to the sauna (alone) to bask in how well it had gone. The sauna TV was showing the Siberian Tiger in post-hunting repose.

The next day then. Could Ovyett move after the first session?
Not initially, but he was okay after a second hot bath.

Was his morale high?
Yes, although still fluctuating.

What did Anastasia do that weekend?
She had the Friday off work so she borrowed her friend Lyudmila's motorbike (Ducati 937cc) and rode to see her grandma at her dacha in the Moscow Region. There was a new calf on the farm which Anastasia hadn't seen yet. Her grandma cooked her an apple pie with apples from the orchard. Anastasia rode around the quiet country roads and deep into the deserted farmland, her private idyll where she felt free from the 'issues' of the city. She thought occasionally about her interesting new client, but honestly not much.

And Ovyett's weekend?
His testosterone production was dangerously high for the next 48 hours. His weekend very nearly reflected this. In the end he resisted the option to 'cash in' on his rejuvenated mojo. He had no current lady friends on the go anyway. The bigger picture of this hormone spike was the extra power it made available again in training.

Did his weekend steady run show instant returns?
Not fully. Some of the aggression was back but this was outweighed by the fact he was a fat fuck. 75.3kg. In February! Now only four months out from the World Masters. This was a disaster. So as you can see, his morale was a yoyo. The Finland dream was over. All he could do was train for fun. Run a bit, slowly. Swim. Train with Anastasia. And hope.

Was Ovyett feeling chipper before the second session a week later?
Yes. He hadn't lost any weight in the intervening week, but he'd completed two steady runs and a slow track session (12 x 300m). He'd also done weights twice.

Had Ovyett seen Anastasia at CCCP during either of his two solo weights sessions in the intervening week? If so, what was her vibe and what was she wearing again? Since we didn't get much action the first time round, about what she… her gear and stuff.
He had seen her. The vibe was very good. A big smile and a wave. She was wearing sports gear but not her official CCCP uniform. Gym civvies: skin-tight Adidas hotpants and a cotton t-shirt with the motif 'EAGLES 33' on the front in collegiate font. Stiv Ovyett's mind raced. She was even more sensational in cotton. And the motif drew him into an underworld of sexual intrigue and boys-own adventure. *Where Eagles Dare. The Eagle Has Landed. All The While An Eagle.* Crack teams of Allied commandos launching daring raids behind enemy lines, with a deadly traitor in their midst. She was on her way to teaching Zumba.

Superb. The second Anastasia session was when and where?
Thursday 14.00. CCCP Fitness. This was a day after she had met with Aleksandr. It had been a beautiful night. Such deep sleep after Aleksandr's thrilling performance.

She didn't mind if she had the lingering scent of *Obsession* from the night before. If Stiv Ovyett smelt it, he would understand her desirability. Ovyett did indeed smell it and did join the dots. He was delighted for her. As he savoured the scent he allowed himself some private extrapolations about how dynamite she would be. He knew it would never happen – he and her – but felt no guilt in the primal human fantasy. This was their second training session and the contact, the face time, the proximity was already beyond his wildest dreams, even within the strict limits he knew existed. Yes, he would somehow become her friend and cherish that. Not seeking more. He would love her as a person, a kind and peaceful Russian soul. There was something special but very fragile about Anastasia Lunovskaya.

[Note: At this point there is an interruption. After the following remarks the discussion is abandoned.]

Wait. Shit! Have you seen this… He's invaded.
What. Fuck. He hasn't! But only Donetsk and Lugansk?

No. Kyiv from the north as well. [from BBC news app] *And he's attacking the south with warships on the Black Sea. He's going for the whole fucking lot.*
So he *is* Hitler after all. That's the end of…

[Fade to silence.]

February 24, 2022. Vladimir Putin has launched a full-scale invasion of the Ukraine. Airports and military bases have been hit by missile attacks. Russian troops have entered the country across borders in the north, and east, and by sea from the south. Unarmed civilians have been shot. Speaking from Kyiv, President Zelensky has vowed that the Ukrainian army will fight fight and fight.

A Russian Navy warship on the Black Sea approaches the small rock of Zmiinyi Island. The island is home to a marine research station, a small lighthouse, and a Ukrainian army garrison. The soldiers are told by the Russians to lay down their arms. They refuse, advising the warship to 'go fuck yourselves!' The ship launches air strikes. The defenders of the island are reported killed.

Day Three. Ukrainian forces defend the corridor north of Kyiv, heroically, against all odds. The West unites to impose the first wave of economic sanctions against Russia. In response Putin announces his nuclear arsenal is on special alert. He's calling on World War Three. At this rate he might get it.

A Donetsk basement. The young man eats his last tin of food. He turns on his phone for the first time in two days. Kyiv is under attack, it says. 3am. What to do? Only six months ago he had travelled to Russia for an IELTS course at an English school in Moscow. His improvement was outstanding. Although a shy person, the student made many Russian friends. He completed all his written assignments, improving his paragraph structure and becoming adept at handling complex academic language. At the end of the three-month course the student passed the IELTS exam with a 7.0 score, high enough to apply for postgrad courses at universities abroad. He returned to Donetsk to finish his degree in genetic engineering. Then the madness. Tanks on the streets where he used to play as a child. Mortars ripping into the building where his grandma lived. The shopping mall razed. His friends had left the basement two days ago and not returned. He was alone. He took the gun the others had left him, the first time he had held one, and quietly left his basement. Fifteen minutes later after killing three Russian soldiers, the student was shot. His body lay inert on the street, just any other young man, no requiem required. A stray cat came and touched a paw on the student's forehead, then left.

In the fields the bodies burning. As the war machine keeps turning. Except this war pig says it's a 'special operation' and no one in Moscow can call it a 'war'. Yet the murder spreads. Millions of refugees flee the Ukraine and are accepted with open arms by Eastern Europeans with long memories. All Russian banks are excluded from the international transfer system. Companies begin to pull out of Moscow. The madman has totally ostracized 'his' country from the modern world. The Ukrainian army and civilians with guns defend Kyiv as Russian tanks rumble forward in convoy. If Putin doesn't get what he wants far worse might follow. And if he does get what he wants he'll just keep going: Moldova, Armenia, Georgia, the Baltics... German newspaper Die Zeit captures it in a simple three-word headline over his mugshot: We See You.

Somebody please shoot him.
Just a wish – upon a Kremlin star.

Spezialnost

★

KGB Archives - Lubyanka
SOVERSHENNO SEKRETNO
File-10778: The Coe and Ovyett File.
Dokument-10778.1b

7th Directorate for External Surveillance

Operation Ace

For the small-scale Coe-Ovyett mission to the United Kingdom the Committee has selected the following field agents.

RYAZANOV Vadim Aleksandrovich
PUTIN Vladimir Vladimirovich

Notes:

Major Ryazanov [25, Moskva] has been promoted in rank to lead this mission due to his expert knowledge of athletics. He is a member of the Dinamo track team and a capable runner of the 800 metres.

Corporal Putin [27, Leningrad] of 7th Directorate will assist the mission with spezialnost in surveillance and data acquisition techniques. His sporting experience in judo may be of subsidiary use.

All reporting duties are assigned to Major Ryazanov. Entry dokuments have been produced for travel to the United Kingdom via Berlin under the guise of the East German Trade Delegation for Industrial Tools.

Operation Ace will commence forthwith.

KGB Archives - Lubyanka
SOVERSHENNO SEKRETNO
File-10778: The Coe and Ovyett File.

<u>Operation Ace: Dokument list</u>

10778.1a	Submission to the Committee
10778.1b	Selection of agents
10778.1c	Percy Coe
10778.1d	Harry Wilson
10778.1e	Health status of Corporal Putin
10778.1f	Price compensation fee [FAO: Finance Dept Lubyanka]
10778.1g	Report from Hove Politzia
10778.1h	The BMX incident

Appendix 1	Stiven Ovyett training files
Appendix 2	Sebastiyan Coe training files

Notes on data acquisition:

Nine days into Operation Ace it was decided [for efficiency] to split the surveillance duties. Major Ryazanov would stay in Sheffield and monitor Sebastiyan Coe, while Corporal Putin would travel on his own down to Brighton to observe Stiven Ovyett in training.

KGB Archives - Lubyanka
SOVERSHENNO SEKRETNO
File-10778: The Coe and Ovyett File.
Dokument-10778.1c

Operation Ace

Major Ryazanov report on Percy Coe, the coach of Sebastiyan Coe.

Confirmed this subject is known as 'Peter'. He is an engineer by trade. Under the cover of a technical instruments conference the subject was approached. His scientific intelligence is high. He also shows surprising political awareness for ostensibly just a capitalist cog. He speaks excellent German. Although he is sympathetic to socialism he appeared too stubborn for future recruitment. A clandestine search of his house revealed excellent training records which were photographed for analysis [see Dokument List: Appendix 2]

For Corporal Putin report on Harold Wilson see Dokument-10778.1d

★

Marlborough Road, Sheffield.

PETER: We've got a friend for tea today, love. This is Vadim.

ANGELA: Hello, lovely to meet you Vadim.

PETER: We're going up to the study for a bit. Any chance of a cuppa each?

KGB Archives - Lubyanka
SOVERSHENNO SEKRETNO
File-10778: The Coe and Ovyett File.
Dokument-10778.1d

Operation Ace

Major Ryazanov reports that Corporal Putin was detected while following the coach of Stiven Ovyett - subject Harry Wilson. This negated further attempts to gain insight into the athlete Ovyett.

The only significant intelligence gained was about Wilson himself, who it seems has a short fuse and is highly proficient in hand-to-hand combat, with an apparent spezialnost in judo counter moves. The DDR Embassy was required to assist 'their' national after Corporal Putin, unaware of his whereabouts, had to be extracted from Royal Sussex County Hospital where he was being treated for concussion, grazes, and a broken nose.

It is also suggested a report from Hove Politzia Constabulary is placed on file. See Dokument-10788.1g

KGB Archives - Lubyanka
SOVERSHENNO SEKRETNO
File-10778: The Coe and Ovyett File.
Dokument-10778.1e

<u>Operation Ace</u>

Health status of Corporal Putin:

Our agent appears to have bounced back quickly from his injuries, which he states were only superficial. He denies having been concussed and says the DDR Embassy involvement was unnecessary. He claims that Wilson just got a lucky one in.

Corporal Putin will lie low for a week before re-commencing surveillance. Major Ryazanov has returned to Sheffield to continue his side of the mission.

★

Radio Times
January 12, 1980
ITV 6.30pm - The Spy Who Loved Me

WOOLWORTHS. Brighton branch.
Security Report January 14, 1980

Shoplifting in the music section.

Three Carly Simon albums were stolen on Monday afternoon. The suspect is a short man with a black eye, possibly in his mid-thirties, seen by staff leaving the store at about the time of the theft. The vinyls themselves remain behind the counter but will now have to be sold on discount without their cover sleeves.

KGB Archives - Lubyanka
SOVERSHENNO SEKRETNO
File-10778: The Coe and Ovyett File.
Dokument-10778.1f

<u>Operation Ace</u>

Major Ryazanov travelled as a matter of urgency from Sheffield to Brighton to mediate a dispute between Corporal Putin and a local man Mr Reginald Price. The man Price is the owner of the PRICE Lotus dealership, and was claiming unpaid damage to a vehicle loaned for a test drive [an Esprit model] which Corporal Putin accidentally reversed into a wall in the car park.

For a period of negotiation Corporal Putin was detained by Price [and his brother Ron who had massive hands and was threatening further consequences]. Fortunately Major Ryazanov was contacted and arrived in time to apply diplomacy. A fair compensation fee was agreed and Price was prevented from contacting the local politzia.

No identities were compromised in the incident.

KGB Archives - Lubyanka
SOVERSHENNO SEKRETNO
File-10778: The Coe and Ovyett File.
Dokument-10778.1g

Operation Ace

Translation of Hove Politzia dokument [obtained]. Due to lack of reference to any facial injury it is thought these events pre-date the Harry Wilson incident [see Dokument-10778.1d]

Hove. 00:45. Domestic disturbance. Resolved without charge.

Following a report of consistent banging on a wall at the Pink Pearl guest house in Argyle Street, two officers attended the scene. An East German national identified by his passport as Mr Hans-Dieter Wangdorf (27) was discovered to be the cause of the disturbance. He was unharmed but naked with [initially] a satsuma impairing his ability to speak. In addition he was attached securely by way of cling film to a bedstead in the attic of the terraced property.

The proprietress of the guest house is known to the police as operating a marginal business from this address. However, her occasional co-operation in investigative matters has allowed her guest house to avoid sanction or closure. She was again most helpful in our enquiries.

In her statement Mrs Ermintrude Bakewell [52] provides a list of the sexual peccadilloes of Herr Wangdorf. Her remark that he spoke Russian in moments of rising excitement has been passed onto other services. While performing unspecified acts upon him as a client she became annoyed at his impoliteness. Since he was already partially attached [at his own request] to the bedstead in the way described, Bakewell suggested upping the stakes, to which Wangdorf agreed. When he was fully secured she placed the call to the police and left the property to visit a nicer client.

Herr Wangdorf claimed his predicament was an 'accident' and since no specific crime had been committed he was released from police custody, whereupon the case was passed onto other services.

KGB Archives - Lubyanka
SOVERSHENNO SEKRETNO
File-10778: The Coe and Ovyett File.
Dokument-10778.1h

Operation Ace: The BMX Incident

Glossary: a BMX is a new style of bike designed for wheelies, endos, and other tricks. They are predictably popular among dilettante kids in capitalist society.

DDR INDUSTRIAL TOOLS DELEGATION - SITREP

Brighton.

DDR delegate TORSTEN DASSLER reports that another unfortunate altercation has occurred. Sketchy details but HANS-DIETER WANGDORF is reported to have borrowed a bike in Brighton town centre. The youth whose BMX bike it was claimed HANS-DIETER WANGDORF had not asked to borrow it and had in fact stolen it. Since the boy was only thirteen he was not deemed a threat.

Delegation abandoned due to serious injury.

★

The Brighton Herald. SPORT.
Palace Pier BMX festival. Feb 10, 1980.
Results: Junior U14s
1. D Evans
2. A Smith
3. C Eubank

Wish Upon a Kremlin Star

★

All direct flights from Moscow to the UK have been suspended. The talk is that all European flights will soon be cancelled too. Indefinitely. A new iron curtain? I buy a flight to Geneva online and pack a suitcase with all my running gear.

5am taxi to Domodedovo. The departures board is full of cancellations. Only Swissair to Geneva is still on. I can go. I'll be out and safe.

Geneva. Check-in Desk 54. I can train with Apollo and the gang at home. I'll still make the World Masters. Training with the gang will make me work harder. The three-mile tempo around Ascot racecourse, sitting on Ray into that wind. Cross-country reps dodging lactic bullets up Hamburger Hill. Track sprint reps with the boys. Taking out Ray on the twelve two-hundreds in spikes and the red vest. The Big O is back in town. *Geneva. Boarding gate D17.* I'll probably get more races in back home too, and better quality. Open graded meets with packs of teenagers all running my time, all trying to scalp me. I'll put down soft predicted times and sit on the leader, responding to attacks, smooth calculated speed down the back straight. The kick. The impish wave. *And he's making it look ridiculous.* Victory after glorious victory at Windsor, Watford, Wormwood Scrubs. The Ovett winning streak. Every training session will require a cool-down lap of honour, milking the adulation, blowing kisses into the crowd. E for Easy. I'll be sharper and more dangerous. If I go now I'm on that plane. *Geneva. Last call.*

But it's not the story.

It's not Steve Ovett versus Sebastian Coe. Clash of the Titans at Central Lenin Stadium. It's not my *Moskva.* All I have is the story. Everything depends on running sub-2 off a 59-second split in the World Masters final, and doing it in majestic Ovett style. I stand in departures knowing I shouldn't stay, but in too deep to leave. To be or not to be? Synapses. My flight disappears from the board. So. We're on again. Sitting on a train back to Moscow hurtling headlong back to the future.

Once upon a time in Moscow.

The train takes me back to the metro where I sit on the brown line for three dazed laps of Moscow. All trains on the circle line are brand new and state-of-the-art. After my third lap I change at Komsomolskaya to get back to my flat. Home.

School. My students are all devastated by the █ that their government has started. Work is suddenly harder. The gloom in the room transcends all my creative activities. They try their best but the wind has been totally taken out of their sails. Moscow looks the same but it doesn't feel the same. The propaganda machine is rolling. It's a 'special operation'. Other terms to describe it are banned. Initially, talk about it happens, being so unavoidable, but soon the topic is a hushed taboo and officially treason.

Most of the other international teachers are leaving because █ really could go nuts and round everyone up. Historical precedent says this scenario is on the table. It sounds like only me and Phil Kimby will stay. He's been here over twenty years and has ties.

After my lessons I walk to the metro. Anti-war protesters are gathered in Pushkin Square, heavily outnumbered by politzia in riot gear. I turn and walk in the other direction up Tverskaya to take a different metro station home, hopefully Mayakovskaya, but a lot of the protesters have headed the same way and the politzia are in force there too. As I walk past Mayakovskaya some young students with scarves around their faces are being herded into empty riot buses to be taken away, to soundproofed cells somewhere. This happened to one of my students once before, even though she was only a passer-by. They'll get beaten up for a couple of days and get a black mark on their record which will cost them in their career. Only the young are brave enough to protest, students and teenagers in hoodies, and there aren't enough of them to take on the politzia batons. Last year the pro-Navalny marches were crushed violently so they know what to expect. The politzia have riot shields, tasers, tear gas, water cannons, and guns; fully weaponised against their own people. I walk past the riot bus and for a moment I'm the closest to getting shoved inside if the politzia wanted to, but a middle-aged man in sensible shoes walking home from work is of no interest to the politzia. I walk all the way to Belorusskaya metro and get the brown line round to my red line for Preobrazhenskaya. Home safely. I never felt scared.

Naïve? I should probably think on a bit. Might just tick over for a few days with steady runs. Only light weights. Saunas to purge the toxins. Focus on being a law-abiding teacher. Not ████████████████ and never mention ███ by name.

CCCP Fitness. It's now March 14th. I ask Anastasia to train me because I don't want her losing income because of a ██ which she hasn't caused. She looks forlorn. Her usually vibrant gym outfit lacks sparkle today. I say let's just stretch on the mats for twenty-five minutes. She can watch and I'll practice my Russian. Nothing more. I don't want her to have to think. I do my usual sequence of stretches and make banal small talk. Riffing about stuff I saw in the park, basically just listing animals: *utka, sobaka, ryba* and some masculine nouns whose accusative endings I don't get wrong. She does her best to smile at some of the sentences I build around such basic vocabulary. After forty minutes we stop. I tell her things will be okay and give her a supportive hug. Horrible, she whispers. Her whole body is shaking like a leaf. We hate him. I wish somebody would…

`Dossier Applecross: Brother killed February 27, 2015, while attempting to protect a political associate [Boris Nemtsov]. Shot. Point black range. Makarov pistol. Assailant unknown.`

Her family, her friends, everyone she knows hates him. They can only whisper their hate through tears. One of Soviet Russia's most famous films is called *Moscow Doesn't Believe In Tears.* Anastasia is a former semi-professional biathlete with a top percentile *spezialnost* in rifle-shooting. Conscription has been mentioned in the news.

Phil Kimby reckons it's a good time to switch to teens and kids classes, who'll be less aware and still fun. This shift happens organically as people become more careful as the sanctions start to bite. The West has dropped the sledgehammer. Does ████ even fucking care?

My advanced class are gutted. Veronika & Natasha et al had dreams of studying abroad which are now shattered. My job is merely to cheer them up in English, which I do. I think it comforts them simply that a foreigner doesn't blame them for the killing. They're looking at options to leave the country, knowing the walls are closing in. Some countries are being expedient towards Russia. Serbia perhaps? Turkey will accept Russian citizens for ninety days. Kazakhstan? Hope for a future. The school admin staff seem less bothered. They say the military action will be over in two weeks and then it will just be 'negotiation'. The flame thrower of propaganda has razed the truth and cleared the way for this so-called special operation. You have to be extremely well-educated, and set your VPN location abroad, not to fall for the ███ lies.

████████████████████████████████ ███ Typing the previous sentence is now worth ten years in prison. I'll delete it and add it back in later.

Cherkizovsky Park. Still too much ice and slush on the paths for a fast 5k time, but there are enough sections of thaw where I can gun it for a fartlek effect. Although I can't 'gun' reps anymore in a Russia at ██ Even my running banter is compromised. Still feeling the remains of my Covid. The breathing is not yet fully back to normal, maybe five percent short per puff. But I'm getting out every day for steadies. Some incline strides for some leg speed. The endorphins are welcome.

I think I'm happy. But safe?

The security guards in the metro look at me differently now. Tourist to terrorist. Even in my sensible shoes they know I'm a foreigner. Something in the face, the tame eyes, not gnarled enough, never been brutalised, too soft to be a Russian. I'm ordered to put my rucksack through the metro x-ray machine every time now, just in case it's full of or weapons-grade Birthday parcel for Mr V.V. If I'm seen as a threat they know who I am and where I live. It wouldn't be a drawn out process. Falsified charges. One signature on a warrant. The knock on the apartment door in the middle of the night. Through the spyhole my neighbours see three men in suits on the landing. Taken away in an unmarked Lada. Hostage collateral. Or I never even existed.

The billboards are changing. Where once was a KFC bargain bucket is now the face of a soldier with a slogan. Eternal glory. Our loyal defenders. Or something about the Motherland and a phone number to call to sign up. Defenders?! The utter

Kuznetsky Most. Incline reps up from *TSUM* department store to Lubyanka. The Adidas flagship store by *TSUM* is closing down. I expected this. After my twelve reps I buy a half-price pair of Supernova in stealth grey. The store only opened a month ago. It had to go. Russia is a pariah. No brands can touch with a bargepole, not now he's Adolf Hitler. Except he owns five thousand more nuclear warheads than Adolf did, and today he's talking again about using them. Hard to see how that isn't the endgame. The West's only other option is to slowly cripple the Russian economy, if it can, but that might also make it worse; make him more desperate and twitchier on the red button. China? They're far too quiet. Just everywhere has gone wrong. The whole world is being destroyed by one psycho. These Supernova won't last until he of natural causes. Or gets off by someone from within? The problem for any attempt is that his entire government is made up of his former goon squad, who are all equally power-crazed scum. And no one else gets anywhere near him. It's common knowledge in Russia that his televised meet-and-greet appearances with the 'public' are staged with hand-picked extras: payroll agents dressed up as priests, nurses, firemen. I love Adidas and this store shutting down is sad, but I also need to see these symbolic scars inflicted on 'his' society. Except he doesn't see his impact. Never will. Never walks the streets. Never does his shoplifting in Adidas. I sit quietly and sip my post-session latte. Starbucks is now called Star Coffee but still has the same cups.

Sokoliniki. 6 x 300m off 4 minutes.

Lefortovo. Cinder track. An 800m time trial. Cross-country spikes. Every millimetre of unevenness on the foot-strike comes through. Noticeable give from the surface on every stride, with grains of track dirt spraying behind with each push off. No explosion off the top. Massively slower than a normal track, let alone a competition-grade Mondo. But it's nostalgic and a beautiful four-laner set amongst trees in a natural bowl, with sixteen rows of seating down the home straight. The Ovett faithful roar me home. Time trial result? 2:11. In my first 'race' of the season. I'll take it. You always take a season's best, especially in the first race of the season. I wouldn't want to run on cinders every session.

Meteor. A 65-second split which isn't comfortable but it doesn't ruin me either. Then picked it up with 300 to go. Solid finish. 2:08.

Krilya Sovietov. Wings of the Soviets has a brand new track surface. Bright lane lines. Committed to it with a 62 split but then died. 2:07. This shit hurts on your own.

Stadion Energiya. An old track with slick black rubber. Six-lanes but faded lines and the top bend is uphill. The downhill first bend doesn't help. 2:07.2. Don't panic. Slow early races happen. You're in better shape than that.

Sviblovo. 2:05.9. Then three fast twos.

Sokolniki. The speedwork and horrible time trials are starting to feed through. Felt some mojo today. 2:04.8. Peroxide Blonde gets a wink on my cool-down.

Luzhniki. The 1980 warm-up track. A random lad paces my first lap in 61 and then cheers me on down the home straight. *Davay!* Extra oxygen swirls in the ether. 2:03.71.

Sokolniki. 3 x 500m off 8 minute rests.

Sportivnaya. The RunLab shop is only a stone's throw from Central Lenin Stadium. It's my go-to running shop for high-end kit purchases, and yes they do have the Nike ZoomX Dragonfly spikes in a UK size 9. Two seasons ago a couple of the top athletes on telly were wearing prototypes of these spikes. Last season a few lads in Moscow races were already wearing the commercial version. The technology is problematic and sparked a lot of debate. They're not carbon but the curved Pebax sole plate does provide artificial lift off the foot-strike. This trampoline effect should definitely be banned, but now everyone is wearing them. All the elite middle-distance boys at Sokolniki have got them. The women's 800m is currently the most exciting event in world athletics and both Keely Hodgkinson and Athing Mu wear the ZoomX Dragonfly. Rinat has a pair and reckons they've knocked two seconds off his 800m times. Apollo agrees on the two-second benefit from what the gang are running back home. Apparently, Ray has two pairs. It can't be denied they're a factor. The price tag in Runlab is eyewatering but they fit like a glove and are neon volt green. I can't strictly afford them, but can I afford to hand over two seconds to the field on the start-line at the World Masters? That's the difference between being in the final and watching it from the stands with a Pot Noodle. The volt green seems to accentuate my beautiful calves. How fast would Steve Ovett have run in a pair of these babies? Just do it. So with the last of my pre-Finland equipment budget, I lump on 1500 roubles. In the end it all happens quite easily. I'm officially all-in.

Torpedo. 2:03.67. A season's best with plenty in the tank. Wow! The ZoomX Dragonfly feel amazing.

Sokolniki. The Moscow Masters Championships. I didn't even know it was happening, but turned up to train and the track was reserved. Two hours and one monstrous finishing kick later and I'm the M45 champion. Ovett wins 800m gold in Moscow. Check. 2:01.98. Race shape.

Yantar. Another cracking track. All these speed sessions are making the difference. Today it's Apollo's 6 x 200m off six minutes. The worst lactic session in the book. I only take three minutes rest before the last rep, because that deep into the session the lactic just gets worse the longer you wait. Slow last rep but drove my arms. Another good day at the office, messages Apollo.

In the Yantar track café I treat myself to a hot chocolate. The journey back is long, but I like the blue line and the funky state-of-the art brown line. I change for my red line at Komsomolskaya. On the red line every second train is of the older rolling stock, refurbed retro carriages with laminate wood-effect interiors, no electronic displays, and long banquettes in brown PVC. The old trains rattle. It makes them feel faster and more exciting. At the end of the carriage there's a wooden frame just below the ceiling with a faded manufacturer's certificate:

Metrowagonmash – Model 81-717.5A. Date: 1980.

★

The key to 1980 is doing the same as usual. Longer races are good to test out endurance. Coe begins his campaign with a 3000m at Crystal Palace and then a 5000m at the Yorkshire Championships. Ovett goes stateside and runs a 3000m in Houston beating Steve Scott. The usual.

Leg speed. 800m runners always like to get a couple of early 400m races in to fire up the engines. In Cwmbran in his third meet of the season Ovett runs a 4 x 400m relay clocking 47.6 for his split. To answer the message three days later Coe runs an anchor leg in 46.4.

Sixty days to go before the Olympics. Coe runs an 800m in Birmingham in even splits of 52.9 and 52.6. His time of 1:45.5 is the second fastest in the world in 1980. Only the 1:44.8 of Andreas Busse in Potsdam has been faster so far. Even splits is hard.

You always need five or six races before you find your race toughness. After your lungs have been stripped out and your legs have been thrashed over race distance a few times: *breaking down the tissues* as Ovett calls it. Then fast gets faster. And faster starts getting easier, until you go even faster still. Repeat.

Fifty-six days to Moscow. Ovett runs 1:46.6 in Bergen. This is already his second 800m race of the season. Speedwork for his fifteen and an eight for his eight. The time is only a couple of seconds off his personal best, but still two seconds off the Coe and Busse season's bests.

Coe runs 1:45.0 on cinders in Loughborough, a new world record for a cinder track. He then runs 1:44.7 in Hull at the Northern Counties. The formbook shows that Coe now has the first, third, fourth and fifth fastest 800m times in the world in 1980, one of which, insanely, was on cinders.

The gazelle. Coe runs the 400m in the nationals, clocking 47.78 in the semi-final to qualify. The following day in the final he finishes last in 47.10 but runs the first 200 in 22 seconds, which is 45-pace. Ominous speed for his 800m rivals. Who's coming past *that* in Moscow?

Crystal Palace. Ovett and his pacemaking entourage line up for an attempt to knock Seb Coe off his 1500m world-record perch. Bob Benn takes Ovett through in 55-point for 400 and then 1:53 after two laps, but it's windy and Ovett finishes three seconds out from the record.

Oslo. The Bislett Games. 4:01 pm.

Sebastian Coe in the 1000m. A rarely run distance which Coe could add to his world record resumé without giving away his exact 800m form, or his preferred split. It's quick. The 400m split is 51 seconds! Crazy for a 1000m. The second pacemaker accelerates off this pace. Despite tying up down the final straight Coe holds on for 2:13.4 to break the world record by half a second. It's twenty-six days to the Olympic 800m final and Seb Coe now holds the middle-distance grand slam: the 800m, 1000m, 1500m, and the mile. Four world records. One hour later he would only hold three.

Oslo. The Bislett Games. 5:01 pm.

Steve Ovett in the Dream Mile. The cheers for Coe's lap of honour become cheers for the Big O's entrance. The track world now revolves completely around the two British stars. Oslo today is a once in a lifetime double bill. The Beatles were great. Enter The Rolling Stones and the world record mission of a street fighting man.

The race goes to plan. At the finish Steve smiles and raises his arms aloft, barely out of breath, and sets off on another lap of honour. He applauds back to the crowd and blows kisses into the terraces. Eventually the time is confirmed. A new world record! Two tenths of a second scythed off Sebastian Coe's best. Ovett is officially the greatest miler in the world.

Ovett returns to Oslo just ten days later for his last warm-up race: a specially arranged 1500m against all the boycott nations. Big John Walker, Thomas Wessinghage, and all the top Americans come to take on Ovett at 'his' Olympic distance. He demolishes them all with a last 200 kick as familiar as the red colour of the track. It's one thing knowing it's going to happen, but another thing to do anything about it. Ron Pickering calls it this time.

Ovett moves away! The crowd going wild. Ovett looks over his shoulder. Unconscious of the time. Conscious of winning. The racer that he is. Ovett relaxed. Ovett full of running. Ovett, his nonchalant wave to the crowd. It's going to be remarkably fast. And the time…

Despite poor conditions and tactical imperatives, Ovett equals Coe's 1500m world record of 3:21.1.

So endeth the prologue.

After four years of preparation, and with all the 1980 warm-up races complete, the Clash of the Titans cannot be more finely balanced. They land at Sheremyetovo to a huge security and media presence, with flashbulbs going off with their every step through the terminal building. Moscow, finally. The matching Team GB kitbags of Coe and Ovett arrive on the baggage carousel simultaneously. They contain three world records apiece.

Coe 800m, 1000m, 1500m (equal with Ovett)
Ovett 1500m (equal with Coe), the mile, the two-mile

Everything is as certain as it is uncertain. Sebastian Coe will win the 800m. His two-second cushion of world-record pace is insurmountable. Steve Ovett will get revenge in the 1500m, inevitably sitting on front-runner Coe and then kicking down the home straight to victory. But no one really knows what they will be like head-to-head. Who will respond better to the pressure? Who really has better tactics and counter tactics? What both athletes are now capable of bears no comparison to their only previous race in Prague 1978. Sebastian Coe is now the greatest front-runner in the history of the sport. He doesn't even need tactics. Steve Ovett is the best pure racer of all-time with the most explosive kick ever seen. Ovett has forty-five consecutive 1500m/mile wins to his name.

Only one thing is certain.
They cannot both win two Olympic gold medals.

★

Threeman was my last client of the day. He tidied away the plates after the third deadlift set. Back to lighter weights now, so near to his big race. While he stretched on the mats I asked him if he was walking to the metro afterwards. Yes. So we took the red line together. He said he would sit with me all the way to my stop then get the next train back to his Preobrazhenskaya. I told him he could also walk me home. He said he could do that too. He was shy on the way to my place, not as talkative and funny as normal. So I held his hand. It was as if we suddenly had less conversation now. We walked the back way home. Silver birch trees between each apartment block. The kids' play area smelling of new paint. A cat watching us cautiously from under a car. Was this just my world or could Threeman be part of it with me? It seemed surreal after all this time denying.

'Why Applecross?' he asked.

'Why Threeman?' I asked back.

We'd never talked about this before.

'Don't know. You get what you're given. There's probably a whole department working all hours thinking up these cover names. Do you know what Applecross is?'

'No.'

'It's a tiny village by the sea in Scotland. Remote. Only reachable over a spectacular mountain pass. A very calm and beautiful place, maybe why they chose it for you. I'll take you there one day. Or you can take me. It would be an amazing ride on a motorbike.'

His voice tailed off. We arrived at mine. I live on the seventh floor. I was hoping he would kiss me in the lift but he didn't. Of course not, he's too gentlemanly to do that. It would be in a park somewhere near some flowers, or on a bridge over a stream, or tomorrow on the grass plateau... or maybe never since it was all business now. Too close to the day. He was probably right to distance me. We sat at my kitchen table and had pumpkin and coriander soup. He said it was vkussno.

'The pumpkin was from my grandmother's dacha. That's where we have to go tomorrow. It's an early start. Would you like to stay here so we can get going first thing? It takes three hours even on the Ducati.'

Was this overly bold of me? Anyway he agreed. So I unfolded the bed and after we had both been to the bathroom we lay next to each other. He smelt fresh. I told him how happy I was that we were friends. I shouldn't have said this. He went cold and closed his eyes, probably thinking about the mission. We weren't friends. We were nothing. He couldn't let himself trust me, or anyone else in Moscow, and I should be less naïve and not trust him either. But that was the thing. I did trust him. He was too layered to be fake. He couldn't possibly be anything other than who I was seeing. I put my arm around him and pressed my body against his. He didn't resist, he didn't respond. He was already asleep. Maybe I would never know him at all.

At 5.30am I was awake. I dressed in light sporty stuff with my leathers over the top. My holdall was already packed. After a cup of tea it was time to wake him. He dressed.

I watched. His physique wasn't a mystery after all our sessions in the gym, but it was still pleasurable the way he moved, so economical and balanced. I lent him Aleksandr's biker jacket, we took the two helmets and left.

He didn't seem comfortable riding on the back, or was there something extra in his squeeze? Once we were out of the city I felt him relax. We only stopped once for gas and some lunch at a stolovaya. He was unusually quiet. I could tell he was already thinking about the rifle.

The N-road became R-roads, then eventually we were on just open country lanes. We rode past the dacha and took a right out of the village onto the farm roads. No houses on the horizon here, and after we had passed over the top of the ridge still none. Another twenty minutes of road and dirt tracks and we were at the barn. The only building for miles. A wilderness touched only three times a year by a tractor and a combine harvester. I lent the bike against the side of the barn, next to the rusty plough and a pile of pumpkins. He was looking at the view from where we had ridden.

'Now I understand,' he said. 'It's the vastness. Russia is so big it feels like everywhere. Could be easy to think everywhere never stops. For some people. Anyway, where is it?'

'Inside.'

The floor of the barn was covered in straw which I swept to the side with my boots. In the corner was the rolled up blanket. Inside it was the Izhmash and two boxes of ammunition. We took the gun, the bullets, and a pumpkin from the pile and walked out into the fields. The rye was still low and green.

'It's not far,' I said.

The path to the tree was dry. From the lowest branch I hung the pumpkin in a mesh bag at about head height. It didn't have to be exact. The elevation to the firing point was the most important thing.

'That way,' I said, pointing to a small hillock.

'Have you paced it?'

'Exactly 202 metres to the oblong stone.'

Threeman paced it himself anyway. It was sensible. The certainty in his mind would help him commit to the shot. To the plateau at the top of the hill was exactly two hundred metres. Two metres beyond it was a large oblong rock which I had put there last time. He agreed with my distance measurement. The elevation was only approximate but it would have to do. On the plateau was a clearing in the rye. Just soft grass. From my holdall I took a picnic blanket and laid it by the rock. The pumpkin seemed tiny from this distance, but I knew the Izhmash sights were good enough.

'Did you get it from here?' he said.

'Six out of six.'

'Prone or standing?'

'Three of each.'

'I won't have space for either.'

He took the rifle and bullets and sat on the blanket. I stood behind him and watched. He handled the rifle well. There was wind blowing through my hair but the pumpkin was motionless. Threeman picked a tuft of grass and threw it in the air. Half an inch worth of wind at this range. He sat in an open-legged stance, both elbows inside the knees, with his left tricep resting on the inside of his left knee as he aimed. He loaded up. One shot, reload, another shot. Then crossed his ankles and aimed again. Two shots. Then crossed his legs. Two shots again. It took less than a minute, although the slick Izhmash reload mechanism would hopefully not be required on the day. Needing a second shot would be a disaster.

'Good sights. Let's see how I did.'

Down at the tree the pumpkin had six holes right through it. He was happy with five of them. The other one was slightly too near the outside.

'One more go. But this pumpkin is bigger than his head.'

Back on the hill aiming at a smaller pumpkin he took one of the dum-dum bullets and loaded the Izhmash. This time I sat on the blanket next to him. He crossed his legs. Probably the most likely firing position in the cramped space he'd be working in. This time he waited much longer in the firing position. Watching the imaginary target walking onto the podium, shaking hands with the VIPs, his generals and sickening political cronies. Some in the front row close to him would be bodyguards dressed up as starred generals. Some along the line would also be women whose hand he might kiss. Threeman needed to be ready for this head movement. One missed shot and the target would be covered in those bodyguards. And it had to be a head shot. Plum Tree would be neck to toe in Kevlar, making his seventy-year-old body look as hench as a forty-year old gym rat. Even his tie would be wrapped around a high bulletproof collar. If Threeman's bullet hit any of that it would cause a significant injury but not death. Only the head got it done. After two minutes Threeman fired. A split second later the entire pumpkin exploded.

It was all done. Everything was prepared. An identical Izhmash and identical rounds of ammunition were already hidden in the firing point in Red Square. Threeman had hit the target seven times out of seven, using the three different firing positions he might need. The hit itself could be done. The only question mark was escape. Threeman would accept his death if it happened, but he couldn't get caught dead or alive and be identified as a foreigner. It had to look like a Russian 'anarchist'. He wasn't happy with the escape plan. He said they would keep everyone barricaded into Red Square, soldiers, politzia, dignitaries, everyone, until the gunman was found, even if it took a week. The security cordon was designed to keep people in as well as out. He didn't believe he would get out of Red Square without detection or without getting killed. So I told him my plan.

'You make your way to the security cordon at the Ulitsa Ilinka exit from Red Square, at the eastern end of GUM. I agree they might not let you out even dressed as a politzia. Everyone is trying to get out, not in. But if I jump the barriers the politzia will chase me and kick me back out, probably straight into a riot van. If you're the politzia who catches me and subdues me, then they'll let you leave to shove me in the van. Once we're outside the cordon, your chances are much higher. You might have to punch me a couple of times, and you might have to leave me in the riot van if we can't avoid getting in, but they'd have to find a rifle buried in a barn three hours away from Moscow to connect me to the assassination.'

'You would do that?'

'He killed my brother.'

This was enough. He accepted that it could work. He accepted they wouldn't dare fire at me in a crowd scene of soldiers and KGB employees. Whatever happened he knew he would need nine lives to escape and saw that this could be one of them.

'Okay. Ulitsa Ilinka.' he said. 'You'll see me. I won't try and exit until you jump the barrier. If I have to punch you I'll make it a glancing blow. Have a blood capsule ready to bite. It's a shame we can only use this Izhmash. If we had an Uzi we could take down dozens of them. Every single one of them on that stage. They'll be taken care of later. Hopefully by the people.'

He was right. This whole plan depended not on one foreign assassin but on the Russian people. The frightened millions who wanted this to happen and would rise up when they saw the chance. How many would die?

Thousands. Tens of thousands. As many bullets as the politzia had with them. Eventually they had to run out.

He kissed me.

I was glad I had brought the picnic blanket, and for the soft grass beneath it. Is a girl allowed to hope for such things? Anyway he obliged. This spy I never knew. This killer. There was raw urgency in his passion. Frantic in the best possible way. I wanted only his power. The once in a lifetime performance of a man who knows the world is about to end. I savoured every heroic thrust he punished me with. And gripped him tightly, as I died in his arms over and over again.

It had finally happened.

Two days later I walked with him from Chistye Prudy along Myasnitskaya towards Red Square. Slowly, just because. We held hands. There was no need to talk, nothing to say. At Lubyanka Square he asked to walk on alone. We both understood. One kiss. Then I walked away. I knew I would never see him again, the love I left in Lubyanka.

May 6. Three days before the assassination.

To: Nevis. Are we green light? Prime Minister requests specifics of the day. Is it soon? From: Gyllyngvase

To: Gyllyngvase. Yes it's soon. Have promised Threeman I wouldn't send any communiqués about the specifics. But if you walk your dog tomorrow I'm happy to give you the outline. You're right, PM ought to know what and when. 8.30am. The lake. From: Nevis

May 7. Two days before the assassination.

EXT. Black Park, South Bucks.

The lake. An unseasonably cold morning. Nevis is wearing an unfashionably patterned and slightly oversized sweater. He is holding two plain coffee cups from one of which he takes a sip. Then -- Gyllyngvase arrives, wearing a black tactical jacket and a trendy newsboy cap.

GYLLYNGVASE: Hullo. Chilly morning, eh?

He looks at Nevis who is not wearing a coat. Considers making a comment about the sweater but doesn't. The suspicion between the two spymasters must be disguised by impeccable cordiality. Their ilk operate their whole lives behind such a cloak.

NEVIS: Coffee? [hands Gyllyngvase the second cup]

GYLLYNGVASE: You're a mind reader. Thanks.

From their meeting bench, Nevis suggests they walk to the eastern end of the lake. Then from the end of the lake they take a popular path further into the woods. Lots of dog-walkers around. No air of danger [it's an exposition scene]. Gyllyngvase takes a sip of his coffee.

GYLLYNGVASE: That's an amazing coffee!

NEVIS: Got you a latte, chum. Thought you'd approve. The park café do their best, bless them, but they refuse to accept my recommendation to switch from a generic blended roast. So I bought these two from the Brown Horse farm shop. They import the finest coffee known to man. That's a Peruvian single malt from Piura. You'll be getting nutty and caramel notes.

GYLLYNGVASE: And such creaminess.

NEVIS: Unpasteurised alpaca milk. Fresh from the teat this morning. The Brown Horse has a herd of them out back in what used to be the beer garden. Cute little things they are. And their wool makes fiendishly warm sweaters.

GYLLYNGVASE: When did the Brown Horse diversify from ales?

NEVIS: Last year. When I acquired a small stake in the business.

A distance away race runners start to appear along the woodland path. Three lads in their late teens are in a small pack in the lead followed closely by a young woman. This leading four are already a distance ahead of anyone else. The Black Park parkrun is a figure-of-eight course. Nevis has positioned them at the crossover where they will see the runners pass twice.

NEVIS: Here they come.

GYLLYNGVASE: Impressive. Who's going to win out of those three?

NEVIS: The girl in fourth.

GYLLYNGVASE: She was ten metres back.

NEVIS: Did you spy the castle insignia on her Lycra? Windsor AC. She also runs for Great Britain. Those likely lads are about to get severely beasted. [chuckles]

The two men stroll a short loop on a more secluded trail where there are no runners or dog-walkers -- privacy to talk shop. A woodpecker yaffles somewhere above in a horse chestnut. Squirrels forage busily. The low-pitched yink of a nuthatch.

NEVIS: So you want to know the plan?

GYLLYNGVASE: You don't have to tell me, but the Prime Minister thinks he ought to be apprised of the timing. He wants to be in public when it happens. To look shocked and offer some sort of faux solace.

NEVIS: It's in two days. Monday May 9. Our H-Hour will be approximately 11:00. Red Square.

GYLLYNGVASE: The Victory Day parade! Jesus.

NEVIS: Indeed. Lone sniper. Plum Tree attends the military parade as he always does, and as he absolutely has to this year, otherwise it's a sign of weakness -- ego is his Achilles heel, chum. He and his slimy VIPs watch the parade from a podium erected in front of the Lenin Mausoleum. Been the same set-up for years. But a security cordon is established around Red Square five days before the event. Only security-screened people allowed in and out. Our asset has been inside since May 3 hiding in the firing point. St Basil's Cathedral -- the interior of the dome of St Martyrs Cyprian and Justinian. The blue and white one.

GYLLYNGVASE: [puffed-cheek exhale] Wow.

NEVIS: A letterbox-shaped aperture incision has been made in the surface structure of the ceramic dome -- cut from inside, but not cut all the way through to the exterior surface. This work was done by Pythagoras many years ago for this or a similar scenario. All the asset has to do is knock the 'letterbox' through for a clear sight at the target.

GYLLYNGVASE: Plum Tree will barely be two-hundred yards away. A sitting duck!

NEVIS: 202 yards. Single bullet. Head shot.

GYLLYNGVASE: So simple. It's genius.

NEVIS: Clever, perhaps. But not so simple. The asset will need to handle six days in such a tiny space, cramped body, minimal supplies, dehydration and hunger will cause inevitable self-doubt, darkness, and the monotony of death. It might break him.

GYLLYNGVASE: If it works it's an absolute masterpiece, chum. Compliments to Pythagoras for arranging the party. What's the escape plan though? I imagine there'll be approximately two thousand Red Army soldiers and politzia in Red Square and the environs. Would like to think our chap has at least a nominal chance of escape.

NEVIS: The asset will carry out the assassination dressed in the politzia SWAT uniform. St. Basil's interior is a maze. After the shot the asset will abseil back into the cathedral from the dome. Short-term concealment in a ground floor priest hole has been pre-arranged by Pythagoras. The asset must only evade the initial entry of the search squad. Banking on full chaos at this point if Plum Tree is down. Pre-rigged smoke bombs and firecrackers will then be set off to create confusion and start a gunfight. The intention is then to merge disguised into the SWAT team itself -- then slip away and exit the cathedral into the crowd scene. As you say, parading troops and politzia will be scattered everywhere. What's one more politzia among two thousand? General hysteria will help the asset get out of Red Square. If he makes it that far he has a change of clothes plus new identity documents in a locker at Kazanskaya Station. Train to Ryazan where our company vehicle is provided in a lock-up.

GYLLYNGVASE: How does he get out of Russia?

NEVIS: Extraction options have been declined. Asset reckons he'll have a better chance alone. South. To the Caucuses. Ski resort called Azau. Then across the mountains on foot to Georgia, where Station G will be standing by.

The runners come round on their second crossing of the figure-of-eight. The female athlete is now twenty metres ahead. The three lads behind are in various stages of demolition as the girl piles on more cadence. Nevis purrs as she opens her palm to him to say hello.

May 8. The day before the assassination.

To: Nevis. Prime Minister impressed nay flabbergasted. Sends a hearty bravo, as well as thoughts and prayers to our man. Even if he doesn't make it, Plum Tree down will be more than worth the sacrifice. An eye for an eye. Prime Minister will be at a constituency school for stage-managed reaction at H-Hour. Prepped with sombre words with an encouraging sub-text for Russian freedom factions. So tomorrow it is... God help us. From: Gyllyngvase

Requiem Required

★

Не Плачь – *Don't Cry*

Не плачь, ещё одна осталась ночь у нас с тобой
Ещё один раз прошепчу тебе: "Ты мой"
Ещё один последний раз твои глаза
В мои посмотрят и слеза вдруг упадёт на руку мне
А завтра я одна останусь, без тебя
Но ты не плачь

Не плачь, так получилось, что судьба нам не дала
С тобой быть вместе, где же раньше я была?
Так поздно встретила тебя, но в этот миг
Я знаю, что теперь твоя и только крик сдержу я завтра
А сейчас побудь со мной в последний раз
В последний раз

Пойми, теперь не думать не могу я о тебе
Сама не знаю, как позволила себе
Чтоб ты любовь мою забрал в тот час когда
Тебя увидела и прошептала: "Да"
Но ты пойми, пойми меня, ведь знаешь
как люблю тебя, Люблю тебя

Так знай, тебя везде я отыщу, где б ни был ты
Я испишу тебе стихами все листы
И если встречу я тебя среди толпы
Ты не свернёшь уже тогда с моей тропы
Я украду тебя от всех, ты будешь мой тогда навек
Ты мой навек

Sung by Tatyana Bulanova

MAY 9, 2022. 08:00 GMT [13:00 MOSCOW TIME]

To: Gyllyngvase

MISSION FAILED.

Just before H-Hour the St Martyrs Cyprian and Justinian dome was shot multiple times by FSB from within cathedral. No external signs of any disturbance. Victory Parade passed off as normal - Plum Tree et al. Threeman missing presumed dead. No sources to confirm how close he got to clear sight at the target or pulling the trigger. Within an ace I suspect, or hope - for his memory's sake. Apologies to Prime Minister for disappointment.

From: Nevis

The Spy I Never Knew

★

Tsentralny Stadion Imeni V.I. Lenina.

After his dominant win in the 800m the bookies were no longer taking bets on Steve Ovett wrapping up the middle-distance double. Five days later, after the heats and semis, it was the 1500m final. Ovett now had everything going for him. The fifteen was his best event. He revelled in the tactical nuances of three-and-three-quarter laps. He had stockpiled forty-seven consecutive race wins at 1500m and the mile, including a world record only sixteen days ago. His 800m performance had been there for all to see. If anyone had doubted his power over the shorter distance he had treated them to a *Magnum Force* second lap of 50.5 seconds. No one was coming past that! The Ovett intimidation factor was off the charts. This was now his third Olympic final. Experience would surely tell. On the warm-up track his opponents couldn't help but imagine the 1500m gold medal already around his neck. But herein lay the irony of fate – the only thing Steve Ovett had no experience of was becoming an Olympic champion.

This was new. An unknown. Dangerous. In an illogical twist it now invisibly handed back some advantage to Coe. For Ovett the euphoria of the 800m win was quickly replaced by mental and physical exhaustion. He suffered a worrying attack of the shivers after the race, almost collapsing in the bowels of the stadium while passing through protocols. Four years of tension being instantaneously released. The body reacts. It shuts down.

Coe was barely in better shape but he went running the next day. Shattered by defeat. Distraught at his meek performance. Suffering the recurring vision of Ovett romping past Nikolay Kirov to victory; the back of another GB vest; seeing #279 and the magic soles of Ovett's spikes flicking up in his face. Coe ran the next day simply to escape. Thirteen miles. Pounding the streets of the Yugo-Zapadnaya district alone. Although he eventually noticed the dubious company of press photographers hanging out of a car. The Coe *Trail of Shame* as they dubbed it, those friendly tabloid newsmen, their fat fingers gleefully typing out the headline. Worse billing even than failure. Shame! But for Coe a long steady run was the best remedy after weeks of nerves, of suffocating media attention, and after such an intense disappointment. Only a run could exorcise being so overwhelmed by the occasion in the 800m. Peter put it to him bluntly: *You ran like a cunt.* Seb had not merely lost, he had handed the race to his arch nemesis on a 24-carat Fabergé platter. Timid, tactically all over the place, laying himself at the mercy of Ovett's stunning fifty-point-five second lap. In the race which Sebastian Coe was ordained to win, Coe was nowhere when it mattered. Even Ovett was privately bemused at how easily he had won. So Coe simply laced up his flats and went out of the front door. On the *Trail of Rediscovery*.

Meanwhile Ovett relaxed. He had to. Both his mind and body required it just to process the relief, to cope with the physical shutdown. There was also the human reality of adulation. Ovett had celebrated. Who wouldn't have? But this was not the preparation for a 1500m he had ever experienced or planned for, and the task he faced was still formidable, even in his favourite event. Double golds are rare. Has anyone going for a second Olympic gold medal ever had to race against an athlete of the calibre of Sebastian Coe – a triple world record holder?

Nine finalists entered the arena on a blisteringly hot Moscow afternoon. Some loosening strides confirmed the conditions. The crucible of Central Lenin Stadium was intensifying the heat at track level. The pressure gravitated in the ether around Coe and Ovett. All the other athletes knew they were part of a bigger story, but one which would not exclude a brave protagonist. Something must be possible, but what? There were two joint world record holders to beat. As they made their way round to the back-straight start-line, the other contenders focused on the fact that Olympic finals are rarely run at world record pace. This at least gave every athlete a shard of hope. Once upon a time in Moscow.

Jürgen Straub	DDR
José Marajo	France
Andreas Busse	DDR
Steve Cram	Great Britain
Vittorio Fontanella	Italy
Sebastian Coe	Great Britain
Jozef Plachy	Czechoslovakia
Steve Ovett	Great Britain
Dragan Zdravković	Yugoslavia

To the spectators inside Central Lenin Stadium and to the watching millions around the world, it seemed irrelevant that there were seven other runners in the 1500m final. The Coe-versus-Ovett rematch was the only story. No one else existed. The others would not be factors when it came down to the crucial part of the race, or so everyone assumed. In reality nothing could have been further from the truth. With Seb Coe and Steve Ovett watching each other like hawks, the race narrative was written by a wholly unexpected author.

So a check on the line-up.
On the inside is Straub of East Germany.
Steve Ovett next to the outside.
Straub on the inside. Jürgen Straub.

```
To: Gyllyngvase. Rather important you walk
your dog, chum. Tonight. The lake. 1am.
From: Nevis
```

Jürgen Straub in the blue DDR vest has drawn the inside. Alongside him the runners stand two paces back from the line, bouncing lightly on the spot, or shaking their legs off, rolling their necks, making tiny adjustments to how much of their vest is tucked into their shorts. Nervous movement just to keep the legs loose and that springy feeling going. The coolest customer might be Jozef Plachy in the red vest of Czechoslovakia. He ran in the 1968 Olympic 800m final as a nineteen-year-old so has been around the block enough times to embrace the nerves. Straub also seems composed.

Steve Ovett wipes his brow with his wrist. It's another hot afternoon, just like the semi-finals only yesterday. Moscow is renowned for its sub-zero winters but the summers are sweltering. Word is that Ovett has been edgy on the warm-up track. Sebastian Coe seems calm and together despite staring down the barrel of a monumental double failure. Coe's tactical decisions are again expected to define the race. Will he revert to what he knows best and front-run the legs off them? Or does he have a secret plan for Ovett? Maybe he'll just sit and see – a racer. Just before the athletes are called to their marks, Coe sets off on a loosening circle a few metres back from the others. He jogs back to the line the very last of the nine athletes. They place their front toe up to the start-line on the back straight. The crowd chatter drops to only hushed murmurs. These in turn quieten as the moment of truth arrives. Silence. Only three-and-three-quarter laps from Olympic gold, or from double Olympic gold.

Vnymanye. BANG!

There's an initial burst of acceleration for a clear run down the back straight. No one veers strongly left for lane one. The nine athletes soon settle into a comfortable pace, with no one seeming too desperate to fight for race positions. It takes them half the straight to even form into a pack. When they do Jürgen Straub of East Germany finds himself in the lead.

Straub on the inside going away and holding the kerb.
Sebastian Coe comes across from the outside.
And Steve Ovett tracking Sebastian Coe.

EXT. Black Park.
The lake. Night. A waning gibbous moon.

Coe's assertive start means his natural position is slotting in on Straub's right shoulder at the front. Straub and Coe are side-by-side after one hundred metres as they approach the first bend, but it's not quick.

NEVIS: Thanks for coming, Alec.

GYLLYNGVASE: Not at all, chum. More grim news I suppose?

All the runners are content with the easy pace. José Marajo of France is behind Straub in third. Ovett is wider, tracking Coe in fourth. Down the home straight

Dragan Zdravković in the blue vest of Yugoslavia moves through past Ovett into third, then tempers his surge to slot into a convenient gap in fourth. Steve Cram has recovered to equal fourth in lane one after a sleepy start. Vittorio Fontanella of Italy – there are five blue vests in the race – is behind Cram. The Italian is heavily boxed, but it's all so slow that his only concern is avoiding the spikes flying around in front of him. Jozef Plachy is chilling out at the back alongside Andreas Busse of the DDR. Positions aren't crucial yet with such a pedestrian first 300 metres. Coe is joint leader but is only following the pace of Straub inside him, and Straub is running well within himself.

Again it's a reluctant pace. Straub being forced in front.
Sebastian Coe putting a bit of pressure on the outside.
Ovett in fourth place and he's watching Coe like a hawk.

```
The two men sit down on the bench by the
lake. Both men are in expensive wool
overcoats and polished city shoes. Nevis has
the collar on his coat turned up and is
wearing black leather gloves. Today he is
not wearing glasses.
```

NEVIS: Yes. Rather grim, unfortunately. Our man has surfaced. Threeman. Reported in -- thirteen hours after H-Hour. Crazy bastard survived after all.

On such a hot afternoon maybe no one wants to risk the effect of the heat. More likely no one in the pack knows what to do. Coe and Ovett have never raced each other over 1500 metres, therefore no one (anywhere) has ever been in a race with both of them. Beating one is one thing. Beating both is quite another. There is no obvious non-suicidal race strategy. Coe and Ovett both have 3:32.1 under the bonnet. A fast race suits both, but likewise both have huge kick finishes off a slower pace.

And the pace is very slow indeed.
It's going to be left to the fast men in the closing stages.
No one wants to sacrifice the chance of a medal.
No front-runner in this race at all.

The seven other runners are jogging and waiting to see what Coe or Ovett do. They know Coe has form as a 1500m front-runner, but they also saw his reluctance to lead Ovett out in the 800m. Despite looking more assured now, Coe is showing no inclination to run off the front and offer himself as a target. Ovett has lost two strides down to sixth.

Straub East Germany leading. And it really is a jog.
Sebastian Coe in second place.
Coming up to complete the first lap. Almost sixty-two seconds.
And Steve Ovett moving through to cover Sebastian Coe.

GYLLYNGVASE: Alive! Good grief. That's wonderful news. But how? I thought they...

Lap two. Down the back straight it's Straub then Coe. Ovett regains his ground, overtaking Marajo to tag onto Coe. Steve Cram is working the inside nicely and has moved into equal third with Ovett. The Soviet sun blazes down on the three iconic Great Britain vests. Coe. Cram. Ovett. With his bouncy stride Busse has followed Ovett on the outside line into fifth.

Busse watching Ovett.
Busse number 296 who was fifth in the 800 metre final.

Coe just checking where everyone is – he's being stalked by Ovett.

NEVIS: Yes, they shot the dome to smithereens. From inside the cathedral, so there was no sign of anything in Red Square. But Threeman wasn't in it -- escaped before schedule -- before the FSB search squad entered the cathedral to get him. They knew he was coming -- but he knew they were coming, and he left the moment after opening the 'letterbox' and setting up his equipment.

GYLLYNGVASE: The Izhmash?

A solid tactic from Busse to move up on the straight. At this slow pace no one is too worried about running wide straights on the second lap. The pack barely churns. One stride gained here, half a stride lost there, nobody making any moves. No major developments at all, apart from the three Brits now clustered behind leader Straub in the dominant race positions. Fontanella is in fifth, still in a nasty box behind Cram. Marajo is to the Italian's right and directly behind Ovett. Busse is now equal sixth on Marajo's right shoulder. Zdravković is keeping Plachy company at the back. Barely five metres separates first and last.

They seem to be going even slower.
So it's turning into an eight-hundred metre race.
We're back where we were several days ago.

NEVIS: The rifle was in place. Yes, an Izhmash... It was in place for everything to tally. But that wasn't his main weapon. His real weapon was a remote camera -- and the 'letterbox', so to speak, was in fact just a pinhole for a fibre optic lens. Which Plum

Tree looked directly into. Lovely footage -- you'll enjoy it. Imagine! Breaking the fourth wall on the Zapruder film. Priceless. That ego. He made it really very simple. Had to boast that he knew it was happening. Too smug for his own good. Especially behind all that bulletproof glass which the FSB had rigged up outside the onion dome. Threeman's bullet would have barely travelled two yards, let alone two-hundred-and-two. We only needed to know he knew. We only needed the look into the camera. Plum Tree even waved at us -- the stupid cunt! By which time Threeman had already slipped out through the sewers and into the Moskva.

GYLLYNGVASE: Curious. In the politzia uniform?

NEVIS: No, he had made other arrangements.

Straub – where he's been all the time. Right on the kerb.
600 metres run. The home straight for the second time.
Jürgen Straub in the blue DDR vest still leads.
He's got no intention of driving for home yet.

It's a now game of chess and the crucial feature of the race so far is precisely that nothing significant has happened. This is hugely significant. Where is the narrative? Every runner in the pack is trying to decipher the plot. They're merely jockeying their positions ready to follow it when it happens. Everyone knows what Ovett does. He sits. He waits. Then kicks. They know Ovett won't set the pace. The whole race is waiting to see what Sebastian Coe will do.

GYLLYNGVASE: I see.

NEVIS: No, I'm not sure that you do -- but anyway, the St. Basil's Cathedral drainage sewer is wide enough to crawl through and comes out directly under the Bolshoy Moskvoretsky Bridge. Hidden from sight, unless you're a fish. Threeman swam halfway across the river and climbed up into the stanchions of the bridge. Some minutes later he lowered himself down into the next gravel barge which came along, going upstream as it happens. All this well before anyone was searching for a fugitive. He took the barge as far as Vorobyovy Gory and then slipped back into the water and swam to the bank under the cover of the metro bridge. Removed his outer clothes and climbed up into Gorky Park. Didn't raise any eyebrows soaking wet in a running vest and shorts. Just any other runner on a hot day. Dry clothes stashed in the woods. Took the red line direct to Komsomolskaya. Fake passport and documents in a locker at Leningradsky Station. He was on the fast train to St Petersburg while the FSB were still climbing up inside the tower of St Basil's to identify his corpse. St Pete to Tallinn. Tallinn to Finland by ferry. He's probably sleeping soundly in a five-star hotel in Helsinki as we speak. Deserves it after days hiding inside an onion dome. Tomorrow he might even manage a loosening run to get back on schedule for the World Masters Championships -- that bit was real, his essential cover story, if you like. Of course, the footage of Plum Tree looking into our lens was with us in real time. At 11.03 Moscow Time today, so we knew the mission had been successful.

The three Britons together. Two – three – and four..

After two laps Seb Coe is happy. He is *not* running like a cunt. Peter Coe's shopfloor language was an unlikely masterstroke in coaching psychology. Honest and enabling. To 'not run like a cunt' simplified the goal – it was small, easy, achievable, and stimulated aggression. The race was no longer about winning. It was only about making sure it cost anyone an arm and a leg to beat you. With the c-word Peter has set his gazelle free once more into the open plains of the Serengeti. His athlete is himself again, and at this pace Coe has every tactical reason to be exceptionally happy. He looks sideways to see Ovett right there. Everyone is waiting for someone else to do something. The jog pace so far makes it virtually a second instalment of the 800m final. Does this give a clear advantage to Ovett who romped the eight in such style? Does it bring Busse into the equation? He was a strong fifth in the 800m. Or Marajo, also a finalist in the shorter distance? Or does it gift-wrap a second chance to the world record holder over 800m? That two-second cushion over two fast laps hasn't disappeared because of one bad race. Coe can hardly believe his luck, and this time he's right on the shoulder of the leader. No drifting today. He's under fierce instructions from Peter to immediately respond to any moves that Ovett makes: *If he runs off to the toilet and takes a dump, you're in that shitter alongside him!* Or words to that colourful effect.

GYLLYNGVASE: Successful? But nobody killed Putin.

Straub leads. Coe second. Cram and Ovett third.
Eight hundred metres. Two minutes five seconds. So it was slower.

NEVIS: Correct. Plum Tree survived -- because he knew we were coming. Knew exactly where and when and how. From this we knew that Russian Intelligence had penetrated us at some level.

GYLLYNGVASE: At some level, yes. How many assets were involved in the mission? The traitor could have been any one of them. Pythagoras. Anastasia -- or Applecross. Ophelia.

The apparent stasis is disguising tectonic shifts in danger. In front the tactical options are rapidly plummeting to zero for Jürgen Straub. He has the dice but has yet to roll them. No one else is showing any desire to take it on. Coe in second. Ovett third. Jürgen Straub's code red beacon is flashing. With every stride the differential is stacking up between his workhorse kick and the dazzling firepower behind him. And he knows it. To stand any chance Straub has to run the finish out of Coe and Ovett. Not to risk it would be the biggest risk of all. With 700 metres to go, time is running out to ask the ultimate question. Finally, the emergency klaxon sounds for Straub. He puts his head down and goes.

And now Straub. Can't wait any longer. 700 metres to go.
He knows the Britons have got the finish so he's got to go – makes the strike for home.

NEVIS: Yes, quite. It could have been any one of them. But only one of them had intimate knowledge of the plan. And was, let's say, intimately close enough to Threeman to betray him.

GYLLYNGVASE: Applecross. The bitch!

The mix is on. Who's in it? The strong change of pace at the front immediately strings out the pack down the back straight. Coe loses three metres but speeds up and is flowing well in second place. One metre behind is Ovett. Cram falls back tamely as Fontanella muscles up lane one. Busse moves on the outside and nudges past the Italian into fourth. Busse is the best of the rest.

Just over a lap and a half left and he's stretching away.
Sebastian Coe in second place looking very comfortable.
Ovett watching Coe all the time.

600 metres to go. Straub pours on more pace.
And they're stretching out now.
There's about ten-twelve metres between first and last.

Coe follows Straub. Ovett follows Coe. 500 metres to go in the Olympic 1500m final and Straub is all-in, knowing his chances are slim, knowing the world-record attack pace that could engulf him at any moment. He has memories of being thrashed by Steve Ovett in Düsseldorf, and thrashed by him again in Prague. He releases more string on his kite despite the two hurricanes on his tail. Jürgen Straub is trying to run the legs off the Clash of the Titans.

NEVIS: She certainly had inside knowledge. Applecross, or Anastasia as you rightly call her -- which is perplexing in itself.

GYLLYNGVASE: The whole thing is perplexing. Do carry on.

Coe second. Ovett third.
Following the East German's pace as they come to the bell.

DING! DING! DING!

East Germany one – Britain two and three – East Germany four. The long run for home is on.

They're in single file now. Straub leads and increases the pace by yet another notch. He grimaces as he tries to annihilate himself and hopefully take down Coe or Ovett, or both, in the process. He works the bend. The runners behind are flat out now to keep up with Straub, even Coe and Ovett. In fourth place Busse clings on. Straub has run the third 400 metres in under 54-seconds. That must be causing damage. Faster than the first lap in the 800m final. Major damage.

NEVIS: Applecross had all the knowledge. But so did the others in their own way. Or at least they would have done, if they had existed -- but they didn't. All figments. Elaborate two-dimensional hoaxes which the FSB hacked into, believed, and passed on. Phil Kimby indeed! I nearly vetoed that name. And Applecross. Anastasia, yes the beautiful Anastasia, who never existed but whose name you seem to know -- which is something of an anomaly.

Straub kicking again.

Straub knows he's got a sniff now. With an empty track ahead and only 300m to go you know you're in the mix. Amazing feeling. Your legs find something extra. Maybe today will be the day it never hurts. Impossibly, Straub increases his leg speed again.

Three hundred to go.

Coe in second place. Ovett is third. Busse fourth.
Marajo is five. Fontanella six. Steve Cram in seventh place.

GYLLYNGVASE: Figments, you say? So, the only people actually involved in the so-called mission were --

NEVIS: Threeman. Myself. The Prime Minister. And you.

GYLLYNGVASE: So.

NEVIS: The Prime Minister thinks we've found our mole. Don't you?

Coe follows the kick. Sebastian Coe is flowing now. Despite the fierce pace there's a calmness to his running, the never-ending gazelle is back. His form down the back straight looks like just another rep floating along the Rivelin Valley Road, and today he's not thinking. It's all synapses. Even three metres behind Straub, Coe is in the outside half of lane one anticipating the overtake, and forcing Ovett wider if or when.

Gyllyngvase reaches into his coat, calmly pulls out a gun and points it at Nevis.

Ovett is also looking smooth but he's two metres behind Coe. Needs to be closer. Hasn't got strike position. The terrific speed being set means Ovett can't pull onto Coe, and he can't kick because Straub has taken them so deep into the red already. Ovett digs in down the back straight and reels Coe into one metre. 200m to go. It's Straub. Then Coe. Then Ovett.

Look at Sebastian Coe there – checking where Ovett is.

And Ovett's watching him all the way. This is the strike we want to see. Can they out-sprint each other? Which one is the faster?

NEVIS: Interesting that you would bring a gun with you to the park, Gyllyngvase. But let's not digress. Would you like to see the footage of Plum Tree staring into our camera? The proof upon which this whole crazy set-up apparently rests.

GYLLYNGVASE: I very much would.

NEVIS: Well, you can't. The footage was a flop. Plum Tree, yes Putin, didn't look into Threeman's camera.

GYLLYNGVASE: The camera didn't exist. All a lie too.

NEVIS: Wishful thinking. As you well know. Your FSB colleagues have presumably reported in the rifle and pinhole camera set-up exactly as I have described. Exactly when it was set up? Well, I'll leave that for you to speculate. No, the final lie was Plum Tree looking into our lens, but of course that was the most crucial and most exquisite lie. The whole story is rather far-fetched, don't you agree? But apparently real enough when deciphered and spoon-fed to you by your dutiful FSB comrades. Certainly real enough to make you pull out that gun. We thought it would be.

As they enter the final bend Coe is within one metre of Straub and has tucked into lane one for the shortest line. This suddenly presents a massive tactical opportunity for Ovett. If he can overtake now and then sit on the DDR vest, he will utterly stuff Coe in the box behind Straub. The box to end all boxes. If Ovett gets on or anywhere past Coe's shoulder, he can pull the trigger whenever he chooses down the home straight, killing Straub and Coe with the same bullet. With 180 metres to go Steve Ovett is the man with the golden gun.

GYLLYNGVASE: So Threeman doesn't even exist?

NEVIS: Yes and no. Threeman is a sleeper I've had in various places for some time. Recruited him in Moscow twenty years ago as a matter of fact -- or coincidence. He's never seen much action, but was my first asset out in Station R, so I knew he was one hundred per cent trustworthy. Latest posting back in Moscow. Mentioned he thought his laptop was being hacked. Was followed around town on several occasions. Clumsy surveillance, he said. Your lot even picked pages of his early story draft out of a Starbucks bin apparently. Bit obvious don't you think? But it gave us great hope that he could reach a certain... desired readership, you might say. So I dreamt up this mission which required someone with a narrative spezialnost. He was the perfect man. Really is a dead spit of Steve Ovett by the way. But not so much a doppelganger on this mission as, well -- a trippelganger. I'm sure he'd approve of the flourish. He really played the whole part rather well, don't you think? Must have been a little soul-destroying for him writing that whole Ovett and Coe thing knowing only one person was going to read it. But then again, they do say the best writers write for one person. That one person was you, Gyllyngvase. Did you enjoy it? Of course, I got excerpts myself when occasionally it was necessary to tally our ends. Very much enjoyed the bits I read. Bonked that Anastasia pretty quickly in the end, didn't he? Have to own up to

```
being the inspiration for the pink jeans and
the banya scene. A rather crude recruitment
ruse. Twenty years ago mind you, before I
was a happily married man. Peter Coe in the
whole Pythagoras plot? I suspect you weren't
seeing the wood for the trees by that stage
-- chum. Maybe your FSB pals will provide us
with the full manuscript at some point if we
ask nicely. Threeman could even publish it.
Under pseudonym of course. Did it not occur
to you that his real name was never
mentioned? Quite skillful that. Almost as
skillful as how I made you point that gun at
me. You are pointing that gun at me, aren't
you?
```

Ovett in the pulling position coming up to attack.
150 metres to go. Track fans around the world watch and wait for the inevitable. Ovett moves out to execute his move. The ultimate tactical masterpiece. But…
And there goes Coe.

Coe kicks. He doesn't even need to hear the footsteps. Knows his fellow assassin too well. The kick edges him closer to Jürgen Straub and swings him out onto the East German's right shoulder. Coe saves himself from getting boxed and the tactical endgame evaporates. The race is now left to raw speed. Everyone has a clear sprint. Who can run the fastest? Coe looks right for Ovett. Coe looks left for Ovett. The sum of all fears. Ovett is directly behind Coe. The shadow.

He's looking for Ovett and wondering where he is.
He's right there behind him.

Straub kicks again and keeps Coe wide on the last ten metres of the bend. Coe is level but can't get past him yet. 100 metres to go. The final sprint is on. Coe versus Straub, with Ovett closing in on both ready for the kill.

Ninety metres to go. Coe edges past Straub.
Eighty metres to go. Sebastian Coe leads.
Ovett gathers himself on the near side. Straub on the far side.

Ovett kicks and gets to within a stride of Straub. But the 700-metre long finish has hurt. The explosion is not there. Ovett cannot pass Straub. Coe has leg speed and the perfect arm drive. He pulls two strides clear of Straub. Ovett digs again, one more time for his last chance… but there's nothing more there. Straub senses a rare chance to scalp Ovett and takes half a metre back in second place.

And could this be Ovett's first defeat?!
Fifty metres to go. Coe – Straub – Ovett.
Ovett is in trouble!

Coe is two metres clear. The finish line cannot arrive quickly enough for him. His legs have nothing left but the arms are still driving. Technique will win him the race. All those sprint reps on dark track nights in Sheffield. The hill reps. The weights lifted. The scientific genius of Peter – and the coaching love of Peter. All the pain of losing the 800m. It all counts for everything and nothing now at the mercy of an Ovett sprint. On the limit, Coe can't pull further clear. There is pure dread on his face. With every stride he expects Ovett to come booming past. Thirty metres to go. Arms. Arms. Arms. Drive! Twenty metres. Fifteen. Ten. One more stride. Followed by another. And another. Steve Ovett is beaten. The Olympic torch above the stadium swirls in mad pirouettes, frolicking with rage, a chaos of flames firing black wisps upwards through its orange tips into the Moscow sky.

And Coe gets the revenge he wants!
Coe wins.
Straub second. Ovett third.

Once upon a time in Moscow two runners won and the same two runners lost. A cryptic tale of majestic disaster and stolen gold. Twin heists each as improbable as the other. The Clash of the Titans ended with the only outcome which nobody had predicted. Steve Ovett won the eight hundred. Sebastian Coe won the fifteen. Ovett tasted Olympic glory but also the bitterness of losing the biggest race of all in his best event. Neither athlete won the double. Neither athlete won the gold medal they were supposed to win. Who was faster? Moscow offered no definitive answer. The single gold star on top of the *MGU* skyscraper remained nameless.

GYLLYNGVASE: Clever. Maybe all a bit too clever. What about the warship technology? The designs you were feeding to the Russians. The Ministry of Defence had you pegged for months. Was about to shop you myself.

NEVIS: Not guilty. Liaising with my Russian oligarch friends, as you well know, was vital to the logic of the project. One cannot simply assassinate a head of state and not have a succession plan in place. Admiral Myod and myself also happen to be kindred model-makers. We build not destroy. Can two men not share the same hobby in this day and age?

GYLLYNGVASE: We'll never know. Personally, it was incredibly gratifying to join the dots of your involvement in the Russian first strike. Admiral Myod and Plum Tree turning the keys simultaneously for Operation Warspite. The red button. Nevis the traitor in our midst, the leather-gloved killer. It's all just mad pirouettes in a flame now. But only the bad guy dies. We both know that.

NEVIS: Agreed. As it should be. Comeuppance is the fundamental plot requirement of the Threeman books.

GYLLYNGVASE: And where is your mythical Threeman now? The spy I never knew. A little bit out of the loop, isn't he? I would have expected him to have had the last word. As it is, it looks like I will. Glock-19, chum. Point blank range. Be a shame to see you go, Nevis. But an exquisite twist that you were the villain all along.

Gyllyngvase pulls the trigger -- a click but no bullet.

NEVIS: You appear to have a malfunctioning gun. I'm very grateful to your polymorphic secretary for that fact. And that's a Glock-23 by the way. I assume you have a blade somewhere too. It won't be required. As to your question, Threeman is approximately 202 yards away and very much in the loop. Wind speed minimal. Clean sight at the target. Single bullet. Head shot. My sincerest sympathies, Gyllyngvase.

A distant rifle shot. Gyllyngvase slumps -- dead. Nevis walks away. The heroic silhouette slowly into the distance under a waning moon.

The burning hows and whys and what-ifs of both finals will flicker on forever. Wisps in the Moscow ether. Victory and defeat are now only mad pirouettes in the same eternal flame. A mystery that made no sense. Did any of it even happen? The Moskva River continues to flow around its giant meander through the city. Wavelets lap against the riverbank wall. Wind. Enough to be a factor. Out over the water an Anguillan gull floats serenely, almost motionless, using only deft wing angle to maintain height. Downstream on the riverbank road there are two slim figures in Great Britain tracksuits. I'm early. I put my rucksack with my racing flats on the slope by the embankment. A scent of autumn leaves breezes down off the woods and along the river. The sky is pale blue with wispy streaks of cloud. An October morning. *Moskva.*

THE END

[roll credits]

The THREEMAN books
Now a major motion picture series

Once Upon a Time in Moscow
Threeman
Comrade Nyet
Winterfold
Fifty Years Of October
The Natalya Rites
If Only Once to Wonder
Anastasia de Lune
Starboard Glove Pylon
Trippelganger
An Ingot for an Eye
Warspite
Espionaut
The Pink Ophelia
Metelitsa
Seventy-Nine Steps
Storm-333
The Applecross Anomaly
Spezialnost
Wish Upon a Kremlin Star
The Love I Left in Lubyanka
Requiem Required
The Spy I Never Knew
Then Beneath a Shimmering Light a Lady

Then Beneath a Shimmering Light a Lady

★

Ratina Stadion. Tampere, Finland – July 2, 2022.

The warm-up straight. Not as many runners as there were yesterday for the semi-finals. Atmosphere more tense. Me? Calmer so far. Knew I would be. I'm good in finals – always deliver. Pressure yes, but it's just go out there and wang it now, isn't it. Dare to die. A lane on the straight is free. I roll into it with one two three four five easy strides and then accelerate into a good cadence. Fast. Yes. Then faster. But still comfortable. Easy arms. Driving hard through the track. My spikes grip into each foot-strike and fire me forward. ZoomX Dragonfly! The GB vest feels great, slightly loose against my torso as I run. *Relaxed*. Then halfway down the straight, smoothly, I unleash my arm drive and sprint eyeballs out, smashing it for ten twenty thirty metres. And… ease down. My momentum takes me all the way to the end of the hundred-metre straight, where I roll through the line. Yep. Felt good. Coordination all there.

Next time I run that fast it will be for real.

The call-room is a set of two gazebos by the warm-up track on the level of the second tier of the stadium. We're allocated specific seats according to our lane draw. Seat six for me. I look around at the other runners. Everyone is seated apart from Kuijpers who has already got up to shake his legs off. Nerves. We'll need them. I prefer to sit and relax my face. The coolest athlete always wins.

Some people talk in call-rooms. Most don't. They've seated the eight runners one-to-four along one row, and five-to-eight along the row opposite. You could eyeball if you wanted to but no one at this level needs that. Mind games show you're desperate. You want relaxed – relaxed is dangerous. Hully is chatting with Norström. Hully seat four. Norström in his seat eight. Both are outgoing personalities. It's not a 'tell' that they're talking. Just banal chit chat. Another way to process nerves. Nice guys. I hope they run well and that I destroy them both.

Bayonne doesn't speak. Confidence. Arrogance? Only he knows. Is he the favourite? Probably. Word on the warm-up track yesterday was that he's run 1:59 this season. He looked value for it in the semi-final, three strides ahead of me. Was I maxed out? Felt like it but any 800m hurts. Fast runs hurt less. If you win.

Stay chilled. Opposite me is the empty chair of Kuijpers. Then Robards the American in sleek half-tinted glasses. He's lacing up his orange ZoomX Dragonfly. My Dragonfly in volt green look fractionally better. 1:59 should win it.

The UK rankings website says Hully ran 1:59 nine days ago at Wormwood Scrubs. Knowing to-the-second how good he is offers me a tactical advantage, and even if the others have researched him too, only Hully and I know that Wormwood Scrubs is a windy track. Arboza in the white-and-sky-blue of Argentina just sits. His face is fixed, unfriendly, a scowl to the extreme pain he's about to inflict upon himself. That's probably what I look like, except colder.

The Italian Mortirolo is tall bald and gregarious. He tries to start a dialogue with Arboza in Spanish. Arboza nods at the remark but doesn't engage, might be too tight. I relax my facial muscles. Mortirolo farts.

Kuijpers has gone right to the back of the call-room. He had to expend a lot of energy to come from behind and win his semi-final yesterday. Kuijpers might feel that today. He's tall too. Stride length.

Arboza is super-slim like a 1500m runner with skinny arms which I envy. Norström is huge. As wide as a decathlete. Next to real decathletes he'd be tiny. Kuijpers and Mortirolo with tall muscular frames look more like 400m runners. So does Bayonne, only leaner. In the middle range, with the perfect 800m race physiques, it's Robards and Hully. And me.

I'm the one who looks most like Steve Ovett.
That contest isn't even close.

Tom Hully. I've raced him twice over the years, which is a lot, both times in the British Masters Champs. He beat me from the front in the M35. And then sat and kicked four years later in the M40. It's annoying knowing he can run it both ways. With these two wins in his race archive, it doesn't even occur to Hully that he might not beat me today. I'm not even a factor. But he must have noticed how lean I am this season. The calmness. My cold eyes. None of my races this season have been on home soil. I'm a ghost on the UK rankings. Nobody knows my form, or my trajectory... Big mistake if Hully assumes he's going to beat me.

Our race is called.

The walk to the track is down an aisle of the back-straight grandstand. Each concrete step is covered in a rectangle of track rubber. I take them carefully. Easy to trip. The future M45 world champion fell head-first and broke his neck. Died instantly. His non-runner friends forgot to attend the funeral. I reach the track with poise intact.

Eight finalists enter the arena. The M45 World Masters final. Never in doubt! The track feels grippy and fast. After all the weights, all the training sessions, all the warm-up races, here we are. The endgame.

Lane 1	Roberto Mortirolo	Italy
2	Maarten Kuijpers	Holland
3	Jalen Robards	USA
4	Tom Hully	Great Britain
5	Arnaud Bayonne	France
6	Richard Weaver	Great Britain
7	Ignacio Arboza	Argentina
8	Stellan Norström	Sweden

Each athlete is middle-aged slim and handsome with a gnarled renaissance beauty. M45 specimens. We have a couple of minutes to loosen the legs off again. Run half a bend easy. Forty metres smooth up the straight. Walk back and soak up the crowd. My nerves have nothing to do with the crowd. I love the crowd. Shouts. One is for me. Brits cheer for Brits. I don't recognise the voice but it touches me that someone is hoping I do well.

The marshall calls us to our lanes.

I'm in six between Bayonne in five and Arboza in seven. We wait. These are the very worst seconds. Not as Kool & The Gang anymore. Our names are announced on the stadium loudspeaker. Each athlete gets cheers. There must be over a thousand spectators in the home straight grandstand. Going to be noisy. Suits me. They might even get an Ovett victory wave. When my name is announced I stay face-forward but raise both arms aloft to acknowledge the ripple of GB cheers, which Hully also got but more, he's a bigger wheel on the GB circuit. Arboza ignores his name. Norström in lane eight milks the crowd more stylishly than me, raising one arm, turning around, and nodding cocksure to the large contingent of Sverige fans going absolutely mental. Fancies this does he? His arrogance empties my legs. I'm all alone. Except for one person thinking about me back home. Athlete and coach are an unbreakable team. We can do this Apollo.

Athletics Club Newsletter - June 2022

And finally...

The club wishes three of our veteran athletes good luck next month in the World Masters Championships in Finland. Representing Great Britain will be Ray McNough (M55 1500m), Richard Weaver (M45 800m), and Mary Clarke (W50 400m).

For more info on elite 400m and middle-distance training, contact: Apollo Nevis.

Me. Was calm earlier. Now not. Now tight. I have to process the nerves with reminders. You've worked hard so you can do what needs to happen. You can dare. Keep accelerating until you reach panic speed and then stay there. Nerves are good, I tell myself, but they've mutated. I'm worried I'm too scared to actually run when the gun goes. Scared of the pain. Or just extra keyed up? Breathe. Loose. My vest needs a small tug at the left shoulder for comfort. Roll my shoulders once. Did some piss just leak out? I adjust the waistband on my shorts. There. Swallow to lubricate the mouth. Nod. Let's do this. Relax. No fidgety leg shaking. Show them all you're Kool & The Fucking Gang. One last chance to psyche out anyone watching you from the inside lanes. Start hard and get yourself in the mix like Ovett would.

On your marks. Somewhere behind me the start marshall raises his pistol to the Finland sky. Get in the mix. Like Ovett would. I leave one millimetre of dark red between the end of my left toe and the white of the start-line, the left toe in volt green ZoomX Dragonfly. My beautiful calves. I crouch over the line. Left elbow back. Right arm forward and high. This is it.

Ovett. Steve Ovett. Ovett. Ovett. Ovett.

BANG!

Short strides. Arms. Drive through the track. Leg speed. I accelerate up to race pace on full afterburners. Sprint for ten. Sprint for twenty. Sprint! Then relax. But I relax too much and lose ground on Arboza who is smashing it in lane seven. Turnover. Swing the arms. Bayonne is killing me on the inside. I'm feeling for the right stride length and a fast cadence, the sweet spot between control and panic. *There.* One two three. The motion of my legs feels momentarily glorious. For three strides I don't even feel the track. Then I snatch at a stride, then I find it again – 'it' the smoothness – as I curve with the bend. Chaos already and we're still in lanes. Drive through the track with the glutes.

Carl Lewis. Glutes. The American legend coaches a drill with his sprinters where they run sixty metres with their hands on their hips. This extends the drive through the track with your hips and backside. You can totally feel it. What's the biggest part of a racehorse? It's arse. Drive through your glutes. Four five six seven strides boom off the track. *And Ovett goes storming off in lane six.* All those deadlifts, squats, burpees, and sprint reps. I've never been stronger. The champion racehorse with a winning streak that broke the bookies. Before my murder they all came: senators, mobsters, movie stars, all visiting my stable just to watch me shit. After romping the Kentucky Derby they studded me out. A whole month at it, nailing filly after filly until my cock fell off. Brutal. Had to lie down in the hay for fuck's sake, too battered to even have a wank. Then she appeared. The one with the cascading honey-brown hair and *Obsession* pheromones. Anastasia's eyelashes flutter before me as we swing round into the back straight. Anastasia. Waiting for her GB stallion. To drive it. Hard. Oceanically deep and – *Nnngh!* – sire her an Olympian offspring. Smash the glutes.

90 metres run.

Bayonne passes my left shoulder but I'm within two strides of Arboza on my outside. I can also now see Norström. Those massive suntanned lats. He's ripped to shreds and has more lustrous hair than is polite in the M45 category. Yellow Sverige vest. Blue shorts in sprint Lycra. He runs a lot of four-hundreds too. Norström is dangerous.

Arboza. Azul-and-white vest. Black split-shorts. Puma.

The break is approaching. Miniature green cones on each lane line mark the 110-metre break. There's also a corner flag either side of the track. Flags. The concept reminds me the back straight is into the wind. My synapses feel this already and I've surged to slice through it, even though it's only the lightest zephyr. Tuck in behind? Negative Ghost Rider. Race position trumps slipstream today. All 800m runners have a built-in wind gauge to measure exactly how much and where the wind will, or won't, affect a race.

Nobody will be cagey today.
This is going to be eyeballs out all the way.

110 metres run. No more lanes. We enter the anti-gravity of the first back straight, the eerie half-world between the start and the real race. Only 800m runners know this. And 4 x 400m second-leg runners, although I'm usually on leg three holding off the American.

Inside me I can half-see Bayonne. And sort of hear him too, but not hear him, because it's only smooth classy silence. There's an extra kinetic sense of another runner, especially a top quality runner. Shit runners you don't even notice, apart from a brief *fuck-off-why-are-you-even-in-the-same-race-as-me?* But Bayonne is poetry. Liquid power. The race favourite with an intimidating physique. He looked phenomenal on the warm-up track in his white ZoomX Dragonfly. The last to arrive and do his drills. Of course he was. He feels easy as he moves from my peripheral vision into my left upper race quadrant. Navy blue France vest and split-shorts. Two strides ahead of me. The disguise of the stagger is over now. France. If I can read the name of a country on a vest someone is faster than me. Or they're front-loading their race more than me. Try to ignore his physique.

My beautiful calves.
His beautiful calves.
His explosive fast-twitch 400-metre sprint calves.
I accelerate.

Arboza is veering left. He's going to get ahead of me in the pack unless I surge boldly now. I'm also veering in and get directly behind Bayonne. Great tactics. That's three seconds out of the headwind zephyr. The millimetres will add up. I click into Bayonne's rhythm and get five strides of free speed. Yes. Bold. This edges me half a metre back up on Arboza. There it is – panic speed. We're at a ridiculous sprint pace that we can't possibly maintain for two laps… *that's* the right pace. I'm in the race. My synapses kick in and start talking. *Relax*. You're good. Leg speed. I take another stride out of Arboza as we drift in, so now I can control him on my right shoulder. This is the pre-battle for the race position we will jostle for in thirty, in twenty-nine, twenty-eight metres. We are forming into a pack.

140 metres. An orange flash to my left.
Kuijpers's vest or Robards's spikes?

The race order on my radar is Bayonne then Robards? Ovett then Arboza. But Norström's late veer in surprises me. For a second I'd forgotten about him. He's ahead of me, but I'm ahead of Arboza now. Where's Hully? I hear contact inside me. Jostling. Only shoulders. Those inside lanes – one, two, three, and maybe lane four – get pinched earliest on the back straight and have to push for places. They can see the walls closing in. We are the walls. I surge for Norström.

Fuck this is going to be a quick 200-metre split.

Arboza is back on me. Shoulder to shoulder. We both have missile lock on the space just behind Arnaud Bayonne's right shoulder. Norström wants the same. Hully moves up on my inside – wants it too. Bayonne is controlling the race already. He smashed it exactly like this in the semi-final.

Foolhardy or in great shape?

In LA 1984 the Olympic 800 metres had an extra round: two qualifying rounds, semi-finals, and the final, on four consecutive days in blazing California heat. The Brazilian Joaquim Cruz ran 1:45 in round one, quick enough to have won the final four years earlier. The next day he ran 1:44. Insanity. In his semi-final he ran super-aggressively again, forcing everyone in his race to dig equally deep, and won in 1:43.82. Sebastian Coe qualified in the other semi-final. In his interview after the semi Coe was asked about Cruz and his startling qualifying times: *Well, he's either foolhardy or in great shape. If he's both we'll all be in trouble tomorrow.* He was both. Cruz won the final in one-forty-three-flat.

150 metres run. Leg speed. Keep that panic cadence.
It has to feel scary to be fast enough.

Mortirolo. The silky *azzurra* vest comes through on the inside. Maybe he'd been ahead all along? Completely bald, cue ball bald, massive nose, rangy stride, arms all over the place. I can't tell if Mortirolo is ungainly or just crazy quick? He was surrounded by an entourage of attractive women in his warm-up today. Again! With his long strides the Italian gets up to Bayonne before the Frenchman has got lane one. Mortirolo now has the choice to lead, or not to lead. Bayonne can respond. If he wants. 160 metres run.

Three vests ahead. Italia – France – Sverige.

The pack is now ten strides from forming. Eight strides. Last chance to hijack a position or pre-emptively escape or launch an insane attack? Six strides. I feel the shape of the box forming around me. I'm running in inner lane two but I'm going to get someone else on my right shoulder. Still Arboza? Four strides. I surge forward into a half-space, then the half-space narrows. Raging bodies around me. Shoulders. Be aggressive. Bayonne's trail legs flick up in front but there's daylight so I don't have to chop a stride, yet.

Sunshine. Hotter than in the semi-final.
The zephyr has dropped or am I tucked in?

Now we're tight and the pack adds to the panic which temporarily negates the escalation of pain. I have to be running this fast. My legs go with all the others. And I'm running aggressively to defend my position with attack, attacking rhythm, smooth attack, Ovett attack, and attack hurts less. What the fuck is this split going to be though? We've run 180m. Keep pushing with them. 190m and through the 200m line.

Twenty-eight.

Fucking hell. Quick. You place unreasonable faith in the person shouting splits. It should be a race marshall but isn't always. Often a coach. Or at Watford a keen mum or dad. Twenty-eight. What if he was lying? An enigma code system in cahoots with Maarten Kuijpers who I haven't seen yet. He might be chilling at the back knowing his Dutch spy is going to call a dodgy split. Two seconds slow, or a second fast, to make the leaders push and blow themselves up, or hold back too much on the second two-hundred. Sabotage? No. Felt like twenty-eight. My pace judgement is exceptional in training but in races I'm never sure. I'll take twenty-eight. If I've run it even paced, twenty-eight is the perfect split.

Trail legs. Careful!

I'm lying – I wanted a twenty-nine split but needed to tag onto Bayonne and get the nudge on Arboza, which I have done. Anyone who's just run twenty-nine is fucked somewhere at the back of the pack with a wall of six runners to negotiate, and the inevitability of running very wide on at least one bend just to get in the mix. I'll take my position.

220 metres run. Mortirolo leads. Bayonne second.
Hully – Ovett – Norström – three abreast in third place.
Then Arboza.

Because I know Arboza's breathing. Then his noise gets lost in the general race roar. Three others are behind me. Or two others? Loud desperate breathing already, times eight. Plus fourteen scratchy ZoomX Dragonfly foot-strikes. Mortirolo is wearing Diadora.

Shoulders with Norström. The friction is horrible extra effort. Norström doesn't want to be wide. To get a piece of lane one (from start lane eight) he only had two likely options: be first or be last. Or a tiny possibility that the pack would be nicely strung out for him. It wasn't. Everyone has gone out hard with Bayonne, including Mortirolo ahead of him. So far I have a great position if Bayonne is as good as he looks.

Italia – France.

I'm watching Bayonne's trail legs. Wary. And yes, he eases off a fraction so I was right to keep an eye downward. Mortirolo must have eased off once he secured the lead. This always happens. Our phalanx in third draws one stride nearer to Bayonne. This tightens the box for Hully. The right side of Hully's box is me. How early will he worry? In Moscow Ovett knew it was a problem before it even happened, and gave a nudge to Wagenknecht to try and save himself, but he still got stuffed. Patience sometimes pay off. Not always.

Hully surges with five strides to get as close to Bayonne as he can. Bayonne is in lane one-two covering Mortirolo's right shoulder, which gives Hully a nice line behind and inside him. 240 metres run. Hully has no trail legs to avoid, and in lane one he is running the shortest distance around this bend. The bastard. His race position is even better if he thinks I'm shit, which he does. Are the two Brits running as a team? Negative. I'm his worst fucking nightmare today. Drive the arms.

Bayonne is sitting on Mortirolo and pressurising. Great position. I'm also good. Or great. Unless Norström pushes on and tries to cut in. If that happens I'm shocking. 250 metres run.

Hully may have a major problem but he can't know for sure. If Bayonne is *The Man* then moving up into the half gap on the Frenchman's inside is the right move for Hully. Because Bayonne is probably going to overtake Mortirolo at some point. Hully's problem is that I also know this, and Norström outside me knows I know. Hully's synapses are in overdrive for options. My Ovett synapses are in hyperdrive not to give him any. I brace myself across the torso. One of his options might be an elbow flick, to gain a quarter stride and morph himself into the gap. Or he can be patient and gamble that the leaders will speed up and open his box, but this gamble involves me not speeding up to follow Bayonne's next surge, which I've just done. Synapses.

No one knows anything about Mortirolo. We only know he gets lots of pussy. Too much? If he was shagging last night he'll be great early, then pay for it on the second lap. Unless shagging is his big thing, his Italian superpower. Truthfully, I don't get much. And alone in bed I have resisted the clarion call for the last six days and six nights: stockpiling weapons-grade testosterone. My balls are exploding. I'll be strong.

Mortirolo is running a great bend – *definitely* a shagger.

265 metres run. It's always risky to lead, but the further we run the bigger an advantage Mortirolo creates for himself. Hugging lane one gains him time-distance on Norström, and slightly on me, and on Arboza if it is Arboza behind me to the right. And metre-by-metre Mortirolo also endangers whoever is at the back.

Robards and Kuijpers must be five metres down on the lead. Five metres to make up with 535m to go is okay. Five metres with only 450m to go is riskier. A five-metre head-start at the bell? You have to bank on being great to get him because Mortirolo might also be great.

No one got David Rudisha in 2012.
Is Mortirolo that good?

Bayonne is taking no chances and edges closer to the crazy Italian. He is poised to attack out of the slingshot. Bayonne wants to dominate. Needs to. That's *his* thing. But despite his subtle surge, no gap grows to joint third. We've responded as one, covering the move every step of the way. No tactical change. Our grouping is giving an armchair ride to whoever is behind. Through in twenty-nine and sitting in a slipstream are Robards and Kuijpers, one of whom also has lane one.

270 metres run.
Robards had a huge finish in my semi-final.
And Kuijpers behind. 280. 290. 300 run. The straight.

Have we been too aggressive on this first lap? My synapses delete the question because Bayonne pushes on. His move onto Mortirolo's shoulder opens the box for Hully, who is pushing into very nearly a far better position. And now that we're on the straight Norström wide is attacking. I've lost half a shoulder of ground on Hully-Norström worrying about Robards-Kuijpers. I respond – not a kick, but a squeeze of sprint speed in my smooth-relaxed continuum. This point in the race feels important. I get my shoulder back on Hully. His 1:59? Those two losses to him? I have no option but to race as if I'm much better than him, because Norström is suddenly the real danger, sustaining his attack and moving ahead in lane two.

Italia – France – Sverige – the two Britons level in four.

Bayonne is all over Mortirolo and going for the full pass on the straight. I knew it. This will leave an Italian right shoulder, probably smelling of expensive cologne, that six runners all want to get on. Norström is closest.

320 metres run. The home straight on lap one. A wave of calls starts from the main grandstand. Inevitably for Mortirolo. *Vai Robby Vai!* Multiple female shrieks, for fuck's sake. The first tier of the stand is raised so that the front row of fans are practically on top of lane eight. We almost catch flying spit from their shouts. *Allez!* The crowd gets denser and louder nearer the finish line. A wave of aggressive noise builds each stride. *Tom! Go Tommy! Come on Tom!* That's too many cheers for Hully. Frenzied fury and it's all anger aimed at me because I get nothing. *Maaaarty!* Hundreds are now shouting. *Vamos!* Loads of Americans for J-Rob. Billions of Swedes chanting for Norström as he moves into third position. More screamy Italian women – how many has he fucking got?!

My aggression doesn't seem to match this atmosphere now. Have I backed off? I can feel everyone else responding to the roars. I'm not good and it's kicking off here. Norström is smashing it. Above the real-life noise in the stadium I have a louder voice in my head.

Apollo – screaming.
C'mon Steve let's rock n roll!

Arboza is going for it outside me. He wants a better position for the third bend. How good is he? Am I bold enough to respond? Questions. Why questions?! The pain has ramped up horrendously in the last fifteen strides. Fuck. Should I hold back and save for a finish? The split is already going to be stupid fast. Norström has tucked in ahead of me. Those lats. I feel small. Weak. Bayonne has now passed Mortirolo into the lead. We're approaching the bell. Hully touches shoulders with me. Grrr. Then he brushes elbows. The Alpha Brit? He wants my space. I might have to relinquish some of it. I'm suffering. Arboza is shoulders on my right. I'm scared of this pain, scared of this speed, and fucking terrified of the second lap. A forlorn grimace is pasted across my face. Let's face it, I'm the least handsome runner in the race. Desperate to hear the bell but also dreading the bell. I'm backing off. Checking out. Giving up. Talk to me Apollo.

C'mon Steve let's rock n roll – This is Moscow!

That means here we go. One shot. One opportunity. It has to happen. This is Moscow. I wake up and attack the last strides to the bell. Waiting for the sideways look at the race timer. Wanting to know that split. Hoping for fast or slow? Either helps. Slow means I'll have a strong finish. Fast justifies how horrific I'm feeling. Fuck you Arboza!

DING! DING! DING!

The bell for Bayonne. I know the race timer stops for him. We'll see his split when we look. Three strides. Two strides. One stride. The bell for me and after one more stride, the look. Relax. Eyes only. 58.1-something. Ffff…

Only 400 metres run. A full 400 metres still to go.

Commit. It has to be all-in now. Fucking all-in Apollo. *Rock n roll!* And I feel my shoulders swing looser which helps the flow. My leg speed goes up one notch. I'm running on my toes now. Knees higher. *Relax*. Here comes the Big O. It's faster and all so much… easier. My house is on fire but now I'm the one throwing petrol bombs through the windows.

Into the third bend. Classic body lean. We curve to the left. Oh, that's beautiful. Nudging back up so Hully is boxed dead again in lane one. Get back in your fucking borstal!

A photographer is crouching outside the track on the bend pointing his camera at me. Big fat zoom lens. Waiting for one moment in time. For artistic perfection. My next glorious high knee. Opposite arm forward. Straight back leg. Such exquisite calf flexion. I'm the photo to end all photos. His guaranteed Pulitzer right there. Now. If his shutter goes. Snap! Majestic. Cover of *Sports Illustrated*: M45 Athlete of the Year. Stardom. I become a thing on the US talk shows. Backstage convo with a supermodel co-guest. Eastern Europeany. Late-twenties, or maybe only mid. She asks about my 400m split. Dinner? Posh restaurant. Then a limo richtung her place, but she can't wait. So I'm drilling away on the backseat.

Work. 380 metres to go. The third bend is all about work, working to earn the rhythm. As the saying goes, your own fucking saying: *It's hard work making it look this easy*.

Bayonne – Mortirolo and Norström.
Hully-Ovett-Arboza – Robards probably – Kuijpers?

If Bayonne went through in fifty-eight-and-bits, I'd have been fifty-eight-high. Nuts. Focus on driving the arms to maintain that leg speed. Concentration! Have to get on Mortirolo and Norström. My synapses trigger five scintillating strides and the order has already shuffled.

Bayonne followed by Norström
Then Mortirolo-Ovett-Arboza – Hully – Robards?
Fuck knows if Kuijpers is still in the mix. 370m to go.

If I overtake Mortirolo here I can tuck into lane one. Feels like it's stringing out, or that it will do, or is everyone equally desperate and equally strong? I pile on extra speed for the overtake but – the absolute fucker – Mortirolo responds to hold me off around the bend. Beautiful move. Pure class. I'll look forward to talking about this part of the race with him and all his friends later. Better to stay smooth and even-paced on his shoulder but maintain that leg speed.

Arboza has gone from my peripheral vision. Must be tucked in behind me. That fucks him if I'm shit. A risk I have forced upon him, but he's gambled because his synapses have said I look superb and told him to stay in the slipstream. More and more of the race is revolving around me. The supremacy fires my next one two three four five strides.

The pack stays super-tight. No stringing out at all. Everyone is in the mix. The volume of our breathing is scary loud now. Like a Boeing 747 on take-off. Except the jumbo is leaking fuel leaving a trail of flammable lactic on the runway. Bayonne flicks open a Zippo lighter. It's only a matter of time before we all explode. Motherfuckers! 320 metres to go in the World Masters 800m final. *Hurting*. But I'm right in the mix.

Anastasia arrives on time at Cherkizovsky Park. I was fifteen minutes early to savour the anticipation of seeing her. It's a thing I do. We meet on the concrete arch bridge over the lake. This is her local park too. She's in all-white in some sort of shorts-but-a-skirt number, slinky, to half-thigh length. Her beautiful thighs. I force myself not to marvel at her too much. Important here to keep intentions strictly under wraps. A false front of easy-come-easy-go. Just play it quintessential. Let the archetype do the legwork. Anastasia's t-shirt is white with trendy cut-out laced-up shoulders and a squarey logo on the front which I don't recognise. In all-white she looks great. All attractive Russian women love a one-colour outfit and as a viewer I'm massively in the fan club thereof, especially on her. I bloody love Cherky Park. The ideal venue for a casual walk-which-is-not-a-date. All attractive Russian women love the casual walk in the park – fan club president *Stiv Ovyett, Esq.* at your service. People and wildlife will give me stuff to riff about in my cute Russian. There are benches every few metres around the entire lake, so we can sit down and my legs won't get tired. We walk one leisurely lap, stopping at the ice cream kiosk for a mint Magnum each. I resist mentioning my 5k splits at the bridge (5:10) at the signpost in the top corner (bang on 9:00) and at the barbecue gazebo (14:30). Actually, we don't talk that much. Anastasia is quiet in the style of an elegant tsarina. Ovett is quiet with the smouldering confidence of a man with an M35 4 x 400m relay silver in his back pocket. I ask her what the logo is and discreetly admire the front of her t-shirt. Givenchy, she says. Oh, of course. There's a path of wooden decking which takes us lower and closer to the lake. We lean over the wooden railing and try to spot fish. I point at one, deftly putting my other arm around Anastasia's slender waist for purchase. She doesn't flinch. I remove the arm straight away, but only slowly and with a deft caressing motion. When one is in Cherkizovsky Park one should delve deeply into its treasures. We walk on. Two ducks paddle by.

300 metres to go. The back straight.

We're level but I'm controlling Mortirolo now. Who's that handsome Ovett-looking guy, whisper his groupies in his ear in Neapolitan dialect. Doubt. His advantage on the bend has just evaporated. We're in equal fourth but I'm basically third. Phenomenal position this now. Arboza is a stride down and can't get anywhere near me. I'm hurting them and myself. It's utterly horrendous in the lungs. And the lactic which won't go away. Stay foolhardy. Everyone will be feeling this pace. Even Bayonne. Especially Bayonne?

I love the back straight. All Apollo's athletes do. Always the place where we cash in. Still with the speed but also the speed endurance coming into play. And the bravery, steeled by so many brutal sessions. The extra 'signature' rep we didn't know was coming. I trained on my own in Moscow all season but never felt for one second that I was alone. Every rep time went back to the UK for analysis and approval: *You're in cracking shape, Steve.* And here we are. The back straight of the World Masters final drawing both guns out of their holsters, fully loaded and ready to blaze away. *Magnum Force.*

Do you like dogs? says Anastasia as a grey pitbull charges towards me. Before Mutley has a chance to bite a chunk out of my leg, I've knelt down with my arms out to greet him. He jumps up at my chest and starts licking my face. *Molodyetz*. I give him a big bear hug stroking his back and muscular flanks. Anastasia squeals with delight. Animal magnetism. Mutley knew. They all do. Dogs and babies, I explain to Anastasia. They love me. Which has been true ever since I took up middle-distance running. I don't know why. Just kind of a soul thing that transmits. Cows, says Anastasia. Her grandmother's *dacha* is on a farm with lots of cows and calves. She has always loved cows, and cows love her. I totally get it.

280 to go. They're all over me.

I know this is too good a field to get rid of anyone. Accepting that is important. So I focus on reeling in Norström and if the rest come along with me then so be it. Norström is good. This is going to take my smoothest most glorious acceleration to hunt him down. I relax my face and start to increase my flow. Close to empty. The lactic is a major factor now, burning like hell, and I can hardly fucking breathe, but by relaxing I can trick my body into thinking it can keep doing this for another forty-two seconds.

Ovett – comfortable! – brushes past, chases the Swede.

Half a stride ahead of Mortirolo. Half his long stride-length. The pack is still clamped together just behind. Noisy. But I'm at the front of it majestically bringing us back to the leaders. Bayonne. Then Norström in second. I now have daylight from Mortirolo! This gives me the new option to cut in and get lane one. Negative!

Norström is two metres ahead but I'm already planning the overtake. Waste of time cutting in only to cut out again. Synapses say Norström isn't going to win, but even if he does he'd have to pass Bayonne which forces me wide anyway. It doesn't look like I'll set foot in the inside half of lane one all race. That's championship finals for you.

As Anastasia and I walk up the steps out of Cherkizovsky Park a cooler seam of air whips up off the lake. I realise this might be where we say goodbye. Not what I want to happen. I pull Anastasia gently towards me and we embrace like life-long friends and of course it is only friends. Deep down I do understand this. And as a friend I invite her to my apartment to see my new racing spikes. She agrees and we stroll in slow-motion along Bolshoya Cherkizovskaya.

Bayonne still. Relentless.
Norström – Ovett – then Mortirolo?
The pack.

I don't make a big deal of my Dragonfly spikes, but Anastasia does lovingly inspect them while I make her a cup of tea. She notices a Russian DVD on my coffee table. An old Soviet film from the 1970s which I've been watching to improve my Russian: *Ironiya Sudby*. The Irony of Fate. A much beloved romantic farce. It turns out this is Anastasia's favourite film. Neither a tactic on my part nor a coincidence; it's everyone's favourite film in Russia. Zhenya lives in Moscow. He gets blind drunk on New Year's Eve (also his stag night) and his nearly-as-drunk mates put him on a plane to Leningrad. He wakes up at Leningrad airport and gets a taxi to his home address. The taxi takes him to the street in Leningrad of that name, an identical tower block to his real home in Moscow. Zhenya's key even fits the lock. The furniture inside the flat is also identical, as so much was in the centrally planned USSR, so he thinks he's arrived home and falls asleep. The beautiful Nadya arrives home soon afterwards to find fully-clothed Zhenya passed out in her bed. This tip-off point leads to arguments, indignation, confusion, relationship break-ups, as circumstance begets unfortunate circumstance, and Nadya and Zhenya end up having to see the New Year in together. The irony of fate is that her hostility is eventually tamed… and they fall in love. The next morning Zhenya reluctantly flies home to his life in Moscow. By the end of the film Anastasia and I are horizontal on my sofa. Both our heads are on the same pillow and my quilt is pulled over us. We have both seen the film before and have both fallen asleep before the happy ending. Nadya flies to Moscow. She finds Zhenya's apartment easily – it's the same address as hers. And her key even fits the lock.

One stride back on Norström.

250 metres to go. A beautiful race. The full majestic power of Ovett is on display now. A masterclass of arrogance and control. Utter disdain for the one-metre gap to Norström and synapse radar is now picking up Bayonne ahead. I have a perfectly clear run. All I have to do is pull onto Norström's shoulder and then track Bayonne. He went hardest and earliest. Now I'm covering his lead with smooth calculated speed. I fucking love the back straight. This is on. And Ovett knows it.

Those blue eyes like chips of ice.

I'm not going to take out Norström before the bend.

Fuck. But I've got footsteps all over me behind so I can't afford to slipstream in lane one around the bend. I have to stay half-wide to avoid a box, and maybe – unlikely, but maybe – get past Norström onto Bayonne. The last synaptic trigger of the race? Nothing else is tactical. Now it's just eyeballs out and whatever shit happens hits the fan.

200 to go. Nobody shouts a 600m split. Thank fuck.

Arboza! Hasn't the guy had enough?! He rolls the dice on me yet again. Attacking exactly as we curve into the top bend. The final bend. Arboza is completely mad, which is seriously fucking dangerous at this desperate stage of lactic. *Relax*. Need to be loose for this warp speed cadence. The cement mixer truck is parking up outside my building. My quads are heavier, slower, with almost no oxygen going anywhere near them anymore. But if I can stay smooth, I'll still be able to drive enough to hold off the rampaging Arboza, which may also get me a nudge on Norström. I have to swing the arms harder. Shit I'm virtually all-in with the arm drive. My neck tightens with the strain. Technique! Internally everything everywhere is impossibly horrendous, but if I make Arboza fail on a wide overtake I gain a stride-and-a-half on him for the finishing straight. If I force him to back off and tuck in behind me I'll also gain a stride-and-a-half. Arboza takes it on, the crazy fool. Swinging wide to try and get past me. 160 to go. Aargh!

Bayonne.
In second it's Norström-Ovett-Arboza.
Then shitloads of footsteps. Everyone else.

I offer to walk Anastasia home. I don't want her to feel

she has to stay. She says she would like to spend more time with me but doesn't want me to misunderstand. I know what's coming. It's the only ounce of emotional intelligence I have with regards women. Call it intuition, a skill if you like, or maybe a gentle curse. I'm happy she's going to tell me. Aleksandr? No, I just made him up. This is something else and I've known it all along.

– I have a partner. We've been together a while. But it's difficult, you know, in Russia for two girls.
– It's very beautiful. And I like being your friend.

My grammar is perfect. Sometimes simple Russian is the best. We hug again. Friends. It's the irony of fate that I only ever fall in love with Anastasias.

140 to go. Absolute horror story in the legs now.

Locked into this Arboza dogfight. He's all over me. At the same time I have to bury Sverige coming out into the straight. As we take the final strides of the bend Norström's head bucks up and down for two strides on the rodeo for more speed which isn't there. The chink! I squeeze my own technique into the tiniest compact shape possible and on the slingshot I've inched myself ahead. The grandstand. Roars. Bayonne leads. Ovett second. Stalking him now. 110 metres to go. Bayonne doing everything he can to shake the tail off.

But the shadow is still there!

By burying Norström, dumping some of my lactic on his driveway, I get momentum for five epic strides. This kicks me half clear of Arboza and finally into Bayonne's world. Only a metre-and-a-half behind him now. Attack again. One metre. Bayonne's technique is perfect but he isn't accelerating. He can't accelerate! I have my last grains of cordite to throw in with my arm drive. It's a puny shithouse kick for what it's worth. The crowd erupts because it looks like a massive kick. *And Ovett goes!* But it's only Bayonne decelerating fractionally as I unleash everything and maintain my speed. The mirage of the finish line appears in front of us for the first time.

100 – 99 – 98 – 97 – 96 – 95 – 94 – 93 – 92 – 91 – 90.

Bayonne is big. So I veer half a lane wider into lane two-three for a clear run. If I can get on his shoulder he might cave in. Pressurise! Hand him his own arse on a plate. He'll hurt. I won't. Winning never hurts. But I'm sinking into this lactic.

As I gain ground on Bayonne I can hear an express train coming down the tracks on my right. Don't look. Just drive. Relaxation can no longer help. I have to swing the arms as hard as I can to hold the footsteps off. I get onto Bayonne's half-shoulder as the orange vest takes half-a-shoulder out of me. Kuijpers! He's got the legs and is killing us. His cement becomes my cement. Dumped into each thigh, into my arse, and into my pecs which tighten up into the neck. This lactic now poisons my arm drive. Focus. All I have left is technique. I can no longer respond and accelerate. I'm eyeballs out and my only hope is Bayonne blowing a gasket and handing me his silver medal. Kuijpers is irrelevant. As disappointing as it should be, I don't give a fuck about him storming away in front for certain gold.

Sixty metres to go.

Acid burn. Quads scarred forever. Running for second place and needing Bayonne to run backwards. Maintain form! Shorter strides to maintain your drive. Punchy arms. One stride down on Bayonne. Three metres down on Kuijpers and getting nothing more off Bayonne. With multiple footsteps chasing me down from behind. A medal even?

Believe in yourself.
Only fifty metres to hold on. Forty-nine. Forty-eight.

A few days later I go to CCCP Fitness to say goodbye. Neither of us say it, but Anastasia has probably guessed that I won't come back to Russia after the World Masters. It's all too complicated – financially, as well as the other stuff. I hope she's training someone in CCCP so we can't make it a long goodbye, and this is exactly how it happens. She excuses herself from her client on the leg press. *Anastasia* and *Ovyett* embrace on the deadlift platform. Where else! She wishes me luck in the race. Oh yes, the race. I'd kind of forgotten about the race. I'll see you when you get back, she says. Definitely, I say and we hug again so I don't have to look her in the eye. She kisses me three times on the side of my neck. I know she knows.

Bayonne looks slow but every movement is still agonisingly perfect. I can't get anything back off him. I'm slowing too. As if we're running up a beach. Bayonne in lane two. Ovett in lane three. Kuijpers way ahead in lane four. The slingshot has thrown us all wide into the straight. Bayonne wide makes my potential overtake even harder. Lane one is totally free but I couldn't have gambled on the inside. Nobody ever wins up the inside! Our beach is getting steeper. Army boots. Drenched uniforms. The sand is drier and softer the nearer we get to the dunes. Ghastly running now. Quads on fire. The charge. On the top of the bluff is a concrete pillbox. A black muzzle protrudes from a slit in the wall. Spandau 57-millimetre. The Devil's Paintbrush. Loaded up with lactic ammunition. It starts. Explosive thuds. Repetitive. Flashes of light and puffs of dark smoke on the horizon. Then high-pitched whistles passing our ears. Bullets are crashing into my shoulders. Drive the arms. Absolute carnage this. Bayonne's cadence is slowing down. He must have taken a couple of shots in the legs. Kuijpers has three metres. Is he extending? Negative. A reload from the pillbox then a furious volley of shots rings out, but not sprayed aimlessly across the track. They rip into lane four. The killing zone. Kuijpers! He's all over the place. His head bucking and rolling. Can hardly lift his legs. Went too big. Too early. Bayonne gets a stride back on him. Even I get a stride back on him. Kuijpers is fucked with lactic.

Forty metres to go. Slam! Kuijpers falls.

His legs go completely from under him and he lands face first on the track. Disaster for him. *And.* Disaster for me. He's almost certainly going to take me out. He lands in a starfish with his acid-poisoned limbs spreadeagled and then bounces across into my lane. No chance to change my stride pattern.

I'm dead. I'll rake Kuijpers with my spikes and then end up on the deck alongside him. My left foot-strike lands six-inches short of his ankle. My right foot then passes over his left leg sprawled across lane three and the right foot-strike somehow misses his body. Now is when I'll surely clip him. My left foot lands on the track again somehow clear of his left arm and my right foot then lifts… *without* contact. The trip never comes. Kuijpers is down! I'm into second place and with the adrenaline shot I'm tearing into Bayonne's lead.

Thirty to go. I'm going to win the World Masters 800m.

I see her one more time of course but not to speak to. On the late shift Anastasia leaves CCCP Fitness at 11:58 at night. She walks alone along Myasnitskaya. From the darkness I watch her. At a distance. Unseen. My last opportunity to protect her. Through the empty streets of Lubyanka where beautiful minds who yearn for peace are no longer safe. The footsteps of her sneakers on the pavement make no sound. A girl born on the last day of the Soviet Union. The beauty of hope. Of a beautiful Russia. It's late now – too late? An old church clock chimes twelve. Anastasia walks through the bright ether shining down from each lamp post. From the shadows I follow, hoping she'll turn around towards me. Then beneath a shimmering light, she disappears.

Twenty metres to go. I need something every stride to reel in Bayonne before the line. Drive the legs. Only need another three inches. His shoulder. My shoulder. Two inches. Harry Wilson's last piece of advice to Steve Ovett before the 800m final in Moscow was: *Run as fast as you can – and keep running until you hit the stadium wall.* All I want is for that stadium wall to smash me in the face. Run. As fast. You can.

Mortirolo! Impossible. He's attacking like crazy up the inside line. He's got my shoulder. We have only ten metres to sprint. Vision blurred. Lactic death haze. Drowning in killer cement. But if I can drive through the track – *majestically* – I might just hold him off and might get Bayonne too. One inch away now. Driving. Dying. I need a rhythm from somewhere, anywhere. Can't feel anything but burn in my legs. I only have arm drive left. Bayonne. Mortirolo. The familiar red of the running track. Drive. We did it Apollo! We got in the mix. Those blue eyes like chips of ice. Ovett. Please Steve, just one more inspirational stride from once upon a time in Moscow. The rhythm of her name. Anastasia. Anastasia. Anastasia.

If you enjoyed reading this, please leave a review on Amazon. I read every review and they help new readers discover my book.

Scan for the *Once Upon a Time in Moscow* Amazon page.

Thank you

Printed in Great Britain
by Amazon

42610785R10209